'Larry Culliford is an im[...] voice in the world of [...]uality. He brings a lifetime's experience from his professional work as a psychologist, integrating this with his understanding and commitment to Christian theology. He has a clear, crisp and easy style of writing, a skill he describes as a "gift". Read this book and your journey towards spiritual maturity will grow. I am so pleased that Larry sees Christian maturity as involving the decline of dualism and a strong move towards holism.'

Arthur Hawes, Archdeacon Emeritus, Lincoln Cathedral, and Vice-President, British Association for the Study of Spirituality

'Reading Dr Culliford's clear conversational prose, I realized I was hearing the voice of a psychiatrist who has mastered wise insights into the day-to-day spiritual experiences of being human. His book embodies the goals of the UK's Scientific and Medical Network. His prose "provides a safe forum for ideas that go beyond reductionist science". He successfully "integrates intuitive insights with rational analysis". His theory of human development "emphasizes an holistic approach". Dr Culliford provides practical paths to continue the great adventure of our living more joyfully and courageously. I value his new book very highly.'

Jonathan Montaldo, former President, International Thomas Merton Society, and Director, Thomas Merton Center, Louisville, Kentucky

'As the fruit of many years of deep thought and reflection, Larry Culliford's unique book deserves to find an appreciative readership.'

Andrew Powell, psychotherapist and founding Chair, Spirituality and Psychiatry Special Interest Group, Royal College of Psychiatrists

'Larry Culliford writes about spirituality with the profound knowledge and insight of being one of the country's leading psychiatrists. This book has much to teach Christians, those of other faiths, and those of no faith. Strongly recommended!'

Sir Anthony Seldon, author, educationalist, historian and Vice-Chancellor of Buckingham University

'Larry Culliford is to be congratulated for writing a book that is both simple and profound. It is refreshing to read about theology and spirituality from someone trained in the scientific discipline of psychiatric care who is rooted in his own spiritual tradition while appreciating the riches of others. This book looks at the human condition struggling to find meaning and significance in life. Bringing together insights from religion and psychology, it strikes a chord with all who long for spiritual growth and full humanity.'

Dominic Walker OGS, former Bishop of Monmouth

'With his intimate knowledge of the writings of Thomas Merton and his acute expertise in the field of psychiatry, Larry Culliford invites his readers to embark upon a profound encounter with the second half of life, inviting nothing less than authentic spiritual transformation.'

Robert Wright, Canon Emeritus, Westminster Abbey
and former Chaplain to the Speaker of the House of Commons

'This thoughtful and challenging book asks the all-important questions that must be addressed by those who want to find the true meaning of Christian maturity.'

John Moses, Dean Emeritus, St Paul's Cathedral, and author of
Divine Discontent: The Prophetic Voice of Thomas Merton

'Being a Christian in a secular world is never going to be easy. But that just makes it difficult, not impossible. Larry Culliford offers to act as a guide who will lead his readers into a form of Christian maturity that is warm, peaceable and transformative. In this book, Culliford offers a fascinating spiritual and psychological interpretation of the Christian tradition, aimed at encouraging both growth and maturity. His openness and awareness of general spiritual needs opens up interesting vistas of spirituality and spiritual change that make sense for liberal Christians, but which may well also touch those engaging in other traditions and ways of looking at the spiritual dimensions of life. This is a most interesting and helpful book.'

John Swinton, Professor of Divinity and
Religious Studies, Aberdeen University

'It is vitally important these days to lead people towards religious life in a different way. Not by pumping religion into them – the old way that has failed – but by drawing religion out of them: the new way that seems to be our only possible spiritual future. To do this requires skill, simplicity and compassion for the divine element in all beings. Larry Culliford demonstrates this skill, simplicity and compassion in *Much Ado About Something*, making him a leading voice in the new religious quest of our time.'

David Tacey, Emeritus Professor, La Trobe University, Melbourne, Australia, and author of The Spirituality Revolution *and* Religion as Metaphor

'Creatively engaging his considerable knowledge of psychology with Christian spirituality, Larry's exploration of growth into spiritual maturity from a specifically Christian perspective is insightful and challenging. He sets the individual's journey of growth and spiritual exploration within universal insights about the human mind and psyche, also the richness of the Christian spiritual tradition.'

The Revd Canon Rebecca Swyer, Director for Apostolic Life (Chichester Diocese)

'As a non-Christian, I found that the insights of this book gave me a deeper appreciation of the spiritual foundations of the faith. With great charm and clarity, Larry Culliford integrates Christianity with the wisdom of modern psychology and Eastern spiritual traditions. Highly recommended for Christians and non-Christians alike.'

Steve Taylor, researcher in transpersonal psychology, author of Out of the Darkness, Back to Sanity *and* The Calm Center

'I so enjoyed this book! Larry Culliford's timely and important study of Christian maturity is a richly compelling read. His blend of the psychological and the spiritual within Christianity, combined with his originality of thought, serve to further understanding *and* experience of spirituality in our lives, at a time when materialism and rationalism seek to dominate. This is an excellent read ... truly wonderful.'

Elizabeth Holmes, author, religious education specialist and lecturer on spirituality

Larry Culliford retired after twenty years as a psychiatrist in the National Health Service to concentrate on writing, lecturing and giving workshops. His books include *The Little Book of Happiness* and *Happiness: The 30 Day Guide* (under the pen-name Patrick Whiteside), and also *Love, Healing and Happiness* and *The Psychology of Spirituality*. For over four years, he has written a regular blog for *Psychology Today* under the by-line 'Spiritual Wisdom for Secular Times'. Larry is a former Chair of the Thomas Merton Society of Great Britain and Ireland. He is a co-founder of the Royal College of Psychiatrists' Spirituality and Psychiatry Special Interest Group and a long-standing member of the Scientific and Medical Network. A church-going Christian, who is also open to the teachings and practices of many world faith traditions, and once taught by Tibetan lamas, he has been a meditation practitioner and advocate for about thirty-five years. Larry lives happily in Sussex with his wife Sarah.

MUCH ADO ABOUT SOMETHING

A vision of Christian maturity

Larry Culliford

First published in Great Britain in 2015

Society for Promoting Christian Knowledge
36 Causton Street
London SW1P 4ST
www.spck.org.uk

British Library Cataloguing-in-Publication Data
A catalogue record for this book is available from the British Library

ISBN 978–0–281–07362–7
eBook ISBN 978–0–281–07363–4

Typeset by Graphicraft Limited, Hong Kong
First printed in Great Britain by Ashford Colour Press
Subsequently digitally printed in Great Britain

eBook by Graphicraft Limited, Hong Kong

Produced on paper from sustainable forests

In memory of Thomas Merton

Born: Prades, France – 31 January 1915
A monk of the Abbey of Our Lady of
Gethsemani, Trappist, Kentucky
Died: Bangkok, Thailand – 10 December 1968

'Life is this simple: we are living in a world that is absolutely transparent and the divine is shining through it all the time. This is not just a nice story or fable … It is true.'

Thomas Merton, excerpt from his final address as novice master, recorded at the Abbey of Gethsemani, 20 August 1965

Contents

————◆◆◆————

Introduction

———————

Spiritus (Latin) = spirit, life-force, breath or wind

Spirituality for a psychologist is where the deeply personal meets the universal. Being personal and subjective, the spiritual dimension of human experience is better thought of as an adventure playground to explore – a vibrant place of fun and learning, of recreation and education – rather than a dying specimen to kill off, dissect, analyse and discard. Furthermore, being universal, this is an adventure park we are all already in.

When writing I often wake with a fully formed idea in mind, sometimes a whole paragraph or passage. Where have these words come from? It is like a gift from the ether, from the spiritual dimension. One day I awoke with the idea to write a book about the source of this gift, the Holy Spirit; to make 'much ado' about this 'little point of nothingness' within.

When ideas arrive in this way there is no sense of personal effort. It is as though your mind has continued its creative work during sleep, reaching throughout its extensive encyclopaedia of knowledge and experiences, often unknown or forgotten, beyond the reach of waking consciousness. The perfect phrase or sentence simply appears, very often to progress what was begun the previous day, completing it and setting off another train of ideas.

Having started Chapter 2, for example, I awoke the following day with the quote from St Paul in mind about the body of Christ (Romans 12.4–5), offering an ideal opening from which to reorientate myself and proceed. Sometimes the emerging ideas are more extensive and complex, having a poetic character, drawing together many strands to encapsulate something greater, something whole. 'We have gifts that differ according to the grace given to us' (Romans 12.6). The gift to me, it seems, has something to do with being able to write.

How do we know things without already knowing that we knew them? Even were there an explanation in terms of brain biology and function, as there might be, the experience remains one of gift and mystery, leaving us grateful and full of wonder. Paul is indicating that we are each touched in a personal way by the grace of the Holy Spirit, according to the will of our loving Father, as promised by his Son, the living Christ. Mindful, however, of Jesus' question, 'Which is easier, to say, "Your sins are forgiven you", or to say, "Stand up and walk"?' (Luke 5.23), it seems important to acknowledge the possibility of more than one way of saying the same thing; and to recognize that not everyone is a Christian. Indeed, living in a broadly secular, materialist culture, heavily influenced and dependent upon the methods, findings and technological fruits of science, not everyone thinks of himself or herself as a religious person at all.

Nevertheless, whether Christian, Jewish, Muslim, Hindu, Sikh, Jain, Buddhist, Taoist or a worshipper from some other religion; whether a pagan, an atheist, a humanist, a 'can't know' agnostic or simply a 'don't know' agnostic, like everyone else, you will have been affected at some level by the dominant impact of Christianity on the Western mind for the past 2,000 years. This is the powerful legacy we have all inherited.

There is a strong argument that mistakes have been made, and continue to be made, in the name of Christianity. The accusation is levelled equally against other world religions. Whenever leaders of religious organizations and their followers lose touch with their spiritual roots, problems arise – especially through inflexibility, exclusivity and associated claims of superiority. Nevertheless the re-emergence of religious expression – for example after decades of repression in former Communist countries – demonstrates the inextinguishable nature of the Holy Spirit. The renewed flourishing of religion speaks of an irrepressible urge within people to feel bonded together, consciously connecting with the divine through worship, Scripture, music and prayers.

This book on Christian maturity is about building understanding, developing faith and growing as a person, whatever your background. It is aimed at Christian clergy and lay people not too entrenched in their ways and ideas, also at anyone interested in a psychological and spiritual interpretation of Christianity, including spiritually minded people from non-Christian traditions. It may be of special interest and value to Christians who are reviewing their beliefs and practices, and questioning their faith; people who may have lapsed from religious practice but remain prepared to reconsider their religious bearings. And it is for ordinary people consciously – and conscientiously – seeking peace, hope, courage, wisdom and the great truths of existence with which to enrich their lives.

Organizations such as the British Association for the Study of Spirituality (BASS)[1] and successful publications like David Tacey's book *The Spirituality Revolution*[2] point to widespread growing interest in spirituality as related to, but distinguishable from, religion. A need to re-emphasize the spiritual dimension of Christian understanding has become apparent: 'God is spirit, and those who worship him must worship in spirit and truth' (John 4.24).

There is also an obvious need to reach out to those whose faith is challenged by scientific rationalism and secular materialism, appealing to them with ideas such as that spiritual development involves facing rather than evading doubt, and that there is a proven way forward – proven to scientific degrees of satisfaction for those prepared to undertake the lifelong personal experiment.

This book is aimed at helping you – whoever you are, think or hope you are, or aspire to become – to get clearer in mind what all the fuss is about. The hope is that anyone interested in Christianity will be stimulated to reconsider both that religion and their own deepest intuitions and beliefs from a perspective broadened by the insights of neuroscience and the psychology of personal development.

The vision offered here reveals that people can be seen to develop from childhood innocence, through a conflicted ego-identity, to advanced spiritual maturity through a series of psychological stages. From this perspective there is an early split between a person's 'everyday ego' (our egoic mind, our habitual, worldly or 'false self') and his or her 'spiritual self' (the 'true self', higher self or soul). Dissonance between these two broadens and deepens during the first half of life, then – after a transition period – the painful split is gradually healed, worldly flesh and divine spirit gradually reuniting as maturity approaches during our life's second half. But not everybody reaches this second half.

Growth often occurs through adversity rather than by avoiding it; through the emotional healing that accompanies grieving and the eventual acceptance of loss, allowing us to set aside both overambitious hopes and crippling fears; to release us from previously distorted perceptions, from desire for control and security; enabling us to relinquish the strength of our attachments and aversions to things – to people, possessions, places, activities, ideas and even beliefs. This is what Jesus offers. 'He went out and saw a tax-collector named Levi, sitting at the tax booth; and he said to him, "Follow me." And he got up, left everything, and followed him' (Luke 5.27–28).

Let go of everything and follow the indwelling Holy Spirit: this is how to become free to live with increasing spontaneity 'in the moment', more attuned also to the sufferings of others. This is how we grow gradually both wiser and more compassionate, our lives richer and more rewarding. This, therefore, is also how we become of increasing value and benefit to others.

Those interested in exploring my credentials for writing such a book might prefer reading the Afterword first. As for the main text, 'Difficulty at the beginning' is a useful aphorism from the ancient, oracular I Ching, the Chinese book of wisdom.[3] Engaging with any new, worthwhile enterprise involving unfamiliar concepts requires both time and effort. There is no way of avoiding the fact that together with an open mind, some determination and perseverance are necessary as a form of invest-ment. Backed by Scripture, by reference to other spiritual writers and psychologists and by some engaging allegories and anecdotes, I hope you will consider what you find here to be a rewarding, authentic, up-to-date, 'holistic' new vision of the timeless message of Christ.

L. C.
West Sussex

Notes

1 See websites (BASS).
2 David Tacey (2004).
3 Richard Wilhelm (1967), pp. 16–20.

1

Much ado about something

Something or nothing?

The title of Shakespeare's comedy contains a brilliant paradox. To create much 'ado', much fuss, much passionate agitation about 'nothing' is irrational, maybe foolish. Nevertheless – and here lies the paradox – this is just what intrigues an audience. As intended, such a title draws people closely into the world of characters and plot. We want to know, 'What is this *nothing* that all the fuss is about?' Perhaps 'nothing' is really 'something' after all.

The 'nothing-that-may-be-something' of this book is human spirituality. At the heart of Christianity is the idea of God as a Holy Trinity of three co-equal aspects. Consequently a vital aspect of human spirituality for a Christian involves intuitive awareness of the majesty and mystery of the Holy Spirit.

The Holy Spirit of God and of Christ, although made of nothing, far from being nothing can be experienced, both directly and indirectly. It is therefore definitely *something*. When experienced at a deeply personal level this 'something' is often life-changing. For Christians, in other words, the Holy Spirit becomes integral to everything.

'Then Moses stretched out his hand over the sea. The LORD drove the sea back by a strong east wind all night, and turned the sea into dry land; and the waters were divided' (Exodus 14.21). Christianity is full of paradox and mysteries. It challenges reason, for example, to accept that the Red Sea could part and let vast numbers of fleeing people through, or that a bush might burn without being consumed (Exodus 3.2). It is hard to credit rationally that Jesus of Nazareth was born of a virgin, turned water into wine, walked on water, quelled a storm and performed many other miraculous feats, and harder still to acknowledge as fact his death and subsequent resurrection. From the perspective of rational science these are absurd propositions; but that is only the first part of the definition of paradox: 'An absurd proposition which, when investigated, may prove to be well-founded or true'.[1] Accordingly riddles like these merit not dismissal but intense further examination and radical elucidation. Many saints and mystics knew this.

The claims and mysteries of Christianity seem irrational and hopeless to many, especially those schooled in the reasoning of science and secular culture. Nevertheless the mysteries may be unlocked from another, complementary, perspective. It usually takes time, however, to discover this other way of seeing things. Becoming a mature Christian is seldom a one-off event. More often it involves continual growth and development. For this reason the mysteries – and the Scriptures relating them – repay repeated appraisal. Even for those who already count themselves Christian, these holy words are worth the expenditure of as much energy, fuss, agitation and passion as a person can muster. First the paradoxes and mysteries are to be penetrated; only then can the wisdom be shared.

'Does Christianity amount to something or nothing?' This is a question best considered not as 'objective', with a single yes/no answer, but as a challenge inviting a prolonged, vital and deeply personal response. The question becomes, in other words, 'Could Christianity possibly hold something *for me*?' No one can decide this crucial point without careful and thorough investigation. Nor can it safely be left to others to decide, not even the saints (much less the author of a book like this), who may make useful guides but should not be accepted as final arbitrators or judges. To benefit, everyone is advised to investigate the subject fully and fairly for themselves.

Shakespeare's genius

The word 'genius', meaning exceptional intellectual or creative power, is derived from a Latin precursor translated as 'attendant spirit present from birth' – like a wonderfully helpful genie. The notion of genius thus invokes the spiritual dimension of human life. Genius depends, at least in part, on its recipient having an unusual capacity for holistic or unitary vision, for seeing things from all six sides – north, south, east, west, up and down – as well as being similarly aware of past, present and future, all at once.

Shakespeare's genius as a playwright includes these elements. He was, for example, a master of double meaning and paradox. The 'fool' in his plays often speaks wisely, but through riddles. The king is foolish and blind. Consider this from the play *King Lear*:

FOOL: If though wert my fool, Nuncle, I'd have thee beaten for being old before thy time.

LEAR: How's that?

FOOL: Thou should not have been old before thou hadst been wise.[2]

In a Shakespeare play everything said from the outset, everything that happens, counts towards the whole, towards completion. If someone sets off, disappears or takes on a different guise, you know that somehow that character will reappear and all will be transformed – usually for the better in the comedies; often for the worse, yet that people are wiser, in the tragedies. Shakespeare always brings a satisfactory sense of resolution, of closure and completion by the final curtain.

His comedy *Much Ado About Nothing* follows such an arc. Two couples are involved: the innocents, Hero and Claudio; the worldlier Beatrice and Benedick. The former come quickly to love each other, but shyly and uncertainly, and are swiftly separated by the selfish duplicity of others. Claudio is devastated, being cruelly made to believe that Hero is wantonly promiscuous. She too learns of this slander and disappears from view, dying (apparently) from shame.

Meanwhile Beatrice and Benedick are already apart, and seem to dislike each other passionately, as in the following from the first scene:

BEATRICE: I wonder that you will still be talking, Signior Benedick: nobody marks you.

BENEDICK: What! My dear Lady Disdain, are you yet living?[3]

Complete disrespect! Yet an experienced audience knows already that these two are destined to be together. The joy and thrill of the comedy involves waiting for the happy ending, while witnessing the gradually increasing rift between Hero and Claudio and the simultaneous – if secret from each other – merging of Beatrice and Benedick; the former heartbreaking, the latter heartwarming. The tension grows as the story unfolds.

There are other goings-on, of course, concerning the top dog Don Pedro and his bad-boy brother, Don John, with his henchmen: two half-siblings in conflict. The climax in the final act resolves all this. Hero is proven innocent of false accusations. She is then revealed to be alive after all, so that she and Claudio may cautiously, then joyfully, be reconciled. Next, in the happy change of atmosphere as their marriage is announced, Beatrice and Benedick are forced to admit their private loves for each other, despite all previous public disclaimers. Finally news arrives that the villainous Don John has been captured and awaits fitting punishment. General celebrations ensue.

The play tells us that love, innocence, courage and honesty – including being honest with oneself – eventually bring resolution, an end to all doubt and distress, advising this as a much better policy than one of selfish possessiveness. The implicit moral says that working together for everyone's benefit is better than striving for control or profit alone.

The play also tells us that this wisdom takes time to acquire and usually comes at the price of many mistakes and wrong turnings. Love, however, will not finally be thwarted. The greater the dissonance and distress in the early phases, the greater will be the reverse pull later towards harmony and resolution. Tension builds up in the first half but relaxes in the second; and this will serve as a useful analogy for the great arc describing the two halves of our lives, as we first make our way in the world then move on towards spiritual maturity.

The arc of life

The Christian writer Richard Rohr, emphasizing this 'journey into the second half of our own lives', says it awaits us all; but he acknowledges that although everybody gets older, not everybody sets out on this second half of the pilgrimage or makes it very far. Rohr calls this further journey a well-kept secret of which too few are aware. 'People at any age', he says, 'must know about the whole arc of their life and where it is tending and leading.'[4] With this knowledge, decisions become easier to make and carry out in both halves of life.

According to Rohr the first half involves 'surviving successfully' by establishing an identity, home-base, family and friends, livelihood, regular pastimes and so on: the essential aspects of community and security. For the majority of people this is all there is: valuing a sense of belonging and prizing what is familiar and habitual. Rohr criticizes:

> Most of us are never told that we can set out from the known and familiar to take on a further journey. Our institutions and expectations, including our churches, are almost entirely configured to encourage, support, reward, and validate the tasks of the first half of life.[5]

In expressing his shock and disappointment the Franciscan priest from New Mexico makes clear in contrast that some people, even young people, do become aware of and accept the challenge to move forward, to escape the gravitational pull of conformity, to take responsibility and work towards spiritual maturity.

Rohr's image of an arc of life, with an upswing followed by a down-swing, is a useful starting point for explaining spiritual development. In another of Shakespeare's plays, *As You Like It*, in the famous speech from Act 2 that begins 'All the world's a stage, and all the men and women merely players', the character Jaques describes seven ages of man.[6] In future chapters Rohr's two life-halves will also be expanded into seven stages, starting with stage zero: before infants begin to experience themselves as separate from their environment, as separate beings. From there we have six further stages: two on the upswing ('egocentric' and 'conditioning'), two on the plateau at the centre of the arc ('conformist' and 'individual') and two on the homecoming downswing ('integration' and 'universal'). We will also focus particularly on the transition process between stages, on how a person's arc of faith goes forward in development and matures over time. Before that we will examine unitary, holistic thinking to show how essential a way of experiencing and appreciating the world it is as we shift into life's second half.

What is a 'thing'? The word is possibly a contraction of the word 'thinking', suggesting the definition of 'thing' as: 'That which may be encompassed by a single thought.'

This asserts the idea that we experience the world primarily through our thoughts and other mental experiences. This is the realm of psychology; and one way psychology can help people grasp theology – to gain an improved understanding of God and his relationship with human beings, with ourselves – is by drawing attention to two different but complementary types of thinking: the linear, rational dualist (either/or) type and the poetic, visionary, all-encompassing, holistic or unitary (both/and) type.

As we shall see, dualist thinking is good for use with what we call 'things' in isolated relation to each other. This includes both 'some-things' and 'no-things'. Unitary thinking is better for use with the same things, whatever they may be, but in their relation to the totality of things, to 'every-thing'.

Everyone is capable of both of these types of mental activity but, better established culturally, dualist thinking is more familiar to people. It is not so easy to explain unitary thinking in terms of dualist thinking, but an attempt here will help make the rest of the book easier to follow. It is an important subject to persevere with and master. Simple arithmetic offers some clues. Consider first the simple equation $2 + 2 = 4$. This is the essence of logical thought. And $2 + 2$ *always* $= 4$. Bingo! End of argument. But think again!

Unitary thinking is 'holistic', related to wholeness. It therefore includes plain dualist thinking but also involves considering matters from the reverse direction as well, indeed from every angle – from all the six directions and from past, present and future. In this case it involves starting with the apparent solution, 4, and thinking about other ways to reach it, of which there are many.

Thus $2 + 2 = 4$, but equally $1 + 3 = 4$. Include multiplication and $2 \times 2 = 4$. Include subtraction and, for example, $7 - 3 = 4$. If we also include fractions, the number of combinations producing the same result becomes infinite, for example: $1.5 + 2.5 = 4$; $0.725 + 3.275 = 4$; $1.67686 + 2.32314 = 4$; $7.2345 - 3.2345 = 4$ and so on.

Because it is impossible to compute all the combinations, or keep in mind all the possibilities from moment to moment, logical thinking is quickly overwhelmed. This can result in an unpleasant feeling and the temptation to give up on both calculation and guesswork – as when stumped by a difficult crossword clue, for example. But for those who gain proficiency at it, unitary thinking offers a better way forward.

As distinct from dualist thinking, unitary thinking involves keeping in mind a grasp or vision of the whole while considering and con-centrating on one or more parts of the whole. To express it differently, holistic experience involves constant awareness of what seems to be missing. It offers the floodlight view rather than the focused spotlight of dualism. Holistic experiences therefore depend more on an opening up of consciousness than a narrowing down, and this takes practice. As we will see in later chapters, meditation, silent prayer and other spiritual exercises are beneficial for improving a person's capacity for unitary thinking and for holistic experience.

To put it yet another way, rather than logical calculation, unitary thinking and holistic experiences involve intuition. This implies that the mind has constantly within its power the ability to access holistic know-ledge; that the required knowledge already lies within the mind somehow, waiting to be accessed. For example, the solution to the difficult cross-word clue might in this way be revealed to a person after he or she has stopped consciously thinking about it. Holistic experiences therefore involve the patient expectation of insight, of revelation, rather than effort towards a goal. On occasion, holistic experiences can have a mystical quality, which brings the conversation back to theology.

The Holy Trinity as an arithmetic problem

The notion of God as Holy Trinity – Father, Son and Holy Spirit – is logically incoherent. Self-evidently, three does not equal one, and this is enough to baffle some people. One way to unravel the conundrum is to go to physics for an analogy rather than arithmetic – in this case

water. Imagine it as solid ice, flowing liquid and invisible gas: in all three
states, into ni liaviga iilili dependiilg on conditions of temperature and pressure, the molecule for water, H_2O, remains the same. Here, once again,
three does equal one.

A much better way of trying to understand the proposition involves
encountering God as three-in-one by opening oneself up to holistic
experience. There are the strongest of clues about God's unitary nature
from Scripture. According to that magnificent, near-hallucinatory vision
of the end of time, The Revelation to John, the final book of the New
Testament: 'I am the Alpha and the Omega, says the Lord God, who is
and who was and who is to come, the Almighty' (Revelation 1.8). And
again: 'It is done! I am Alpha and Omega, the beginning and the end
(Revelation 21.6).

Alpha and Omega, the first and last letters of the Greek alphabet, here
represent an all-encompassing symbolic vision of the cosmos, of creation.
The passage also says something about time and timelessness. Here is
reference to past, present and future, together with a note of finality: 'It
is done!' But, we might wonder, how can that which is rolling from the
past towards the future already be complete, finished? The logical, dualist mind cannot compute this. It takes another type of vision – unitary,
mystical vision – to understand. While growing in maturity, Christians
are called on to develop the capacity for this kind of holistic vision.

The term 'mystical' applies when the entirety of the universe is under
consideration. Returning briefly to arithmetic, the concept of unity can
help elucidate this further. Suppose we take the number 1 instead of 4
and similarly think back towards the fractions that might add up to the
whole number. There is again an infinity of them; the combinations are
numberless. All the worldly fractional units therefore add up to the one
Great Unit. A unitary God is therefore both the sum and the source of
countless components, seamlessly interlinked through him. The words
for God, the supreme being, the highest divinity, in Semitic or Middle
Eastern languages – *Elohim* in Hebrew, *Allah* in Arabic and *Alaha* in
Aramaic – are said to denote 'sacred unity' or 'the one with no opposite',
which translations lend themselves better than the word 'God' to a unitary or holistic interpretation and understanding.[7]

The English word 'God' is problematic because it is associated with the word 'good' and therefore implies the existence of its complement 'bad', even 'evil'. Here lies the essence of the distinction between dualist and unitary concepts. Dualism, as the name implies, divides everything into two, into polar opposites: black/white, up/down, hot/cold, dry/wet, close/distant, positive/negative, right/wrong, good/bad and so on. The two poles are complementary. They define one another, each depending on the other for its existence and meaning. They may seem to describe 'absolutes': black is black, the total absence of any white or light, for example, and vice versa. However, these two, and all conceivable polar opposites, can only exist 'relative' to each other. As such they risk incompleteness. Missing are the broader aspects of human experience; in the case of black and white, for example, not only of an array of greys but also the glorious experience of colour.

Another important set of complementary pair-words are 'masculine' and 'feminine'. The Holy Trinity risks misleading people by two of the three identities – Father and Son – being male. A corrective idea would be to consider the Holy Spirit as holding a more feminine, maternal character. This is supported by the Latin word for soul, *anima*, which is a feminine word.

Truth

We read, in the Gospel of John, these words of Jesus to Pontius Pilate: 'For this I was born, and for this I came into the world, to testify to the truth. Everyone who belongs to the truth listens to my voice' (John 18.37).

Pilate famously replied with a profound question, 'What is truth?' No reply from Jesus is recorded; but no reply is possible because the truth, absolute truth, is unitary, and words cannot fully encompass it. The great truth is indivisible, thus requiring a holistic type of sensitivity to experience and know it. The nature of absolute truth is divine. Christian maturity involves success in the search for experience of this divine absolute.

In contrast to the absolute, 'relative' truths are mundane, partial and transient; that is, they are 'of the world', of the material universe and subject to both the order of the universe and its vicissitudes. In people, relative truths are subject to the patterns and vagaries of biology and human psychology – both personal and social or group psychology. Relative truths are always incomplete but often erroneously presented as if they were absolute. This is often ignored by people thinking dualistically, notably those finding uncertainty problematic and (relatively) hard to bear.

The search for certainty, and for comfort, the avoidance of confusion and distress, is universal. In our immaturity all of us err in this way on occasion. As we grow we are able to tolerate paradox and uncertainty much better. We are better able to retain two or more apparently opposing ideas in mind at the same time: water simultaneously as solid, liquid and gas, for example; a good-hearted person who, from time to time, may speak or act with indifference, even cruelty. Accepting *both* this *and* that rather than insisting on *either* this *or* that occasions less anxiety and allows us to be much more tolerant. This is another key aspect of human maturity.

Maturity

It is unpleasant to be called immature but when we begin to think of ourselves in that way – capable of further development – we open ourselves to a satisfying period of growth and ripening. For that is all the word 'immature' means: unripe, like a fruit or wheat or a seedling tree, in need only of more water, sunshine, nutrients – and time. Ripening, becoming mature, is a natural process. Christian maturity involves moving from dualist thinking towards holistic experience, thereby gaining an increasingly clear grasp of Christianity's blessed mysteries. St Paul's oft-quoted reflection seems to confirm this: 'When I was a child, I spoke like a child, I thought like a child, I reasoned like a child; when I became an adult, I put an end to childish ways . . . Now I know only in part; then I will know fully' (1 Corinthians 13.11–12).

Paul is here arguably favouring unitary over dualist thinking and experience. Christian maturity depends on the influence of the Holy Spirit. Often when this is felt, 'something happens'. This special phrase will appear again a number of times in this book: it is again the 'something' about which we are bound to make 'much ado'.

Whenever 'something happens', a transformation, an important developmental change, occurs. In the positive sense it refers to a kind of beneficial, hard-to-explain, transcendent experience that is potent, meaningful and has a lasting effect in someone's life. There is also a complementary, converse aspect to this. Some 'somethings-that-happen' have less positive, even destructive, effects, turning people away from the Holy Spirit. Fortunately, although potentially enduring, they are susceptible to corrective experience.

Paul's first letter to the people of Corinth contains plenty that is useful when considering the concept of Christian maturity. However (as Paul admits in the following passage), these matters can be hard to comprehend – until you are ready.

> Yet among the mature we do speak wisdom, though it is not a wisdom of this age or of the rulers of this age, who are doomed to perish. But we speak God's wisdom, secret and hidden, which God decreed before the ages for our glory. None of the rulers of this age understood this. (1 Corinthians 2.6–8)

Paul explains:

> these things God has revealed to us through the Spirit; for the Spirit searches everything, even the depths of God. For what human being knows what is truly human except the human spirit that is within? So also no one comprehends what is truly God's except the Spirit of God. Now we have received not the spirit of the world, but the Spirit that is from God, so that we may understand the gifts bestowed on us by God. And we speak of these things in words not taught by human wisdom but taught by the Spirit, interpreting spiritual things to those who are spiritual. (1 Corinthians 2.10–13)

Paul says – as Richard Rohr has repeated – that not everyone desires or is ready to understand this message: 'Those who are unspiritual do not receive the gifts of God's Spirit, for they are foolishness to them, and they are unable to understand them' (1 Corinthians 2.14).

There are, though, people capable of discerning things spiritually; and these, says St Paul, have 'the mind of Christ' (1 Corinthians 2.16).

A dualist response to these passages would be to think of Paul describing two kinds of people: spiritual and unspiritual. The former are blessed, favoured by God; the latter less fortunate, in the dark, even 'doomed to perish'. But Paul clearly does not condemn such people. Calling the Corinthians brothers and sisters, he refers deliberately and kindly to their immaturity by calling them 'infants in Christ' (1 Corinthians 3.1), adding figuratively that they continue to need feeding milk rather than solid food. He writes: 'Even now you are still not ready, for you are still of the flesh. For as long as there is jealousy and quarrelling among you, are you not of the flesh, and behaving according to human inclinations?' (1 Corinthians 3.2–3).

The question is rhetorical and the answer is obviously yes. Paul is applying the holistic approach, which offers the wisest interpretation of the matter. The distinction between unspiritual (of the flesh, immature) and spiritual (of the spirit, mature) does not reflect an absolute division but relies on the understanding of a relationship between them. The two are not finite, polar opposites but on a dynamic continuum. Depending on time and conditions, and on the influence of the Holy Spirit, the one may lead to the other.

Does the Holy Spirit exist?

For a psychologist the idea of 'the mind of Christ' represents an exciting challenge. How might it properly be understood, and in such a way that makes it easier to acquire? Some insights from the discipline of developmental psychology will help clarify the stages and processes involved, offering a vision of Christian maturity – of individuals in a developing relationship with God, the Holy Spirit – that remains fully compatible with the teachings of Jesus and St Paul. We human beings cannot be separated from the whole. Christians accept that they are somehow integral to God's creation.

All human experience is mediated by human consciousness, by the minds of men, women and children. These observations render so-called 'objectivity' limited. The sciences of physics, chemistry and biology are necessarily selective and partial, dominated by dualist thinking. Their findings are always and forever incomplete. Whenever one scientific question is answered another set of questions arises immediately.

The dualist thinking of science can answer only 'How come?' questions: explaining phenomena under investigation in terms of phenomena already understood. It can offer partial explanations for the origin of life – in terms, for example, of asteroids acting as crucibles, creating and transporting organic material through space; or of lightning strikes on soups of protein-like organic chemicals millennia ago when conditions were favourable. It is much less well suited to elucidating 'Why?' questions, such as, 'Why did life appear on Earth? What is its purpose?' – the type of questions that contribute much to the greater existential search among humankind for a sense of meaning and a serviceable set of values.

Science and technology have resulted in marvellous achievements and are immensely valuable. It is hard to conceive of modern life without their benefits but it seems naive to expect that all existing problems – related to physical ill-health, mental illness, overpopulation, global food, water and energy requirements, ecological habitat management on land and sea, safe waste disposal, global warming and climate change, for example – can be resolved by science and technology in time to prevent massive levels of human deprivation and related suffering. Indeed for some of those problems, science and technology are major contributing factors. How to minimize that suffering, or to grow through it, become equally valuable questions.

Even were humanity's material problems solved, the big existential questions would still need addressing, if only because rather than offering solutions, science and technology also contribute to the problems of human conflict, man-made destruction, warfare and resulting human displacement: migration and consequent problems associated with extraordinarily tragic numbers of refugees.

Limited supplies of land, food, water, fuel and other resources divide people against each other. Is it possible that a better understanding of human psychology might help? Unfortunately, whereas the basic sciences are already problematic, allowing different interpretations of results, with psychology and social psychology the degree of uncertainty escalates. First, the minds of investigators – and their possibly unconscious biases – are unknown and scientifically unreliable factors. This makes it difficult even to agree and decide upon useful questions, to find appropriate methods for elucidating them and then to interpret results fairly. Second, the risk of being misled is high when the subjective personal experiences of many are 'operationalized'; that is, put into categories, aggregated and analysed in the quest for 'objectivity'.

In science we try to reproduce and so verify results. This is difficult in psychology and sociology. Each individual values most his or her own deeply personal experiences. It is a problem for psychologists that these are often hard to describe accurately and in detail; also the sequence of thinking about and trying to describe them has a way of altering them, by the addition of complicating associations, memories, conditioned responses and so on. There can be no certainty here. Spiritual solutions are necessary.

The holistic approach, focusing on personal experiences, avoids these problems, offering the opportunity to avoid much sterile debate about 'objective reality'. 'Does the Holy Spirit exist?' is a question seeking an objective, dualist, yes/no, answer. There is less equivocation, however, about a similar question: 'Do human beings ever experience the influence of that which many recognize as the Holy Spirit, whether called by that name, something else or given no name at all?' Even those claiming no personal experience of the spiritual dimension are obliged, with reference to the self-reports of others, to reply in the affirmative to this. Even the most sceptical person must admit that it could at least be possible.

Due to natural reticence on the subject, finding out about the spiritual experiences of ordinary adults can be difficult. Such people need prompting with questions, and need especially to have the opportunity to speak about themselves without feeling uncomfortable. Researchers David Hay and Kate Hunt, for example, once interviewed about 30 people chosen because 'They never went to church'. All responded fully and all could definitely identify spiritual aspects to their lives, but they were initially afraid of two things: being ridiculed and laughed at; and being proselytized or preached at. When they were sure that neither was happening they opened up and spoke freely. None had any subsequent regrets and most felt they had profited.[8]

In 1969 the Oxford zoologist Alister Hardy set up the Religious Experience Research Centre.[9] Advertisements in the media resulted in thousands of replies to the question, 'Have you ever been aware of or influenced by a presence or a power, whether you call it God or not, that is different from your everyday self?' In 1987 David Hay and Gordon Heald looked at the Hardy archive and selected the commonest experiences. They defined several subcategories for use in subsequent research. Questions about six of these were to be included in the BBC's year 2000 *Soul of Britain*[10] review of the spiritual state of the nation. This was the largest ever survey of the personal beliefs and attitudes of the people of Britain. As Hay reports in his book, *Something There*, religious or spiritual experiences were reported by more than three-quarters (76 per cent) of the sample.[11] The six types of experience from the survey are:

1 'Awareness of a patterning of events: synchronicity'. Over half (55 per cent) of respondents said they were aware of a patterning of events, convincing them that they were 'meant to happen'
2 'Awareness of the presence of God' (38 per cent)
3 'Awareness of prayer being answered' (37 per cent)
4 'Awareness of a sacred presence in nature' (29 per cent)
5 'Awareness of the presence of the dead' (25 per cent)
6 'Awareness of an evil presence' (25 per cent).

In a celebrated example that seems to combine the fourth type of experience with another identified by Hay and Heald but not used in the survey – 'Awareness that all things are one' – the Apollo 14 astronaut Edgar Mitchell, returning from the moon in February 1971, said he was:

> filled with an inner conviction as certain as any mathematical equation he'd ever solved. He knew that the beautiful blue world to which he was returning is part of a living system, harmonious and whole – and that we all participate, as he expressed it later, 'in a universe of consciousness'.

Apparently 'something happened' to Mitchell on that occasion.[12] He appears to have had a life-changing holistic experience; and his attribution of it to 'a universe of consciousness' speaks of a moment of direct insight, a conscious connection to the spiritual dimension of human life. Mitchell went on to found the Institute of Noetic Sciences in 1973. According to the website from which Mitchell's description of his experience is taken,[13] the word 'noetic' comes from the Greek word *nous*, which translates as 'intuitive mind' or 'inner knowing'.

To use an analogy, just as a person who is born (or becomes) totally blind cannot see, and a person born (or becoming) totally deaf cannot hear, so there may be people who are born or who become totally insensitive to the influence and experience of the Holy Spirit. It is not necessary for everyone to experience this influence. If the answer is yes in even one case, then the Holy Spirit falls within the totality of human experience. Aspects of human brain biology and function have been found to support the idea of people being hardwired for spiritual experiences and for some to be better adapted – therefore more sensitive – to these than others. The findings from neuroscience will be discussed in more detail later, as will further examples of human spiritual experience, including those occurring in childhood.

At the end of this chapter we need only be aware that there is 'something' about which to make much ado, something that has no physical substance, something of a spiritual nature that it is possible to experience directly, inaccessible to dualist consideration but readily available, in contrast, to the unitary approach. Thomas Merton put it like this:

> At the center of our being is a point of nothingness which is untouched by sin and by illusion, a point of pure truth, a point or spark which belongs entirely to God ... from which God disposes of our lives, which is inaccessible to the fantasies of our own mind or the brutalities of our own will. This little point of nothingness ... is so to speak His name written in us ... It is like a pure diamond, blazing with the invisible light of heaven. It is in everybody, and if we could see it we would see these billions of points of light

coming together in the face and blaze of a sun that would make all the darkness and cruelty of life vanish completely.[14]

Nothing – Merton's 'nothingness' – could really become a big 'something' in our lives. Each of us has the opportunity to try proving this for ourselves.

Notes

1 From the *Oxford Dictionary of English*, 2nd edn (revised 2005), Oxford: Oxford University Press.

2 *King Lear*: Act I, scene V, in *The Complete Works of William Shakespeare*, Oxford: Oxford University Press, 1962, p. 917.

3 *Much Ado About Nothing*, Act I, scene I, in *Complete Works*, p. 120.

4 Richard Rohr (2012), pp. vii–viii.

5 Rohr (2012), p. xvii.

6 *As You Like It*, Act 2, scene 7, in *Complete Works*, p. 227. The stages are: 1 infant; 2 schoolboy; 3 lover; 4 soldier; 5 justice (magistrate); 6 pantaloon (retiree); 7 in second childishness (senility).

7 See Neil Douglas-Klotz (1999), p. 27.

8 David Hay and Kate Hunt (2000).

9 Now the Alister Hardy Religious Experience Research Centre at Glyndŵr University, Wrexham, Wales.

10 *Soul of Britain*, written and presented by Michael Buerk, was broadcast on BBC2 in nine episodes in June and July 2000. See websites (BBC2 *Soul of Britain*).

11 David Hay (2006), p. 11.

12 It seems wise to be cautious about attributing so deeply personal an experience to someone else. More confident personal spiritual experiences appear in the Afterword: My Christian journey.

13 See websites (Edgar Mitchell).

14 Thomas Merton (1966), p. 142.

2

Members of the body of Christ

Flesh and spirit

St Paul told the Corinthians: 'Now you are the body of Christ' (1 Corinthians 12.27). Similarly he wrote to the Romans: 'For as in one body we have many members, and not all members have the same function, so we, who are many, are one body in Christ, and individually we are members of one another' (Romans 12.4–5). This is a rich metaphor that serves well to introduce this chapter by reminding us of the seamless relationship between parts and the whole, between the constituent 'members' (the limbs and organs) of the human body and the whole body, between each other as embodied beings in the world and between our bodies and the divine, spiritual dimension.

Earlier in the same letter to the Romans, pointing to an apparently dualist phenomenon, a distinction between 'flesh' and 'spirit', Paul also wrote: 'But you are not in the flesh; you are in the Spirit, since the Spirit of God dwells in you . . . it is that very Spirit bearing witness with our spirit that we are children of God' (Romans 8.9, 16).

Obviously we are made of flesh, but Paul is emphasizing here that for true and mature followers of Christ, the Holy Spirit takes precedence.

Five seamless dimensions

There is no reason why Paul or any other well-educated person living in the Roman Empire 2,000 years ago should know as much as we do today. Setting aside for the moment the moral aspects of the discussion, we have the advantage of understanding his binary description of 'flesh' and 'spirit' rather more comprehensively.

Using the unitary approach this involves consideration of the entirety of human everyday experience as comprising four seamlessly interconnected dimensions: **physical**, **biological**, **psychological** and **social**. These four, consisting of atoms and energy, life, consciousness and society, make up Paul's 'flesh'. The fifth – **spiritual** – dimension (the 'mind of Christ') equates to Paul's 'spirit'. These five dimensions of human experience – dynamic and indivisible – take care of everything. It is worth taking time to consider this step by step.

The physical dimension

This refers to all inanimate matter and energy of the vastness of the universe. We understand much about the laws of physics and chemistry, including the remarkable discovery by Albert Einstein that, according to the equation $E = mc^2$, energy and matter are interchangeable.[1] Like much of physics and chemistry this unvarying connection between energy, mass and the speed of light is an unfathomable mystery. Eventually we are obliged to acknowledge and accept it; to say simply, 'This is how it is.'

A great mystery, approachable through the wiles of science to within milliseconds but still ultimately unreachable, concerns the origin of the universe from the apparent starting point of a singularity – the so-called Big Bang. A vital point often ignored is that with the sudden arrival and rapid expansion from a single instant, with the birth of three-dimensional space, so also was born a fourth physical dimension: time. It was Einstein again who elucidated the irrevocable connection between time and space. As a result the phrase 'before the Big Bang' has no meaning. It is not logical to attach a dualist concept, time (which depends for existence on its relationship to three-dimensional space), to an unformed unitary whole within which it cannot exist independently.

Even if we have not witnessed an explosion, we are accustomed to the role of observer – from a safe distance – from films and documentaries. But this is profoundly misleading where the origin of the universe is concerned. Whatever we are now also began its existence *within* the exploding expansion, not outside it looking passively on. The phrase 'outside the universe' cannot therefore have real meaning for us. Each of us is an integral part of the whole; the matter and energy of which we consist have always been part of the cosmos from the Big Bang expansion. For many this forms the basis of a deeply personal sense of connection with the whole of existence.

The first atoms – helium and hydrogen – formed the first stars, which eventually exhausted their energy, collapsed inwardly then exploded to form second-generation stars and with them the more complex atoms of the periodic table, including those most important for life: carbon, oxygen, nitrogen, chlorine, calcium, iron and so on. This is all part of a new creation story, to be understood alongside rather than replacing earlier traditional accounts, including that of the book of Genesis. To many it is no less poetic and visionary.

This unformed, timeless unitary whole, out of which the Big Bang and the universe emerged, cannot be made to fit into dualist thinking. It cannot be divided. Nor can it be placed: not in time (past, present or future); nor in space. It has no location but it does exist in the human mind and imagination, if only – for some – as a conundrum. It is therefore not 'nothing' but genuinely 'something'.

This pre-existing 'something' may be ineffable, impossible to describe in material terms or human language, but it can be appreciated by people through creative imagination and through direct holistic experience. In other words this 'nothing-that-is-something' is there to be experienced and valued as the central aspect of humankind's existence – and that of everything else. There is no true break between the material and spiritual dimensions of being, between flesh and spirit. Awareness of this invokes for Christians not so much the minds of men and women but the Holy Spirit of the one God and creator, which is the 'mind of Christ'.

The biological dimension

Complex atoms and molecules combine to form life. Biologists and geneticists have offered highly plausible explanations for the emergence of life on earth – possibly seeded from some other planet elsewhere in space. Simple organisms came into being through favourable conditions, multiplied and changed form, adapting to different environments, becoming ever more complex and varied.

Despite this evolutionary account there remains for many people a fundamental mystery at the heart of living matter: the spark that took what was inanimate, gave it life, caused it to grow and directed it to develop coherently into magnificent abundance. There is an equivalent sense of mystery also concerning the reverse processes of degeneration and death, the withdrawal of life. These same mysteries have always been connected with human spiritual experience and wisdom, which envisions the animal and plant 'flesh' of the living planet and the 'spirit' of the universe as indissolubly linked.

Here is a further updating, through the mirror of another dimension, of the Genesis story, albeit employing a much lengthier timescale. In the original, after first creating the heavens and the earth (the universe), the waters of the planet earth and the sky, God created vegetation and living creatures. Next, in Adam and Eve, he created humankind. Finally, he rested.

The psychological dimension

The 'added extras' of biology over the physical dimension are life and death. The 'added extra' of psychology over biology is human consciousness, which includes the following faculties:

- cognition (thinking, calculation, factual knowledge and belief)
- emotion (painful and pleasurable)
- sense perception (sight, hearing, touch, taste, smell and so on)
- impulse (to action and inaction, speech and silence)
- additional faculties like memory, imagination, creativity and intuition.

Personal growth towards maturity very often follows a period of emotional healing from loss, and through weathering episodes of other forms of emotional pain. Some of the most powerful reactions to loss and the threat of loss concern separation from loved ones; from other people, family and friends; even from strangers with whom we have come to feel a particular bond. There will therefore be more on relevant aspects of the psychological dimension (notably in Chapters 3, 4, 6, 7, 8 and 9), especially regarding the emotions and particularly where these focus on personal development throughout life – as achieved through facing adversity and by engaging in spiritual practices. Here, though, it is already worth noting the particular intimacy between the psychological and spiritual dimensions. That proximity is often mediated through emotional experiences such as awe and wonder; sometimes through terror, as in a thunderstorm; sometimes through beauty, as at a sunset; often through sublime calm, contentment and bliss.

The social dimension

The added extra of the social dimension over the psychological involves love and fellow feeling or empathy. The words 'sympathy' and 'empathy' are similar and often used interchangeably, but it will be helpful to make the distinction between 'feeling for' (sympathy) and 'feeling with' (empathy).

To clarify this point: anyone can feel sympathy for anyone else who has suffered, is suffering or will suffer. There is sadness, regret and the wish to improve the situation, whether close or distant in time or place. See, read or hear about anyone who is sick or hungry – perhaps battered by natural disaster or a victim of man-made aggression (as we do every day in the news media) – and sympathy is a natural response to human suffering, whenever or wherever it occurs.

Empathy – as we will use the word here – is more localized and specific. It involves being with and communicating directly with another person; actually feeling how they are feeling, moment by moment. It is a form of immediate emotional telepathy that operates throughout the emotional spectrum, covering pleasurable feelings as well as painful ones. When groups of people are together, strong emotions are often in this way contagious. Empathic transfer is holistic, operating dynamically backwards and forwards between two or more people. At times some people make us feel good just by their calming presence. Some people similarly transmit mainly anxiety and anger.

Empathy is allied to intuition, operating 'here and now' from instant to instant. As such, empathic ability offers those who are open to and aware

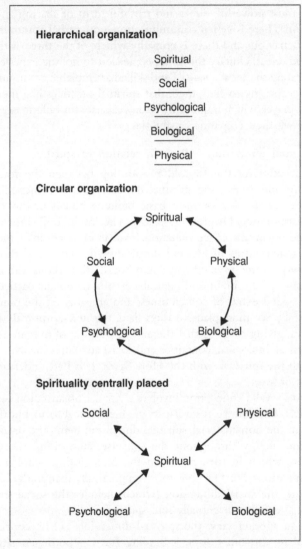

Diagram 1 Five dimensions of human experience[2]

of it the most powerful, direct and truthful form of sharing and communication. There is verbal communication, non-verbal communication through behaviour and there is empathy which, of the three, is the most honest and direct. Unitary thinkers, people alert to holistic experience, are usually among the most aware of and skilled at empathic communication. It is not surprising to find, then, that spiritual practices like meditation and silent prayer, which improve a person's capacity for holistic experience, also improve their empathic capabilities.

The spiritual dimension – flesh in relation to spirit

One conception of the fivefold relationship between the four 'flesh' dimensions and 'spirit', the spiritual dimension, is as a hierarchy, with the apparently simplest or most basic building blocks of the 'physical' at the bottom (see Diagram 1, p. 27). The 'biological' dimension of organs and organisms, of reproduction, involves more complex molecules and the added extras of life and death, growth and decay. Biology in turn underpins the 'psychological' and 'social' dimensions, through the mechanisms of the brain and central nervous system in particular but with the added extras of consciousness and empathy. At the pinnacle of the hierarchy we must place, as does Paul, the non-corporeal 'spiritual' dimension, giving the idea that the aim or purpose of human existence with physical, biological, conscious and social attributes involves seeking unity with the spiritual, with the Holy Spirit. It is best understood as a hierarchy of love.

An equally valid conception involves a circular organization (see again Diagram 1). The pattern is similar to the hierarchical form, but this adds the idea of the non-material, spiritual dimension being the origin of all matter and energy throughout the universe, comprising the physical dimension, which in turn results in the biological, psychological and social dimensions. Furthermore, more emphatically than in the hierarchical picture, the social dimension (which includes the social structures of religion) devolves eventually into spiritual reality.

Third, in another view the spiritual dimension can be conceived of as central to the other four, a binding force – both generative and degenerative, creative and destructive – linking them seamlessly together.

This model offers the clear interpretation of the spiritual dimension as responsible for the added extras of the other four: for matter and energy at the beginning of space–time; for biological life and death; for consciousness and wisdom; for empathy and compassion (see again Diagram 1).

From the spiritual perspective a vital aspect of the step-change from biology to psychology, with the arrival of higher powers like memory, imagination, creativity, intuition, evaluation and discernment, involves the capacity of human beings to contribute to change and development within our physical, biological, psychological and social environments, within the world and the universe of cosmic creation. This explains why the spiritual dimension holds the key not only to the meaning and purpose of human life and death but also to all notions of human responsibility and values. Like it or not, accept it or not, human beings are all destined to be participants as well as observers in life. We are each other's co-creators. The moral question, 'How should we best live our lives?' is therefore prominent for each of us. Once aware of it as an imperative, demanding a response, we are ready for the next move – towards growth and maturity.

The spirit within

Before looking into human spiritual development there is one more point to establish and emphasize. Paul obviously considered the people of Rome more mature than the people of Corinth. In an extraordinarily rich chapter, Paul expands for them on the distinction between flesh and spirit: 'The sufferings of this present time', he says, in other words the sufferings of the flesh, 'are not worth comparing with the glory about to be revealed to us' (Romans 8.18).

The important point is his assertion that the Holy Spirit dwells within people and finds an echo there in the spiritual nature of men, women and children: 'that very Spirit bearing witness with our spirit' (Romans 8.16). The one Spirit bears witness to the other and does so through a direct form of communication that is an immediate, an empathic ability to access holistic knowledge.

Many names, in addition to 'spirit', have been given by many writers over many centuries to this aspect of each person that is aware of and communicates with the Holy Spirit, with the spiritual dimension. For Christians it is a personal 'soul', a word helping distinguish it from the heavenly Spirit. Psychologists and other writers have also referred to it as the 'true self', 'higher self' or simply the 'self'. The term used for preference in this book will be 'spiritual self', allowing a contrast and distinction between this and the 'everyday ego', the latter used to indicate rather what Paul refers to as 'flesh'.

The Cistercian monk, writer and poet Thomas Merton preferred the terms 'true self' and 'false self'. Christian maturity, for Merton, involves the human search for authentic identity. About himself, for example, he wrote: 'There are great illusions to be got rid of, and there is a false self that has to be taken off . . . There is still much to change before I will really be living in the truth.'[3]

Merton also wrote: 'Buried and hidden within, the true self is who we really are. The true self knows its Source in the God who is Truth, and in so doing recognizes its unity with others whom it meets on a common ground of spiritual truth.'[4] This 'common ground', the spiritual dimension, therefore links each person to everyone else and similarly to nature, to every aspect of the living geography and biology of our planet home, to its varied landscapes, seascapes and the extraordinary diversity of plant and animal life. Such insights, whether conscious or otherwise, serve to inspire the heart of the ecologist within us all.

It becomes a mark of Christian maturity to *realize* – to make real – the 'little point of nothingness', to kindle the spark of a personal 'soul' within ourselves; to make it our constant guide. As it was for Merton, so it is for others the aim and substance of the second half of life to which Richard Rohr refers (see pp. 8–9). It will soon be time to look more closely at how we get to the starting point and what is involved in moving forward from there. First we will clarify some of the points already discussed and set the scene by also focusing in more detail on the biological, psychological and social dimensions with reference to what others have already written about them and their relations with the spiritual dimension.

The body of human knowledge

Like science, Christian maturity also depends upon human curiosity being relentlessly persistent, but in a different way. It entails curiosity about the Holy Trinity, about the entirety of God's unfolding creation, and the kind of curiosity that seeks both knowledge and deeply personal experience. This is human curiosity coupled with a sense of adventure.

Although strong tension, even frank opposition, between science and religion has occurred through recent history (prevailing yet in some minds), this is unnecessary according to the mature, unitary (both/and) paradigm. Consider how Christian institutions – monasteries first and the earliest universities – were the major repositories of knowledge, enquiry and education.

The split that developed as science became an increasingly secular pursuit is arguably spurious. Christians need not be averse to, much less fear the explorations, investigations and findings of science. Mature Christianity will show an eager willingness to appreciate and assimilate new knowledge, as it has in any case been obliged to do since the time of Galileo and before. It matters little, for example, that fossil records do not seem to tally with the seven-day account of the creation in the book of Genesis. The Scriptures still offer a faithful allegory of the truth. The trick is to read them creatively, imaginatively, as you might do poetry and other forms of great literature; to appreciate them holistically, rather than with the right/wrong, true/false logic of dualist thinking.

Ideally the open and welcoming attitude of the mature Christian to science is matched by a comparable readiness among scientists to acknowledge the awe-inspiring scale, mystery and beauty of the unfolding cosmos, the dazzling fecundity and diversity of evolved life forms on this planet and the astonishing wonder that is the human mind. In support of this proposition the philosopher Ken Wilber lists several pioneering geniuses of science (including Albert Einstein, Werner Heisenberg, Erwin Schrödinger, Max Planck, Niels Bohr, Wolfgang Pauli and Sir Arthur Eddington), reporting each as having 'a profoundly spiritual or mystical worldview'.[5] Those great physicists are by no means unique. Comparable to Edgar Mitchell's Institute of Noetic Sciences, the Scientific and Medical Network, for example, is an international forum of scientists, doctors, psychologists, philosophers and others, founded in 1973 with these aims:

- To provide a safe forum for the critical and open-minded discussion of ideas that go beyond conventional paradigms in science, medicine and philosophy.
- To integrate intuitive insights with rational analysis in our investigations.
- To encourage a respect for Earth and community which emphasizes a spiritual and holistic approach.
- To challenge the adequacy of 'scientific materialism' as an exclusive basis for knowledge and values.[6]

A quote from the science writer and particle physicist Jeff Forshaw adds weight to the idea of a superlative – in other words spiritual – dimension to human experience:

I am struck by the astonishing beauty of the central equations in physics, which seem to reveal something remarkable about our universe ... The natural world operates according to some beautiful rules ... We are discovering something at the heart of things ... It feels like a personal thing – like we are relating to something very special.[7]

Max Planck[8] has also been credited with writing: 'Science cannot solve the ultimate mystery of nature. And that is because, in the last analysis, we ourselves are part of nature, and therefore part of the mystery that we are trying to solve.'

So science and religion are both members of the greater body of human knowledge. There is science and there is something beyond science. There is the incomplete, material knowledge of things and there is wisdom – sacred knowledge – about how to be and behave for the best. As we look more closely at research from neuroscience and the social sciences, this distinction between material and sacred knowledge seems worthy of extended consideration.

The divided brain

Keeping in mind St Paul's metaphor about one unified body having many members, let us consider the human brain while remembering that it is not an isolated structure.

This organ, the brain, interests us particularly because of our mental capacity for both dualist and unitary types of thinking and experience. Parts of something and the unified whole of that same thing may be appreciated simultaneously. This depends on both sides of the brain – left and right – working together.

Neuroscience, concerned with the anatomy and physiology of the brain and central nervous system, clearly has much to tell us about ourselves. The human brain is not much to look at – just a pinkish-grey aggregation with jelly-like consistency – but it is concerned with human consciousness and contains upward of 100 billion densely interconnected nerve cells, each one receiving, processing and passing information to other cells. According to the psychiatrist and highly accomplished author Iain McGilchrist, 'There may be more connections in the human brain than particles in the known universe.'[9] Even more remarkably, the brain's two hemispheres, while similar, are different. The brain is asymmetrical, and the significance of this is highly revealing.

The two halves – left and right – are connected to each other by a band of between 300 million and 800 million fibres (the *corpus callosum*), yet only about 2 per cent of neurones in the cerebral cortex on each side are linked by these fibres. Furthermore it turns out that many of the connections in this transverse bundle are inhibitory. They are designed to stop the other hemisphere from interfering. Thus to a considerable extent the two brains are capable of operating separately, in parallel. They are structurally similar but have significant differences of emphasis and function. And here is a paradox: although they work independently they continuously maintain some contact with each other. Simultaneously, in other words, they work both separately and together. Indeed in the right circumstances they function as if one, working as a united whole.

According to the principle of 'contra-laterality', the left side of the brain controls the right side of the body and vice versa. In Western society almost 90 per cent of people are right-handed. The speech and semantic language centres – related to words and their meanings – are in the left hemisphere of the brain. Of the remaining 10 per cent of people who are left-handed, about three-quarters still have their speech and language centres in the left hemisphere. Of the others, some have a simple inversion of the two sides, with everything that normally happens in the right half happening in the left and vice versa.

Although brain organization does vary from individual to individual, regarding left–right distribution of hand-dominance and the contra-lateral location of the speech area, there is therefore considerable consistency. The small minority of people who differ in this regard have only partial inversion of the standard patterns of organization. This seems to increase the risk of developing psychological problems (including schizophrenia, autism, Asperger's syndrome and dyslexia), but this group need not further concern us here.[10]

That the speech centres of the brain are in only one hemisphere forms part of a design in which the left brain tends to deal with 'parts', with pieces of information in isolation, and the right brain with whatever is under consideration as a 'whole'. It has also been found that in general the silent right brain is attuned to whatever is new while the speech-capable left depends rather upon what is familiar. The right, in other words, attends to things on 'presentation', the left when they have been encountered before and are already known, on re-presentation (hence on 'representations' – images, maps, models and facsimiles).

In order to appreciate things whole and in their context, the right hemisphere has been found consistently to exhibit breadth and flexibility of attention, compared to the focused intensity of which the left hemisphere is more capable. The left half discerns things removed from context and divided into parts – parts it is able to name. From these it then reconstructs a 'whole', a paradoxical whole that is not really whole. This concocted whole is of a qualitatively different nature from the seamless whole of unitary holistic perception.

It follows that there is a hierarchy of attention, starting with the right half, which attends to what is new. Attention then passes to the left to categorize the parts of what the right perceives, according to familiar groupings. The right, picturing the whole, may broadly understand living vegetation, for example, but the left is required to pin it down to 'flower', then 'rose', then perhaps 'bush rose', 'climbing rose' or 'rambling rose', identifying and naming its colour at the same time. While attention is held on the flower, the process continues back and forth at lightning speed as description and categorization by the left side gets increasingly fine-tuned. Repeated reference back from left to right serves an important grounding and integrating purpose. The right brain is the one that always holds on to the bigger picture, to context.

McGilchrist's book about the brain is called *The Master and His Emissary*.[11] The master is the right brain, he says, but in Western culture it has been destructively deposed and usurped by its emissary, the left brain. This is a powerful argument, worth bearing in mind.

So far the two types of thinking mentioned in Chapter 1 – dualist and unitary – seem separately located in the brain's two halves: dualist to the left; unitary to the right. Further observations from neuroscience support this conjecture. In general terms the left hemisphere is concerned – even in birds and mammals – with providing narrow, focused attention, like a spotlight. The right hemisphere simultaneously provides a complementary broader and more openly vigilant type of attention, like a floodlight. How useful – such as when feeding – to be able to fix a target (like a single seed or fruit) with the left hemisphere while remaining alert through the senses using the right half-brain to changing conditions (both favourable and adverse)! This might alert an animal or bird, for example, to the appearance of predators or the disappearance of support from the pack or flock. We humans, going to a supermarket for example, require the focus of the left brain to make a shopping list, to seek and select specific goods on the shelves, while using the broader awareness of the right brain to keep track of what's going on around us, particularly perhaps what other shoppers and their trolleys are doing.[12]

According to McGilchrist, the human brain must attend to the world in two different ways at once:

In the one, we *experience* – the live, complex, embodied, world of individual, always unique beings, forever in flux, a net of interdependencies, forming and reforming wholes, a world with which we are deeply connected. In the other we 'experience' our experience in a special way: a 're-presented' version of it, containing now static, separable, bounded, but essentially fragmented entities, grouped into classes, on which predictions can be based. This kind of attention isolates, fixes and makes each thing explicit by bringing it under the spotlight of attention, In doing so it renders things inert, mechanical, lifeless. But it also enables us for the first time to know, and consequently to learn and to make things.[13]

The two halves of the human brain mediate this. They bring two different types of world into being. The left brain has been found to prefer whatever is mechanical, impersonal and abstract. Being associated with right-hand dominance, as well as the seat of speech and language, it is concerned with making and using tools and machines.

The right brain, in contrast, which sees nothing in the abstract, only things in context, takes primary interest in what is living and personal. Appreciating things as whole, it is responsible for recognizing that faces are faces, not just juxtapositions of disconnected eyes, nose, mouth and so on, as the left brain would see them. It therefore recognizes people as individuals and it appreciates even extremely rapid changes of facial expression.

The right half of the brain is therefore central to satisfactory social intercourse, and to those functions and abilities that enable we human beings to form bonds – bonds of both attachment (affection) and aversion (dislike) – through emotional understanding and interplay. The right brain, by extension, is also the seat of morality and our sense of justice, these matters being closely bound up with our emotional sensitivity to others. Patients with damage affecting the brain's right frontal lobe are less able to see another person's point of view and are therefore found to behave more selfishly. The explanation is that this part of the right brain, when healthy, inhibits our natural impulses towards selfishness. Stimuli related to fellow feeling and co-operation capture the master's right-brain attention, while those related to rivalry and competition are treated in preference by the emissary on the left. Humanity clearly benefits most when the master remains in control.

As well as identifying with others, and powers of empathy, the right hemisphere is concerned with self-awareness. On it also depend the intrinsically human capacities for humour, poetry and metaphor – and the use of parables. Consider Jesus' parable beginning, 'A sower went out to sow' (Matthew 13.3–9; also Luke 8.5–8). The left brain, capable only of literal understanding, would think it simply a tale about a farm worker being rather careless about where his seed ended up: 'some seeds fell on the path ... other seeds fell on rocky ground ... other seeds fell among thorns', and only, finally, 'Other seeds fell on good soil' – what a foolish fellow!

The left brain without the moderating influence of the right is like people who 'will indeed listen, but never understand, and ... will indeed look, but never perceive. For this people's heart has grown dull, and their ears are hard of hearing, and they have shut their eyes' (Matthew 13.14–15).

Jesus compassionately adds, 'and I would heal them'. In terms of their origins the words 'heal', 'whole', 'holistic and 'holy' are connected through a common Germanic and Old English root. The word 'heal' means to cure symptoms and make well but it also means 'to make whole'. The remedy for an overbearing left hemisphere involves a corrective balancing influence from the right. The whole brain needs to be in play for full understanding and wisdom to be achieved, because only the right brain can fully grasp the metaphor, as here: that the sower is the teacher, Jesus himself; and 'The seed is the word of God' (Luke 8.11).

Jesus' explanation of the parable to his disciples helps those who have not immediately grasped the hidden significance of the tale. The story holds in two contexts: in the farm fields and in the hearts and minds of the teacher's audience. The left brain is required to distinguish the different categories of seed-outcome (path, rock, thorns, good soil) and the right brain does the rest, putting it all together to make sense of, and learn from, Jesus' message: 'as for that [seed] in good soil, these are the ones who, when they hear the word, hold it fast in an honest and good heart, and bear fruit with patient endurance' (Luke 8.15).

Humour, including irony, satire and sarcasm, also depends on understanding the context of what is said and done. The left brain attends only to words as labels, to the literal aspects of language. It cannot grasp whatever may be implied by a communication, only what is concretely explicit. It is therefore poor at grasping higher levels of meaning, being thus confined slavishly to follow the internal logic of the given situation. Repeat the joke over and over and it just doesn't get it – ever! Make fun of the isolated left brain with sarcasm and it will not even realize it is being teased. You need the right brain for that.

> BEATRICE: I wonder that you will still be talking, Signior Benedick:
>   nobody marks you.
> BENEDICK: What! My dear Lady Disdain, are you yet living?

Benedick realizes he is being teased and returns it likewise, in spades![14]

The right brain appreciates that words that denote things can also have a wider connotation. It therefore recognizes the importance of, and even takes delight in, ambiguity and – by extension – paradox. Double meanings, triple meanings – the right brain lives contentedly, so to speak, with change and uncertainty. The left side in contrast is so averse to uncertainty and intolerant of doubt that it can only cope by picking one interpretation as correct. It is impatient with all others, which it thinks must therefore be wrong.

This insistence on being right, despite comprehensive ignorance of the much broader information available to its right-brain partner, is itself paradoxical. The left brain commonly insists it is right when it is blatantly wrong. It uses logical steps of reasoning that, because based on incomplete information from the outset, lead to irrational conclusions. It would be funny if poor inferences did not lead to unwise choices (as they often do), to destructive consequences and a great deal of suffering. While *unconscious* awareness and intuition (promoting wisdom in speech and conduct) are features of the right brain, *conscious* self-awareness and the associated capacity for expressing personal choice, will and intention is sited mainly in the left.

Surprisingly neuroscientists report that very little – less than 5 per cent – of brain activity is conscious and that, every day, people make decisions, solve problems, make judgements, discriminate and reason as it were 'automatically', without resorting to conscious involvement.[15] This alone means that the person we are conscious of being is rather less than who we actually are (for example to an outside observer), thus adding weight to the notion of a 'false self' and a 'true self' side by side (see p. 29). The process of becoming mature thus involves becoming more conscious of what's happening, giving us greater discernment, more choices and the opportunity to be more deliberate in terms of sensible, judicious speech and action. Similarly, and at least as important, improved self-awareness enables us better to refrain from unwise or hurtful speech and behaviour.

We can learn more about the false self from the observation that the pattern of tyrannical left-brain-dominated false logic is seen in people who have suffered damage to the right hemisphere as a result of a stroke. When they do not have an answer to a question they frequently con-fabulate – make something up and insist they are right even when confronted by clear evidence to the contrary.[16]

The left brain is unadventurous. It prefers what is familiar, only dis-covering more of what it already knows and doing more of what it is already doing. It avoids what is new, unfamiliar and strange. In contrast the right hemisphere prefers what is new. It is constantly vigilant for change and anomalies. Also, it is the right brain that, through shared experience, allows us to attribute thoughts and especially emotional content to another person. This is how we can appreciate what someone is thinking and how they are feeling. The left hemisphere supports only 'a blanket disregard for the feelings, wishes, needs and expectations of others'.[17]

The evidence firmly suggests that all forms of emotional perception and most forms of emotional expression depend on the right side of the brain. In psychopaths and other socially destructive people the part of the brain concerned with emotional experience and expression is significantly smaller than average. In altruistic people (such as those who have donated kidneys to strangers without payment) the same part (the amygdala) is consistently found to be larger than in normal research subjects.

The left brain mediates only the more superficial, social forms of emotional expression: the perfunctory smile of acknowledgement, for example, the slight shrug or almost imperceptible raising of the eyebrows. Of the commoner emotions, it notices only anger.

In the context of this book, left-brain activity seems to form the basis of human immaturity and right-brain activity likewise underpins maturity. A number of other observations appear to support this, such as that addictive behaviour involving intoxicating substances and gambling, for example, may be features of the left brain, having been found by researchers to be associated with damage to the right hemisphere. On a cautionary note, though, this kind of knowledge is derived from experiments that artificially separate left- and right-brain functioning, whereas they work partly in tandem most of the time. It may be better, then, to think of the two sides as functioning similarly but running on markedly different agendas. Over time these each support and encourage ways of being in the world that are mutually antithetical. There is, in other words, an apparently perpetual tension or dissonance between the two. The tension may be reduced, however, during certain spiritual practices, which we will return to and examine more fully in Chapter 9.

As noted already, exercises like meditation and prayer help promote 'unitary' over 'dualist' thinking. Although he does not use these labels, McGilchrist makes a clear distinction between two ways of thinking or knowing, attributing one to the right hemisphere and one to the left.[18] The first, he says, mediated by the right hemisphere, is knowing as *experience* in the sense of encountering something (especially someone – a unique living person) as a whole, with one's whole being, in a particular context. This kind of knowledge is hard to put into words in a way that fully conveys the experience. The second, McGilchrist suggests, mediated by the left hemisphere, is knowing *about* something or someone, second-hand so to speak, from a list of impersonal facts and observations about them; for example, date of birth, height, weight, eye colour, skin colour.

Broadly speaking, people tend to favour a left-brain world view during Richard Rohr's first half of life, adding a complementary right-brain world view during the second. Eventually, as we shall see better in Chapters 7,

8 and 9, with full spiritual maturity left–right reunification becomes increasingly complete.

Both kinds of knowledge – unique and general – can of course be applied to the same object or person. Everyone 'knows about' clay, for example, but only a skilled potter or sculptor 'knows' clay well enough through experience to become one with it and use it as almost living matter to create a distinctive object – a simple bowl perhaps – that is both utilitarian and beautiful at the same time.

According to one enduring metaphor we human beings are made from the earth's soil, from clay; and God is the great cosmic potter responsible for fashioning us 'in his own image'.

Then the LORD God formed man from the dust of the ground, and breathed into his nostrils the breath of life.　　　(Genesis 2.7)

The Lord created human beings out of earth, and makes them return to it again . . . He endowed them with strength like his own, and made them in his own image.　　　(Sirach 17.1–3)

This makes clear that we too are potters, imaginative creative artists. The Holy Spirit knows no boundaries; so we are wise to consider this as referring not only to those who count themselves Christians but to everyone. We are all, without exception, members of the body of Christ.

Notes

1 Where E = energy, m = mass and c^2 = the speed of light in a vacuum, magnified by itself.
2 Diagram from Larry Culliford (2011), p. 49, with permission from Jessica Kingsley.
3 From a 1963 letter to the theologian and mentor Jacques Maritain, in Shannon, Bochen and O'Connell (2002), p. 496; original in Merton and Bochen (1993), p. 39.
4 Also quoted in Shannon, Bochen and O'Connell (2002), p. 496; original in Merton and Cunningham (1996), p. 273.
5 In Ken Wilber (1991), p. 17.
6 See websites (Scientific and Medical Network).

7 Jeff Forshaw (2012).

8 Max Planck, physicist, 1858–1947.

9 Iain McGilchrist (2009), p. 9. This book is a scholarly masterpiece, highly recommended for those readers interested in discovering more about our left and right half-brains, the interplay between them and the consequences for the history of human society.

10 McGilchrist (2009), p. 10, for more information about people with this anomaly.

11 McGilchrist (2009), p. 14.

12 People working at the checkout, performing repetitive work, are at risk of exercising mostly their left brains. Engaging with them as people, saying 'Hello' to them by name, commenting on the weather or joking about something, gets their right brains active again and gives them a break from machine-like existence.

13 McGilchrist (2009), p. 31.

14 This expression also needs spelling out for the left brain: it is a reference to the game of bridge, where the suit of spades always trumps (trumpets over; that is, triumphs over) the other suits: hearts, diamonds and clubs. 'Spelling out', incidentally, is also a metaphor.

15 McGilchrist (2009), p. 187.

16 McGilchrist (2009), pp. 79–83.

17 McGilchrist (2009), p. 58, quoting L. E. Schutz, 2005, 'Broad-perspective perceptual disorder of the right hemisphere', *Neuropsychology Review* 15:1, pp. 11–27.

18 McGilchrist (2009), pp. 94–9.

3

Growing through adversity

The challenge

'No one can serve two masters; for a slave will either hate one and love the other, or be devoted to one and despise the other. You cannot serve God and wealth' (Matthew 6.24). What a challenge to contemporary Western values, to the desire for wealth, status, fame and power! In Matthew we read again of the rich young man who asked Jesus what he must do to have eternal life.

Jesus said to him, 'If you wish to be perfect, go, sell all your possessions, and give the money to the poor, and you will have treasure in heaven; then come, follow me.' When the young man heard this word, he went away grieving, for he had many possessions.

(Matthew 19.21–23)

Ouch! Sell my house, my car, my smartphone, my games console, my computer, my wardrobe, my music collection? Take the rest to the charity shop? Give it all away – 'Are you serious?' But yes, Jesus is serious. Give away your attachment to all these, he says, also to the fine trappings of office, even of religious office. He speaks the truth. Jesus is the embodiment of truth.

Like the young man we may well lament our situation. So how are we materialist consumer types, fiercely attached to what we have, to deal with such an enormous test? There is only one way: with wisdom – with maturity. It is no good naively saying we do not want to be perfect, despising perfection for being so impossibly out of reach, because rather than 'flawless' the word 'perfect' is better understood here as 'whole' or 'complete'. As we will see later, it is an aspect of our human nature at the deepest level to strive for personal wholeness.

So how can we benefit and grow through giving up attachment, through grieving, pain and loss, especially when adversity forces these upon us? How can we find meaning in suffering? Put simply, we do so by discovering our true nature, by letting go and allowing ourselves to be healed, made whole. Obedience, submission, surrender and acceptance are therefore important attitudes to cultivate for emotional healing and growth to occur, to obtain maturity and wisdom. For Christians this means through submission, surrendering ourselves through obedience to the will of God, aided by the irresistible, loving influence of the Holy Spirit, the ultimate source of our faith.[1]

Understandably in a culture that prizes individuality and personal striving, this is too challenging for some – for those who are not Christians, perhaps, and for those who were raised Christians but no longer find it easy to accept the teachings and promises of our Lord, the Apostles and the Saints. It may be of particular value for these, then – appealing to intelligence rather than blind belief – to look into the relevant findings from psychology. Both left brain (intelligence, reasoning) and right brain (intuition, imagination, empathy) are needed to understand first the origins of emotional pain then the processes of emotional healing, which in turn result naturally and spontaneously in growth towards maturity.

Natural laws

Science has uncovered many of the natural laws of physics and chemistry, proposes widely accepted theories about biology and has revealed consistent trends and patterns in psychology and sociology. We do not usually consider obedience to these laws, theories and trends as matters of choice or as leading particularly to happiness; but where human emotions and relationships are concerned this is a possibility worth considering. 'Happy', for example, is the first word of the first psalm:

> Happy are those who do not follow the advice of the wicked,
> or take the path that sinners tread ...
> their delight is in the law of the LORD,
> and on his law they meditate day and night.   (Psalm 1.1–2)

Another psalm tells of obedience bringing joy and prosperity (see Psalm 128.1–4). The question arises, 'What are these laws to obey, and on which to meditate day and night?'

Christians begin with the Old Testament, with the Garden of Eden and with the book of Exodus, where we find the story of God giving Moses the Ten Commandments on Mount Sinai. Here they are: you shall have no other gods before me; do not make or worship any idol; do not misuse God's name; remember the Sabbath day and keep it holy; honour your parents; do not murder, commit adultery, steal, tell lies, or covet what belongs to another (from Exodus 20.3–17).

The first commandment serves as a reminder that we are wise to think of God as a sacred unity, the one with no opposite, the entirety of being and the great whole. It is not arrogance but absolute truth, and therefore kindness, to assert this point. To accept as 'God' anyone or anything less than this totality is to break the second commandment too – to make and worship as an idol something less than the whole. From the perspective of maturity (and its associated unitary patterns of thinking), this would obviously be a mistake. One way of recognizing such an error is to catch ourselves thinking or saying, 'I need that – I've set my heart on it. I must have it!' The truth is more likely to be that we desire, rather than need, whatever it is. Most of us mix up desire with need very often.

The third commandment is about having proper respect for the sanctity of creation and creator; although with 'Holy Moley',[2] Gee Whizz,[3] 'OMG',[4] 'For Goodness' sake' we break this one frequently with barely a thought. The fourth commandment has a similar intention, deliberately setting aside time for worship. Keeping the Sabbath also helps us maintain a healthy work–life balance and positive family relationships, giving precious time to recharge our physical and emotional energy supplies, also to reflect meaningfully on our personal life-goals, standards and values. Together with the remainder this commandment makes up a list of sensible, almost essential rules, social conventions and guidelines for keeping any community healthy and together. A number of them appear as precepts at the heart of other, non-Christian cultures too.[5] In general they also form the basis for the rule of law in many countries.

Adhering to the advice underpinning these commandments gives everyone a better chance of happiness and fulfilment. The Lord Jesus knew this. He said he came 'not to abolish but to fulfil' the laws and commandments of the Old Testament (Matthew 5.17–20). When asked by one of a group of Pharisees and Sadducees 'Which commandment in the law is the greatest?' he proceeded in masterly fashion to condense and simplify the matter, emphasizing how all the law and words of the prophets depend entirely on the following:

> 'You shall love the Lord your God with all your heart, and with all your soul, and with all your mind.' This is the greatest and first commandment. And a second is like it: 'You shall love your neighbour as yourself.'   (Matthew 22.34–40)

Here lies the heart of Christian maturity. As the psalmist says, it is worth contemplating 'day and night', spelling out the true nature of our relationship with God and with each other, based upon pure love; importantly the same love we can and must find in our hearts for ourselves.

'Blessed are the pure in heart, for they will see God' (Matthew 5.8). Purity of heart and true self-love are comparatively rare. From the point of view of a psychologist, pure love is also the key to human happiness and contentment: mature, unconditional, selfless, non-possessive love of self, others, of nature and the entirety of creation. Paradoxically, selfless loving does not feel like living in obedience to a tyrant, like servitude or slavery. It feels, rather, like joyful freedom. How may it be achieved? By following natural laws and patterns, as we shall now try and see.

The psychology of emotions

However complex and unpredictable they usually seem, our emotions do follow natural laws. They depend on a circuit of fibres in the brain called the limbic system,[6] a central part of a larger dynamic and integrated system. Like colours on an artist's brush or notes emerging from a musician's instrument they are closely related and flow into one another, sometimes harmoniously but also potentially discordantly.

As we explore this wonderful spectrum of feelings, anger is a good place to start because anger frequently indicates resistance – non-acceptance – of something. If there is any way in which we may be avoiding or rejecting anything, any aspect of God's will and natural law, we do well to be aware of it. Anger will often flag it up.

Frank anger has a gentler but no less destructive form: irritability, which is frequently accompanied by both impatience and intolerance. These arise in situations where the self-serving 'everyday ego' is dominating the more altruistic and loving 'spiritual self'. The left brain seems to be overriding the right. Anger, though, often conceals – and distracts us from – other painful emotions, as the following story reveals.

In the mid-1980s I was privileged to spend a half-day per week for more than a year in the children's department of a specialist London hospital. The paediatricians had noticed high levels of stress, and particularly strong tension between nursing staff and some parents, usually mothers staying in the hospital hostel to be near their sick children. From the start I found a great deal of anger, barely suppressed and readily flaring up at apparently slight provocation.

The initial work involved lengthy interviews with a number of parents. Once the mistrust and resistance settled I unearthed a consistent story. Complaints about the accommodation – plumbing problems, room-temperature control and so on – came first, then gave way to angry criticism of nurses and other ward staff. Comments like 'They never seem to have any time' and 'They never tell me anything' were common. Curiously the very senior nurses, doctors and surgeons were seldom the targets of criticism. Suspecting they were being protected, and that there was a deeper level of concern operating, I continued my questioning as sensitively as possible. Two further levels of problem and sources of emotional pain usually emerged.

The first concerned whatever was going on at home while one child and one parent were at the hospital. Many of the families lived far away.

Some had financial problems, and while one of the parents was at the hospital unable to work the other also had to take time off to keep house and look after the sick child's siblings. Many wives found the separation difficult and worried about how their husbands were coping. Before the days when everyone had a mobile telephone, communication was also a significant problem. The mothers wanted to inform the fathers about the sick child and what the doctors were saying but were anxious that they had not understood properly or might convey incorrect information.

Finally, present all along but seldom mentioned directly in order to stave off grieving, there was the fact of the child's ill-health. Always a serious, often life-threatening matter in this hospital, it was frequently discussed at interview by the mothers with understandable displays of great anguish and tears. Basically, in the face of a possibly tremendous loss, they were frightened. Beneath the anger, contributing significantly to it, were other strong, painful emotions: anxiety, bewilderment, doubt, guilt (feeling to blame for things going wrong), shame (feeling bad about themselves) and, of course, sadness.

As a result of discussing these matters with a sympathetic nurse-tutor, ward sisters and one of the senior social workers, the unit began holding weekly 'psycho-social' ward rounds. During these the plight of each visiting parent and their whole family was reviewed and their questions were answered by the staff team. Sometimes a staff member would agree to speak on the phone to the distant parent. This new approach seemed to help all concerned.

Before this was put into effect, observations about the parents made it easier to understand the ward staff and their needs. I began running a weekly support group, attendance at which was voluntary. Everyone was very busy so only a few came each time – mainly nurses – but this was better than nothing.

One day some trainee nurses spoke about how they managed to cope with the severity of the children's conditions, and the fact that a number of them – with heart malformations undergoing corrective surgery, for example – failed to survive. When the subject first came up there was a heavy silence in the room. 'Do you ever cry?' I asked. One young nurse said, 'We are not allowed to cry'; so I asked what they did with their feelings when unhappy things happened. Cautiously, one by one, they answered:

'I cry in the sluice room.'
'I cry on the bus on the way home.'
'I cry later, when I'm with my boyfriend.'

How natural! They *all* cried! They also made clear that they were pretty fed up at having to behave differently, to suppress their grief as if they were machines rather than human beings. In other words, their sadness was mixed up with anger.

On another Monday afternoon a few weeks later, the room was unusually full. Something distressing had clearly happened but at first no one spoke. The tension grew. Looking around at eight or nine down-cast faces, male and female, I finally had to ask, 'Is there someone who would like to tell me what has been going on?'

A boy of nine, Darren, a favourite among the nurses, had died that morning during surgery. He had been visiting the hospital for a long series of operations on his heart since infancy. Many of the nurses were angry about it. They blamed the surgeon for the decision to operate. Some wanted to blame Darren's mother for allowing it to go ahead. Another said how obvious it was that he was very ill, and how she wished they had simply put him back on the ventilator, allowing it to continue breathing for him, unaware apparently that this could only be a temporary solution.

The discussion continued for several minutes. Almost everyone present had feelings to vent and wanted a say. Eventually the room quietened again but the silence remained uncomfortable. Some minutes later, though, a new voice spoke up. Debbie had known Darren and his mother longest. She knew how much they had gone through over the years and how hopeless – despite the surgeon's efforts – was Darren's case. His heart and lungs were barely functioning. His health was deteriorating. That day's operation had been a final – as it happened fatal – attempt to make at least some improvement. 'Sadly,' Debbie said, 'it didn't work. I'm sad about it . . . But maybe his dying was for the best.'

It was brave of her to oppose her colleagues but no one argued or spoke against her. This was a long time ago but my strong recollection is that 'something happened' in the following moments. The anger departed and a wave of sorrow filled the room. No one said anything. We simply sat for a while, as if held together by the sadness. One or two people shed tears. The bustle elsewhere throughout the hospital was forgotten. Time seemed to stop as we shared a sense of loss and each became inwardly absorbed momentarily by the process of grieving.

To me this felt natural and healthy. Wonderfully too, as the process continued, we all began feeling better. Intuitively the full context of Darren's recent death after lifelong difficulties and major impairment became clear. So too did the compassionate nature and value of everyone's attempts throughout his nine years to put things right, trying to give him as normal a life as possible. All anger and blame and all unspoken self-recrimination disappeared. People in the group were able to start feeling good about themselves and each other again, and about the noble and difficult work they were engaged in doing. The team was reunited. Hope and the possibility of happiness were renewed.

A psychiatrist is not a chaplain. Nevertheless during those quiet, emotion-filled moments it felt as if we were gathered in prayer, and the subtle, healing influence of the Holy Spirit was among us. For me as well as for the group they were certainly moments of transformation. This experience started me thinking about the way grieving leads to healing. That anger and resistance are transformed into acceptance and acquiescence, via the experience and expression of sadness, seemed somehow to hold the key. This is a form of meekness in the face of the inevitable but it is certainly not weakness – 'Blessed are the meek, for they will inherit the earth' (Matthew 5.5).

On the contrary, facing adversity and loss on a regular basis is an inescapable part of everyday life's work in the service of others, requiring considerable moral strength and emotional stability. This is another sign of maturity.

What is it like in heaven?

One of the first dualities mentioned in the Bible, in the book of Genesis, juxtaposes 'heaven' and 'earth'. They are intimately related and give meaning to each other. In the New Testament, however, something is different. Jesus refers frequently to something unitary, 'the kingdom of heaven', likening it to a field sown with both good seed and with weeds. He uses other metaphors too: 'a mustard seed', 'yeast', 'treasure hidden in a field', a 'pearl of great value' and 'a net that was thrown into the sea and caught fish of every kind' (see Matthew 13.24–47).

These metaphors do not refer to any duality but to an otherwise indescribable absolute, to attain which is the supreme goal for those who follow Christ's teaching. However, calling heaven a 'kingdom' is also a metaphor. Our Lord's words and the remarkable descriptions to be found in the book of Revelation conjure up a vision that is much more, and more glorious, than the realm of any earthly king or queen.

> Our Father in heaven,
>   hallowed be your name.
> Your kingdom come.
> Your will be done,
>   on earth, as it is in heaven.
> (Matthew 6.9–10)

In giving us the prayer beginning like this, Jesus himself is using the word 'heaven' metaphorically. He is not literally referring to the great skies above our heads, neither to an actual place, a location occupying space–time. Even the appellation 'Father' is metaphorical, for God is no corporeal parent like our own fathers. He is the divine whole, the sacred, timeless and invisible totality of being.

The language expert Neil Douglas-Klotz says that Middle Eastern languages, like the Aramaic Jesus spoke, allow for many different translations and interpretations of words and phrases – especially when spoken by a prophet or mystic – that in Greek, Latin or English become much more limited. As an example, the first line of the Lord's Prayer – in Aramaic *Abwoon d'bashmaya* – can be rendered as follows:

> Father-Mother who gives birth to unity,
> Vibrating life into form in each new instant ...

Or:

> O Parent of the universe,
> From your deep interior comes the next wave
> Of shining life ...

Or:

> O fruitful, nurturing life-giver!
> Your sound rings everywhere
> Throughout the cosmos ...[7]

How poetically these phrases conjure up for us a truly spiritual reality. So what is it like in God's kingdom, in heaven? Although most of us can only imagine it, we can do so by employing both left-brain intellect and especially right-brain imagination and intuition. We can, in other words, imagine what heaven is like more convincingly through our emotional experiences than according to the unfeeling use of cognitive appraisal, intellect and theorizing.

The emotions best associated with a heaven in which there is no pain or further risk of suffering will surely include joy, calm and contentment associated with meekness (acceptance), with renewed clarity of mind and sensations of certainty, purity and self-worth that extend, wave-like, indefinitely and universally outwards.

By the same token, having been celestially transformed the following emotions will be absent: sadness, anxiety, anger, bewilderment, doubt, guilt and shame. Gone also will be desire and antipathy – therefore all attachments and aversions. In heaven there will be no more wanting what we like and trying to avoid what we dislike. Free of these painful emotions; full of joy, calm and contentment – this is the best brief description a psychologist can offer of life's ambition and goal, of what it might feel like in heaven.

Attachment, threat, loss, grieving and healing

Anger involves resistance to the threat of loss. It therefore indicates that we are holding on to something. The nature of this holding on is 'attachment'. The nurses were attached to the person, Darren, and more particularly to his well-being and, finally, to his life. The remedy is always to let go.

Every desire is accompanied by a related antipathy; every attachment by an aversion – in this case an aversion to Darren's suffering and death. The two, likes and dislikes, which seem like opposite sentiments, are therefore paradoxically similar. We may hold on to our aversions as tightly as we do our attachments. This is the basis of prejudice.

Attachments and aversions are associated with feelings of desire and attraction, antipathy and repulsion. We shall see later how this plays out through the arc of life, with its two halves and six main stages. For now it is worth identifying that people form attachments and aversions naturally and blamelessly to many categories of thing, among them people, places, possessions, activities, sensory experiences, values, beliefs and belief systems, ideas and ideologies; also to many other things, real and/or imagined.

We can even be attached to one or more of the emotions, such as anger, for example, which can give us feelings of strength and energy, together often with a powerful but dangerous sense of being right and therefore 'in the right', whether that may truly be the case or not. Attachment to anger, as we shall see later, is a sticking point inhibiting progress towards maturity.

Similarly we often hold aversions to one or more of the emotions. We do not enjoy feelings of anxiety, doubt, guilt, shame or sadness, for example, and regularly seek to avoid them, consciously or otherwise. This, the discovery of the ego's defence mechanisms (denial and repression chief among them), was an important aspect of the work of Sigmund Freud and his followers.[8] Likewise nurses being forbidden to cry on the children's ward indicates an official, cultural aversion to expressions of sadness. Traditions of holding a 'stiff upper lip' and 'boys don't cry' offer further examples of this, which – in the light of what follows – could usefully benefit from revision.

Pain free	Painful
Contentment	Desire/aversion
Calm (inner peace)	Anxiety (dread)
Clarity	Bewilderment (confusion)
Certainty	Doubt
Acceptance (acquiescence)	Anger
Innocence (purity)	Guilt
Worth	Shame (worthlessness)
Joy (happiness)	Sadness

To back up the earlier statement that they follow natural laws and logic, it helps to consider the emotions as operating in a kind of dual spectrum. Each positive or 'pain-free' emotion is balanced by a complementary negative or 'painful' one, as shown in the table above.

The pain-free emotion on the left arises when the complementary painful emotion on the right is absent and vice versa. These descriptive terms are preferable over 'positive' and 'negative' because the so-called 'painful' emotions can have positive effects. Anxiety, for example, is a useful stimulant to alertness and readiness for an adrenaline-fuelled 'fight or flight' response when genuine danger appears.

The logic inherent in this system of seamlessly interconnected emotions begins with desire, with wanting some things and wanting to avoid other things.[9] As we shall explore and explain in the remaining chapters, no one is exempt from wants and wishes – and therefore from every form of emotional pain – from infancy onwards; from whenever we are born as flesh. 'What is born of flesh is flesh, and what is born of the spirit is spirit' (John 3.6).

From birth into fleshly existence our egoic minds and worldly instincts are attached to life and survival. From the onset of desire and attachment – to warmth and comfort, to people, places, possessions and so on – the emotional spectrum can be seen to unfold logically in response first to threat and then to loss.

The threat of failing to get what one wants or of losing it once attained gives rise to *anxiety*. That is what anxiety is: the unpleasant feeling that things are not right and that you need to do something – to flee or protect yourself and your possessions in some way or get protection from elsewhere. Anxiety is in addition closely related to both *bewilderment* and *doubt*. With increasing anxiety our minds easily become confused and muddled. We cannot work out, for example, whether it will be safer to go forwards or backwards in our attempt to avoid a threat. Doubt and uncertainty follow.

Very naturally, depending on a person's innate temperament, when a threat grows increasingly evident or powerful, anxiety, bewilderment and doubt frequently give way to *anger*. Now our thoughts, words, actions and energies are given over to holding on and to resisting the loss. This can be very successful, but not always. In due course we all experience actual losses as our defences against a threat begin to fail. If we have any tendency to blame ourselves, rightly or wrongly, feelings of *guilt* and *shame* characteristically take over from anger.

(We may ask: 'Surely some losses must be resisted; some things are worth fighting for?' On reflection, however, this is a question of values and priorities, which we will address as we go along, especially in Chapter 7.)

Finally, when all struggles against loss fade and eventually cease, when the loss is experienced as inevitable or as having actually happened, when the situation feels near complete and irrevocable, *sadness* arises and takes over from the other painful emotions.

As I discovered with the nurses in the aftermath of young Darren's death, sadness and acceptance of loss herald the start of recovery. Surrendering to inevitable fate, emotional healing begins by attachments being loosened. (The process of release, of letting go, is called lysis). When attachments are reduced in intensity or, better, relinquished altogether, there is a spontaneous release of emotional energy previously invested in the attachment, usually in the form of tears. (This process, purging, is known as catharsis.)

Lysis and catharsis, letting go and freeing up emotional energy by crying, weeping and wailing – this is the essence of grieving, leading to healing. Tears and other manifestations of grief are a healthy sign that the emotional healing process is working towards resolution. With maturity, emotional release can also take the form of laughter, when attachments are lighter and loss is felt less painfully, even with a sense of relief.

By this stage in life we may realize an important if subtle distinction: that the healing process involves letting go of our *attachment* to things. Therefore it does not necessarily involve losing the object of attachment entirely. This insight allows mature people to continue the enjoyment of specific objects, places, ideas and even people without being as self-ishly rigid, controlling and possessive about them as before.

Growth

Darren had died. At the start of the meeting, people wanted it otherwise. Their anger hid other feelings. Their resistance to the fact of the loss hindered their progress towards healing, until Debbie's intervention gave them a new, broader and wiser perspective. The loss had to be acknow-ledged and accepted; then people were able to stop blaming themselves and each other. We all felt the sadness for a time but it was not sustained. Somehow we began to recover ourselves.

Some losses, however, are too sudden, too unexpected, too great to assimilate quickly. The grieving and healing process is prolonged and may even stall completely, leaving the suffering person enduringly impaired emotionally, full of anxiety ('What if it happens again?'), angry (for example, with those causing the loss: 'I will never forgive them!'), sad, guilty and ashamed ('I will never forgive myself!'). But hope is always possible. Time may allow further spontaneous healing. Life may bring consolations: a new puppy to follow an old dog who has died, for example; a child or grandchild as a vivid new being to fill something of the vacuum left by losing a parent, daughter or son.

'Corrective emotional experiences' engineered through therapy might also help. Natural healing works quickest and best in an atmosphere of pure, unconditional love: 'God's love', as a Christian would say, working in our hearts, mind and souls through the blessed influence of the Holy Spirit. There was love in that room at the hospital but it could not stay focused as love of Darren or of anything mortal, worldly, of the flesh. It needed transforming, to mature into something infinite and timeless, not tied to this outcome or that. St Paul said something memorable about mature love:

> If I give away all my possessions, and if I hand over my body so that I may boast, but do not have love, I gain nothing. Love is patient; love is kind; love is not envious or boastful or arrogant or rude. It does not insist on its own way; it is not irritable or resentful; it does not rejoice in wrongdoing, but rejoices in the truth. It bears all things, believes all things, hopes all things, endures all things.   (1 Corinthians 13.3–7)

To experience pure love like this, when facing adversity, threat and loss, promotes not only healing but also personal growth. Love brings satisfaction and contentment; it brings calm and joy; and it brings people a great sense of their own purity, innocence and worth – not for *doing* what they do and achieve but simply for *being* who they are. Contentment, calmness, joy and self-worth give powerful protection against desire, hatred, anxiety, bewilderment, doubt, guilt, shame and sadness – also anger, for in a state of grace and contentment no loss threatens; anger is therefore wholly redundant.

Peace reigns in the kingdom of heaven, but few among us have experienced it – not yet! We continue to experience desires and aversions and so be susceptible to the painful feelings associated with attachments and the threat of loss. Nevertheless as time goes by and as we experience and endure more adversity, we naturally develop increasing equanimity, emotional resilience and stability. We grow wiser, calmer, clearer in mind, more certain of ourselves and our world, less angry, guilty and ashamed and less frequently sorrowful.

Each episode of loss from which we are healed leaves us less fearful of what might happen in the future, less regretful of what has happened in the past, less anxious generally. We become more spontaneous and better able to live in the moment, ready to engage anew with people and places, with activities; and better able too to sit still and quietly contemplate our life's path and values.

Similarly we are naturally more aware of the plight and suffering of our fellow human beings, susceptible as ourselves to attachments, losses, accidents, injuries, mental afflictions, ill-health, ageing and, finally, death. This new awareness of the context of our own life, as just one among countless others, brings life and energy to our natural faculties of empathy and compassion. This too is what makes us wise. Wisdom without compassion is false; compassion without wisdom quickly leads to exhaustion. Even Jesus could not bring healing to everyone. The nurses in the children's hospital finally knew that all the medical skill and technology in the world could not revive and sustain young Darren. We are born to die, as 'dust to dust, and ashes to ashes'. We must eventually lose all our possessions, relinquish all our attachments. Growing in maturity involves preparing ourselves for that.

The nature of belief

Belief is no more than an intense form of attachment – to an idea, an ideology or some form of theology.

I believe in God the Father Almighty, maker of heaven and earth:

And in Jesus Christ his only Son our Lord, who was conceived by the Holy Spirit, born of the Virgin Mary, suffered under Pontius Pilate, was crucified, dead, and buried, he descended into hell; the third day he rose again from the dead, he ascended into heaven, and sitteth on the right hand of God the Father Almighty; from thence he shall come to judge the quick and the dead.

I believe in the Holy Spirit; the holy Catholic Church; the Communion of Saints; the Forgiveness of sins; the Resurrection of the body, and the life everlasting. Amen.

(Slightly adapted from the Book of Common Prayer)

This, the Apostles' Creed, is said by worshipping Christians at every service of morning and evening prayer. If we take only the first four words, 'I believe in God', there is already much to discuss, three separate concepts: 'I', 'believe in' and 'God'.

The first question, asked infrequently but with much to commend it, is: 'Who is the "I" that is affirming belief?' In other words, we do well to ask ourselves from time to time: 'Who am I? What is my true nature?' This is a real challenge to think about. In everyday circumstances we define ourselves by our name, where we live, where we come from, our language and dialect, gender, physical appearance, likes and dislikes, including our sexual orientation and political affiliation – and by our religious (or non-religious) beliefs. We arrive at a long list of attachments and aversions. If we can agree that the 'I' is defined in part by what we 'believe in', an element of circularity has crept in. The question remains: 'What does that imply?'

According to the dictionary, 'believe' has two similar meanings but one stronger than the other. The first is 'To accept that something is true, especially without proof'. The second, weaker, is 'To hold something as an opinion'. To 'believe *in*' is slightly different again. This means 'To have faith in the truth or existence of something or someone'; also, less robustly, 'To have confidence in something or someone'.[10]

This all seems to boil down to the strength with which the 'I', the egoic mind, is attached or wedded to the idea under consideration, ranging from utter conviction to a relatively weak opinion. This is all based on the 'I', the 'everyday ego'. The question has changed from one seeking an *absolute* yes/no answer ('Do you believe?') and has become one with a *relative* answer ('How strong is the belief?'). On the other hand, for the 'spiritual self' there is no question of belief or disbelief. It knows. The knowledge is based on deep personal experience. It does not know how it knows; but, beyond all argument, it does.

Because it is a matter of personal experience rather than scientific or philosophical deduction, this is a point for which no proof is available. To pit one strongly held opinion against another is futile. One way round it, for a Christian, instead of arguing might be to say, 'I live by (or try to live by) the idea that the Christian message summarized in the creed is true.' No one could argue with your intent.

For the everyday ego the possibility of doubt accompanies every credal statement. This may seem paradoxical because doubt makes us feel uncomfortable, but just as anxiety can be useful, so can doubt.

Doubt is necessary for growth. Many people who once learned the Apostles' Creed, saying it regularly and religiously, eventually stop doing so. Could they be acting out of wisdom? Doubts having arisen in their minds, they no longer choose to ignore them. The strength of their belief, of their attachment to the ideas expressed in the creed, becomes weakened. It feels wrong to keep repeating what no longer seems to them unequivocally true. It may seem more honourable, if we find ourselves in that predicament, to stop saying it and to stop attending services where it is said.

Thinking and taking responsibility for ourselves instead of unthinkingly conforming to the patterns of thought, speech and behaviour set by our family and community, including our faith community, is an essential aspect of the transition from the first to the second part of life. It is only the beginning, however, because when we relinquish hold on a belief we have a choice to make: to continue defining ourselves according to a negative, to what we do not believe; or to go in search of something more satisfying to believe in and live by. As we go along, chapter by chapter, we will look again more closely at how people grow increasingly mature by dealing positively with choices like this.

The psychology of sin and repentance

The Book of Common Prayer version of the Lord's Prayer (based on Matthew 6.11–13) continues from the opening quoted above as follows:

> Give us this day our daily bread.
> And forgive us our trespasses,
> As we forgive them that trespass against us.
> And lead us not into temptation;
> But deliver us from evil.

'Trespass' is replaced in other versions by either 'debt' or 'sin'. A psychologist will note keenly, then, the implication here that someone is deemed to have done wrong to someone else. In other words 'sin' refers to an aspect of human relationships: either with other people (in whose debt we are or who have trespassed against us) or with God.

Problems people have with sin particularly concern the apparent futility of attempting sinless engagement with a deity who is perfect. Despite wanting to behave well we are all bound to fail. We are bound, therefore, frequently to experience anxiety, bewilderment and doubt (about how to think, speak and act correctly in God's eyes), also shame and guilt when we feel we have fallen short – or sense that we are about to. This is all very exasperating. No doubt we will get angry too – either with God, with Jesus, the Church, the ministers, the faithful, with ourselves or with 'all of the above'!

Sometimes we will also truly lament our actions – or failure to act – and feel sad. This sadness and the accompanying emotional release of catharsis, just as in the process of emotional healing described earlier, heralds the restoration of contentment, calm, clarity, certainty and acceptance, accompanied by renewed feelings of worth, purity and joy. These ideas therefore fit with the broader translation of the Aramaic word for 'forgive' which, according to linguists,[11] can also mean to 'set free', 'let go', 'loosen', 'leave out' or 'restore something to its original state'.

When we lament and feel genuine remorse in this way it fits logically that the relief we feel is accompanied by a spontaneous sense of being forgiven. This in turn might bring with it a strong feeling of gratitude, also the robust intention both to make amends where possible and to improve our behaviour in future. In addition, aware of the effect of our transgressions on other people, natural compassion will ensure that we become more considerate in what we say and do. This is how we grow wiser, learning from our mistakes. This is a brief account, then, of the psychology of repentance.

Many people, however, consider sin an either/or, black/white, guilty/innocent matter. Even today, in some religious communities, the Ten Commandments are enforced rigidly, leading to situations, for example, in which young unmarried women who fall pregnant are ostracized and ejected, leaving them with a lasting burden of isolation, suffering and shame. This is the regrettable antithesis of forgiveness.

A more mature, less accusatory way of looking at sin, based on psychology, invokes the idea of dissonance, which we have already met in this book: the dissonance between the lovers Beatrice and Benedick, for example; also between the brain's rational left hemisphere and its imaginative, intuitive right hemisphere, and between the false, incomplete everyday ego and the true, whole spiritual self. The word 'dissonance' refers to a combination of musical notes sounding as if they need resolution; and it is used metaphorically here to suggest deliberately an unstable situation seeking the restoration of harmony.

For most of us, much of the time, there is a split between the conflicted everyday ego and the serene spiritual self. Put simply the ego, influenced by material goals (success, celebrity, wealth, power and so on), tends towards selfishness in thought and behaviour; while the soul, under the influence of the Holy Spirit, tends wholly towards selflessness and altruism.

In life, as we mature there is a constant, dynamic tension between the two. Imagine a length of thin wire, like a guitar string, strung horizontally between two points. Immobile it forms a straight line; set in motion by plucking it vibrates rapidly in a way that makes it impossible to see the string except as a blur. Eventually the energy from the plucking motion dissipates. The amplitude of the vibration reduces until the string becomes motionless and clearly visible again. While in motion the string's vibration results in the air around it vibrating too. In other words it causes a disturbance, a wind that, carried to our ears, becomes translated into sound. The nature of the sound depends on the degree of tension in the wire. Its volume depends on the force with which it is plucked. When it is plucked repeatedly, with the tension varying from moment to moment, there is a strong possibility of discord.

Life is like that. From infancy we are each subject to various needs, desires and aversions of varying strengths from one minute to the next. The still, silent soul-string, so to speak, is set in motion. The dissonant, sound-producing everyday ego is like the moving wire. As it follows natural laws, God's laws, including the laws of physics, energy dissipates. Unless and until it is triggered once again its tendency is always to return to its resting state. In this case the energy concerned is emotional energy invested in our attachments and aversions. Once these are relinquished the dissonance naturally collapses: resolution, healing and growth are achieved.

According to this description, 'sin' equates more to tension, to the dissonance *within* as we follow our desires, than to the breaking – deliberate or otherwise – of externally imposed commandments. Jesus said much the same. Without diluting the Old Testament laws he gave them a vital new and loving interpretation. Here is a wonderful example:

The scribes and the Pharisees brought a woman who had been caught in adultery ... they said to him, 'Teacher ... Moses commanded us to stone such women. Now what do you say?' ... Jesus bent down and wrote with his finger on the ground. When they kept on questioning him, he straightened up and said to them, 'Let anyone among you who is without sin be the first to throw a stone at her.' When they heard it, they went away, one by one ... Jesus ... said to her, 'Woman, where are they? Has no one condemned you?' She said, 'No one, sir.' And Jesus said, 'Neither do I condemn you. Go your way, and from now on do not sin again.'   (John 8.3–11)

This is mature love in action. Love begets compassion, kindness, tolerance, understanding and wisdom. Imagine this woman's sense of relief and gratitude! Through his gentleness and patience Jesus had, we could say, healed the dissonant split in her psyche. Doubtless he had also won over a committed and devoted follower. He gave the scribes and Pharisees – and us – something to think about too.

Notes

1 The name for the religion 'Islam' translates into English as 'submission', submission in particular to the will of Allah, of God.
2 'Holy Moses!'
3 'Jesus!'
4 'Oh my God!'
5 The five precepts of Buddhism, for example, include avoiding the following: destroying life; stealing; sexual misconduct (including adultery); telling lies; intoxicating substances (including alcohol, nicotine and other drugs). See Rahula (1959).
6 The limbic system includes the amygdala, mentioned in the previous chapter.

7 Neil Douglas-Klotz (1999), p. 20.

0 Other common defence mechanisms include projection, displacement, distortion, dissociation, reaction formation and somatization. See Anna Freud (1937); also George Vaillant (1992).

9 This is given substantial emphasis in Buddhist teaching. According to the second of the Four Noble Truths, suffering is due to unrestrained desire – often described as craving, passionate greed or thirst – particularly for existence itself and for sense-pleasures during life. See Rahula (1959), ch. 3.

10 Definitions from the *Oxford Dictionary of English*, 2nd edn (revised 2005), Oxford: Oxford University Press.

11 Douglas-Klotz (1999), p. 45.

4

The arc of life

---◆---

Going with nature's flow

Some tropical plants have stems covered with thousands of downward-facing little spikes to deter climbing insects. Run your hand up these stems and the resistance is strong, even painful. Alternatively, grasp the stem and run your hand downwards and the feeling is completely smooth.

St Paul's account of his conversion on the road to Damascus includes his description of seeing a light from heaven and hearing a voice that says to him, 'Saul, Saul, why persecutest though me? It is hard for thee to kick against the pricks' (Acts 26.14 KJV). Other versions substitute 'goads' for 'pricks' but I prefer this one because it brings to mind those plants and their spicules, the little pricks that cause resistance and pain in one direction only. In effect God was saying to Saul (who became Paul), 'Go with the flow of your true nature and all will run smoothly for you.'

To use a comparable metaphor, it is hard to swim upstream. It is much easier to relax, letting the current decide our direction and carry us along – until we reach rapids or a precipice of course.

Traffic lights

As people leading everyday lives in a turbulent, pressurized, consumerist society we often find ourselves experiencing unpleasant tension or stress. So it was with Peter, a successful man, always busy on behalf of his employer. When his two young children, Patrick and Susan, had started school, Peter's wife Evelyn resumed part-time work as a nurse.

They were a Christian family but on Sundays Peter excused himself from church, saying he needed the time to catch up with chores around the house and in their small garden. He admitted that, of the two, his wife's faith was stronger.

Evelyn had been aware for several months that Peter was unhappy. His mood was often irritable, seeming to improve at the weekends and deteriorate again as the week approached. One nightmarish Sunday evening he erupted in anger over a trivial matter, shouting at Evelyn and frightening the children. The following morning, driving along his regular route to work, Peter became angry and impatient as the traffic built up at an obstruction. He yelled at a driver whose vehicle was moving slowly, and undertook a sudden, dangerous manoeuvre to get past it. Having done so he was even more furious when the traffic light in front of him suddenly changed to red, forcing him to brake hard.

During the 60 seconds he was sitting there before the light changed, aware of the slower driver coming up behind, Peter felt guilty and ashamed of his actions. He also remembered his wife saying, the night before, that he was behaving out of character and asking what was wrong. He had denied any problems but now began to think about the situation more objectively. He began, for the first time, properly considering his present anger and his general unhappy mood. After the lights changed he pulled safely off the road to consider the matter for a while.

Asking himself what could have been going wrong, Peter closed his eyes for a moment. His boss had been promoted and replaced a few months earlier. The new manager was very efficient. He seemed fair and likeable to most of Peter's colleagues but the change of personnel had upset him. The new boss reminded him of his authoritarian father, who always seemed to demand more effort and seldom gave any praise. Peter realized he had been dreading the Monday-morning managerial meetings. Despite improving results each month he felt increasingly exposed, imposed upon and frustrated.

As he sat in his car Peter gradually began feeling calm and in control again. When he opened his eyes the first thing he noticed was the small wooden crucifix Evelyn had put there. Dangling from the rear-view mirror support it made him think of her, and he smiled. Armed with new insight into what had been troubling him he formulated a plan. First he called Evelyn to apologize for his recent bad temper; also to arrange a dinner date with her the following Friday and a special treat day out with the children on Saturday. He was going to apologize, explain and compensate them too. Peter was determined that family life would regain priority over his work, even if it meant switching jobs.

The second part of the plan was to follow up the morning meeting by saying something, calmly and privately, to his new manager about how he had been feeling overstretched and undervalued. This began a new and happier phase between them. It started with his boss, Jack, admitting he was in awe of Peter's record of success at work and that he had been thinking of him as a rival rather than a colleague. In the days after their discussion Jack took Peter into his confidence and asked his advice more frequently. They were able to work much better together and soon set about ensuring that others among the close-knit workforce felt fully appreciated, no longer taken for granted. The productivity level of their department quickly improved to superior levels, to everyone's satisfaction.

A decade or so later Peter was an altogether happier man. To mark his fiftieth birthday, together with Evelyn, Patrick, Susan, his elderly parents and a group of close friends he took a ride on the giant London Eye Ferris wheel. It was a crisp, bright day and the views of the city were tremendous. The experience was invigorating. Peter felt at the time, too, that it was somehow symbolic. He noticed that the great wheel's rotation never stops. You enter one of the pods and it begins to carry you up. You rise slowly, higher and higher, so that it is a challenge to pick out exactly when you have reached the arc's zenith. At some gentle changeover point, though, you begin your graceful descent. At the bottom you have to hop or shuffle off again and leave.

As they circled and went down it occurred to Peter that he was now descending comfortably from a high point in his life. Surrounded by people he loved and felt loved by, it was a happy thought. He no longer needed to work quite so hard to set and achieve worldly goals or to achieve the goals set by others with whom – he was now able to see – he was barely in tune. Time has passed and there have naturally been numerous problems for Peter (a certain amount of adversity and many difficult decisions), but since turning 50 he has felt the force of a kind of natural gravity, gently ensuring that he continue to move forward in the right direction while maintaining his equilibrium.

There was no specifically discernible moment of change, other than that time at the traffic lights, but he had gradually begun realizing how futile it was to try to oppose the natural way of things and the way God seemed to want him to be. Now, for example, he joins Evelyn in church on Sundays – and the teenage children, when they can be persuaded. Still uncertain of his beliefs, Peter has nevertheless accepted that he belongs as a member of the Christian community. In addition he coaches a schoolboy football team and sometimes plays piano favourites at a nearby care home for the elderly. Being increasingly true to his deepest inner 'spiritual self', Peter is now firmly in the second half of his life and an asset to his community.

Psychologist pioneers

William James (1842–1910)

William James was the first psychologist to take a major interest in religion and spirituality. His book, *The Varieties of Religious Experience*, based on the Gifford lecture series delivered at Edinburgh University between 1900 and 1902, was highly influential and remains relevant today.[1] Asserting that something within people seeks meaning in life beyond everyday concerns, James defined religion as: 'The feelings, acts and experiences of individual men (people) in their solitude, so far as they apprehend themselves to stand in relation to whatever they may consider the divine.'[2]

This deeply personal interpretation seems more consistent with what, in this book, we call 'spirituality'. James had a background in medicine and philosophy. He thought of himself as a pathfinder, intent on applying the scientific methods of the time. To justify his enquiry into a then neglected topic he wrote: 'To the psychologist, the religious propensities of man must be at least as interesting as any other of the facts pertaining to his mental constitution.'[3]

James's even-handedness, plus a naturalistic style of observation and description, ensured a degree of compatibility with the aims and methods of the science of his time, such that he is now considered one of the founders of modern psychology. His book has almost 500 pages of description and analysis of deeply personal experiences (under headings that include 'Healthy-mindedness', 'The sick soul', 'Conversion', 'Saintliness', 'Mysticism' and 'Repentance'), followed by a short chapter of conclusions. A brief summary of his findings is worth repeating here:

1 The visible world is part of a more spiritual universe from which it draws its chief significance.
2 Union or harmony with that higher universe is our true end.
3 Prayer or inner communion with the spirit thereof is a process wherein work is really done, and spiritual energy flows in and produces effects, psychological and material, within the phenomenal world.
4 Religion brings a new zest, which adds itself like a gift to life, taking the form either of lyrical enchantment or of appeal to earnestness and heroism.
5 It brings an assurance of safety and a temper of peace, and, in relation to others, a preponderance of loving affections.[4]

Although James's work linking psychology and religion was new and impressive it was not taken up directly in academic circles. Psychologists of the time considered it too religious; theologians found it too psychological. Other spiritual writers met similar obstacles to gaining widespread acceptance.

Pierre Teilhard de Chardin (1881–1955)

Teilhard de Chardin was a Jesuit priest. Nevertheless his controversial written work was rejected in his lifetime by the Roman Catholic authorities. His defining books, *The Divine Milieu*,[5] an essay on the interior life (written in 1927), and *The Phenomenon of Man*,[6] an evolutionary alternative to the traditional creation story of the book of Genesis (written in 1938), were only published after his death.[7] Initially a teacher of physics and

chemistry, Teilhard de Chardin later became a distinguished palaeontolo
gist and geologist. Given his scientific training, and experiences searching
and excavating in the field, it is understandable that he thought religion
and science, 'must necessarily meet at some pole of common vision'.[8]

Setting out to explore this intersection he developed the idea of the
cosmos as God's 'evolutionary creation'. According to Teilhard de Chardin
this universe, bringing love of God and love of the earth together, consists
of unified 'spirit-matter' and is evolving towards the spiritual fulfilment
of consciousness and human personality at what he called 'Omega Point'.
In summarizing his observations and reasoning it would be easy to make
errors of oversimplification. In terms of psychology, however, the following quotations point us towards his conclusions:

> Love alone is capable of uniting living beings in such a way as to
> complete and fulfil them, for it alone takes them and joins them
> by what is deepest in themselves.
>
> All we need is to imagine our ability to love developing until it
> embraces the totality of men and the earth ... A universal love is
> not only psychologically possible; it is the only complete and final
> way in which we are able to love.

Teilhard de Chardin's contributions are particularly noteworthy for extending William James's ideas from the personal to the collective, from individual
spiritual growth to the psychological and spiritual evolution of humanity.

Carl Jung (1875–1961)

A Swiss psychologist and psychiatrist, Jung also decisively linked the
personal with the collective. His father was a Protestant minister. However,
Jung, like James, was interested in but did not support organized religion.

Many of Jung's relatively well-known ideas have entered contemporary folklore.[9] He wrote extensively throughout a long life and, like
Teilhard de Chardin, developed a forward-looking psychology incorporat-
ing ideas about human spirituality. A translated collection of his essays
is called *Modern Man in Search of a Soul*.[10] Unlike his former teacher and
collaborator, Sigmund Freud, Jung took a favourable interest in the
spiritual lives and development of his patients. He made links with the

symbols and myths of many cultures, including indigenous cultures, observing widespread similarities. His influential theories about 'arche-types' and 'the collective unconscious' grew from these observations.

Jung relates the human conscious and unconscious minds according to a pattern of development. The conscious mind starts as the domain of the habitual, personal 'I' (the 'everyday ego' of this book). According to Jung, as this limited self-awareness grows it comes to relate first to the personal unconscious and then to the collective or universal uncon-scious, bringing them increasingly into personal awareness.

Jung calls the personal unconscious 'the shadow'. Each conscious everyday ego has its unconscious shadow, a term used to represent all drives, idiosyncrasies, attachments and aversions at odds with prevailing social standards and peer pressures. In the early stages of development each of us forms, and tries to hold on to, an ideal image of our own identity, the perfect person we hope – and try to convince ourselves – we are. The 'shadow' is always at variance with aspects of this, wherever and whenever we fall short of our ideal.

Naturally, finding our shadows unacceptable we repress them. We automatically banish them into unconsciousness because they include everything concerning ourselves we are ashamed of and do not want to admit. In everyday life, therefore, we hide our shadows behind a kind of mask, which Jung called the 'persona'. We then have a strong tendency to 'project' our shadows on to others, to see faults in them we deny in ourselves:

> how can you say to your neighbour, 'Let me take the speck out of your eye', while the log is in your own eye? ... first take the log out of your own eye, and then you will see clearly to take the speck out of your neighbour's eye. (Matthew 7.4–5)

The way forward is for each ego gradually to become aware of and confront its shadow, to accept and integrate the painful components. This means letting go of attachment to the false ideal we have been trying to maintain.

As with the healing process, letting go is likely to be followed by the release of emotional energy through tears – tears of shame as well as sadness but tears eventually, too, of relief. When reconnection with our true nature is achieved and becomes firmly established, the false mask or 'persona' can – either abruptly but usually gradually – be discarded. Then we will seem more natural, transparent and friendly to others than before, better capable of intimacy in relationships. We will find other people's masks more transparent too in return.

This is how our narrow personal everyday ego expands into what Jung called simply the 'self' (in this book, the 'spiritual self'). It is this self that communicates with the collective unconscious. A Christian way of putting it is that each individual 'soul' remains directly in communication with the universal 'Holy Spirit'. According to Jung, the 'self' is a much less inhibited version of each person than the 'ego'. As we grow to inhabit it we feel and appear far more relaxed, content, intuitive and spontaneous. Communication between Jung's self and the collective unconscious is mediated, he says, through 'archetypes' shared by all members of humanity, whatever their personal history or cultural background. These archetypes are found particularly in art, literature (including Scripture), symbols (including religious symbols, icons), myths (including tribal and cultural myths) and in dreams. Jung reports that in dreams the archetype of the self often appears as a magical or golden child.

These archetypes also include a feminine principle, the 'anima', and a corresponding masculine principle, the 'animus'. The self has access to both, bringing balance to the personality. Women can assume male characteristics when necessary; men can take on female attributes – the unitary principle of wholeness is thereby maintained.[11] Importantly, according to Jung the self involves a person's awareness of his or her unique nature, and of having an intimate relationship with everything, with all life (people, animals and plants), with the inanimate too and so with the entirety of the cosmos.

The value of a map

The ideas generated by James, Teilhard de Chardin and Jung are consistent with the scheme of spiritual development outlined in the following pages. It can be summarized in a diagram (see Diagram 2). However, when

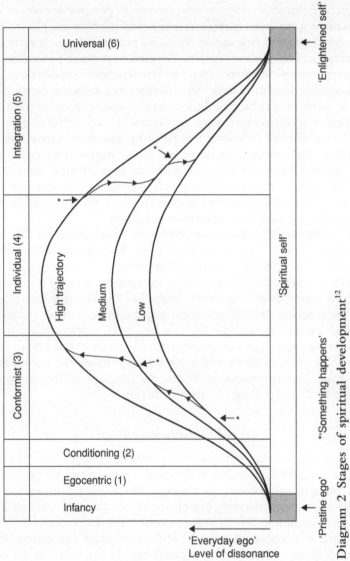

Diagram 2 Stages of spiritual development[12]

examining this static, diagrammatic account of personal growth towards maturity it is important to remember its potential limitations. The multidimensional reality of each human life it aims to represent will, in every case, be richer and much more complex. We speak in terms of 'personality' and of 'temperament', of inherited traits and environmental conditioning. Our lives are filled, from before birth, with countless major and minor factors affecting who we are and become. People are the same in many ways but also different in others. We have much in common but each one of us is unique.

Having said that, wherever we start from and wherever we hope to travel on life's spiritual journey, a serviceable map will be useful. The diagram is offered as a structural guide for both personal and general enquiry into human development, acknowledging ourselves and each other as beings of seamlessly interconnected physical and spiritual dimensions, of 'spirit-matter', of both bodies and souls.

The explorer Alexander von Humboldt[13] said something like this: 'To find out what a place is really like, you have to stop reading about it in the library. You have to actually go there.'

These words offer advice on how to make the most of this chapter and the whole book. It is not the manual of a technical machine but a sketched outline of life's path for living, breathing, sentient organisms, human beings, you and me. So it is best read as preparation for the continuing journey, and of deeply personal relevance. It is best to learn from and use it creatively and imaginatively – to use the right side of the brain, in other words, as well as the left. Ways of improving our ability to do this will be covered in Chapter 9.

The bottom line

The shortest distance between two points is a straight line. The two points along the bottom line in Diagram 2 are 'onset of life' on the left and 'full spiritual maturity' on the right. The journey from one to the other is not straight: it describes an arc, the endpoint of which is back on the bottom line. We do well to examine this more closely.

When does a human life begin? At the moment of conception, when a man's sperm first fertilizes a woman's egg? In the womb as the early embryo develops into a viable foetus? At some other point during gestation? Or only at the moment of birth? This has become an important moral and ethical question. However, as readers will have reached adulthood, past these early landmarks, the matter is no longer so important here. A psychologist will be more interested in when consciousness and memories first begin. Before that moment, according to another pioneering psychologist, Donald Winnicott,[14] we are each blessed as infants with a 'pristine ego', which he defined as 'a component of self which possesses a purity, wholeness, untarnished innocence and spontaneity'.[15] This pristine ego is therefore the forerunner of the spiritual self, staying with us and influencing us all our days.

There are various ways of describing full spiritual maturity. Christians will think in terms of 'sainthood' or 'sanctity'. In popular culture the term 'enlightenment' is used. The psychologist Reza Arasteh, another important contributor to the discussion, developed a theory of personal development leading to the goal of what he called 'final personality integration'.[16] We will examine more closely what spiritual maturity involves later. The bottom line – both in this diagram and in our lives – is essentially unchanging and timeless. Our soul, the spiritual self, remains tuned in to the spiritual dimension, to the divine, eternal, infinite, inexhaustible, ineffable Holy Spirit throughout each earthly moment of life – but this is not how we experience it.

Trajectories

Consider the part of the diagram showing low, medium and high 'trajectories'. It might be helpful to think again about lengths of wire like guitar strings, strung between two points. But this time imagine that some lengths are shorter and thicker than others; strung at higher or lower tension; made of different material, say nylon instead of steel. Pluck or hit any string with the same force and you will get different amplitudes of vibration and will therefore hear different sounds. Stimulate different strings repeatedly, varying both the force and the interval between plucks, and there is the basis for infinite variety. In the scheme of this book each pluck represents an impulse of either desire or antipathy, prompting a person towards new or stronger attachments and aversions. Each pluck threatens, in this way, to disturb the equilibrium of one's calm and joyful contentment.

Each note that arises from plucking the string moves it away from the baseline of silence and stillness. This represents the split or 'dissonance' between the noisy everyday ego of daily life and the silent, enduring spiritual self.

Temperamentally some people are liable to react minimally to distraction, provocation and temptation. Strongly influenced by the spiritual dimension, they are less likely to form attachments (and corresponding aversions) than other people, and to do so with less force – so that these attachments are more easily relinquished later. People like this are said to be on a *low* spiritual trajectory. They stray less from the ideal and their life experience is smoother, riding life's challenges, threats, losses and other vicissitudes relatively easily, with good grace.

In the story about Peter, he seems at first to be on a medium trajectory, irritated by aspects of his life outside his control. Later, wiser and more mature, the amplitude of dissonance – and the entire spiritual trajectory of his life – has declined. Moving forward on the arc of life he has become decidedly more contented.

Life on a *medium* trajectory involves significant tension in the separation of flesh and spirit. The goals of worldly ambition, once adequately achieved, are associated with the risk of settling into a comfort zone that involves strong continuing attachments – to loved ones, places, possessions, activities and so on; also to beliefs and opinions. This, in summary, is attachment to a comparatively rewarding way of life, which it might not occur to us to challenge, much less to change. We prize stability; nevertheless challenges inevitably arise. The threats of misfortune, accident, injury, ill-health, ageing and, finally, death are stacked against us and those we love, threatening any form of contented equilibrium and worldly success. Even in this apparently satisfactory steady state it is important to recognize that we have more growing to do. Awaiting us is the journey of life's second half.

Sadly some people follow a *high* trajectory and fail to find any form of enduring satisfaction. Their lives are more chaotic and they are less likely than others on lower trajectories to feel in control. Such people are likely to be conscious constantly or repeatedly of absences in their lives. They are driven by strong appetites, by craving whatever they imagine to be missing, even to the level of addiction.

Lady Luck – a story

Veronica, born in England during the Second World War, was the child of a young woman and a man she liked to think was an American soldier. She grew up in state care, however, knowing neither parent. Sometimes she was fostered out from the orphanage in the hope she would be adopted by a family. She was always returned. 'Nobody liked me enough,' she once said during several months of therapy sessions. At the age of 18 she was abruptly released from the institution to make her own way in the world. She found work. With some money in her pocket one day, she put a few sixpenny pieces into a 'one-armed-bandit' machine. When she won, and coins started pouring out of the machine, she felt for the first time that 'Lady Luck' had smiled on her, that she was now somebody special, someone of value. It was rather meagre compensation for feeling so utterly unloved in her life, but for a short while it worked. Veronica felt great, so the next day she tried her luck again. Quite soon, after another jackpot success, she was completely hooked.

Veronica was both intelligent and a hard worker. She survived. Later she met her 'Dependable Dave' and they married. Dave was affectionate and offered security. Taking advantage of a government-sponsored im-migration scheme the couple moved to Australia. Dave started a job in Mildura. In time they had two children. Everything seemed fine but for Veronica something was still lacking. She started playing the jackpot machines again. Her addiction escalated once the children reached school age and she had time on her hands. She was soon outspending the allowance Dave gave her for housekeeping. Unknown to him she remort-gaged the house at the bank, forging his signature on the application. To help with the extra repayments she took a part-time job; but always hoping for further affirmative visits from Lady Luck, still unable to keep up with the demands of an insatiable need to gamble, she began stealing cash from her employer.

It was only a matter of time before she was suspected of theft. When her boss spoke to her about it, knowing she would soon be arrested and that Dave would be told, she formed a desperate plan. Veronica took the overnight bus to Adelaide, checked in to a cheap hotel, visited a pharmacy to buy some pills and took a large overdose with the aim of suicide. The next day, in the afternoon, hotel staff went into her room. Finding her on the bed in a coma they called for help. She was treated successfully at the hospital and later transferred to the psychiatric unit. She was depressed, deeply ashamed and still wanted to die.

It took time for trust to develop between Veronica and hospital staff but excellent nursing care pulled her through the early period of her stay. She felt positive about art therapy, in particular, where she made spiky sculptures in clay. She said the spikes represented the awkward, ugly, unwanted aspects of herself. As the weeks went by, and her story unfolded, she was able to see herself differently, to grieve for the love and esteem she had never experienced from others and to see how poor a substitute was her reliance on Lady Luck. Fortunately Dave – who made the long journey and visited the hospital several times – was entirely supportive. He reassured Veronica that he had repaid her employer the money she had taken, so she would not now be prosecuted. He also reassured her that his pay was enough for the family to pay the mortgage instalments and to weather their financial problems. Veronica could hardly believe it when he said he still loved her, and so did the children, and that they all just wanted her well and back home again. She cried copiously as she spoke about it and said she felt much better for doing so. The tears gave welcome authenticity to the experience. She felt she could trust it as genuine and know she had a family who really did love her. This made her able at last to love them properly in return, and to love herself likewise.

Before returning home, well again, happy and optimistic, Veronica completed a final artwork: an attractive – and completely smooth – abstract clay sculpture. 'This is my new self,' she explained. 'I've managed to get rid of the spiky bits! I've never believed in God,' she added, 'but for the first time in my life I feel somehow blessed, and I'm grateful.'

Fatal attraction

Like Veronica, who found some comfort at first in her marriage and domestic stability, people with addictions tend to find eventually that what they want – or think they want – fails to satisfy them indefinitely. Satiety, getting enough of whatever it is, finally results in boredom, leaving them to continue their restless search for more: for stronger or more frequent rewards; for something new and more stimulating. Chief among the objects of many people's desires will be money: 'For the love of money is a root of all kinds of evil, and in their eagerness to be rich some have wandered away from the faith and pierced themselves with many pains' (1 Timothy 6.10).

In his first letter to his follower Timothy, St Paul warns not against money but against attachment to money – 'the love of money'. Money is useful. We need it to provide for ourselves and our families in daily life. But money is currency. It flows. It is intended to flow, not to be grasped and accumulated.

Strong attraction to money brings problems and pain, both when it results in the gathering of wealth and property as an end in itself and when it is used as a means of acquiring other things to serve as distractions from the core feelings of emptiness, powerlessness and insignificance that always, deep down, accompany the everyday ego's split from the spiritual self.

Such things include intoxicants – nicotine, alcohol and other so-called recreational drugs, drugs of abuse – that serve to oust, divert or numb temporarily the prevailing emotional pain. Excessively exciting and pleasurable activities, such as sex and adventure sports (which trigger the release of the body's equivalents – adrenaline and endorphins), are also indulged in, but these provide only similarly transient relief. Gambling is another example. Worldly power and fame also offer the illusion of protection against feelings of helplessness and unimportance, and may be desperately striven for, held and defended. These are all things to which people readily become addicted.

Also, because people on the highest and most painful of trajectories often feel isolated and lonely, they naturally seek out – and may easily grow dependent upon – company, camaraderie, friendship, affection and love. True, selfless love, of course, should they find it, can heal the dissonant split and be transformative. Too often, however, sexual attraction, dependency and possessiveness in relationships – the latter fuelled by jealousy and the fear of loss – distort the situation and deny those involved the blessings of genuine, mature, unconditional love.

Shakespeare's Othello, for example, gripped by sexual jealousy, cannot see the purity of Desdemona's heart, with tragic results. He murders her. In Flaubert's celebrated novel *Madame Bovary* the young Emma is raised by her father following her mother's death. She flirts with Charles Bovary, the recently widowed doctor attending her father, and eventually agrees to marry him.

> Before the wedding, she had believed herself in love. But not having obtained the happiness that should have resulted from that love, she now fancied that she must have been mistaken. And Emma wondered exactly what was meant in life by the words 'bliss', 'passion', 'ecstasy', which had looked so beautiful in books.[17]

Charles was Emma's 'Dependable Dave', but she does not remain faithful. A beautiful woman, attractive to men, she embarks on a series of adulterous affairs. Psychologically speaking, deprived as a young child of maternal love, of non-threatening and non-sexual affection, Emma developed the kind of coquettish behaviour necessary, in the childhood years before sexual maturity, to get successfully the attention of the only possible mother-substitute, her father. With puberty the ploy aimed at filling the void of maternal love now risks finding the wrong targets and achieving the wrong kind of response. Men do not respond to the needy child within, only to the provocatively sexy adult – the 'persona' – they see before them.

The matter becomes complicated by Emma Bovary's own sexual desire and by her evident enjoyment of intimacies with handsome and exciting partners. But beyond, or at a deeper level, than physical relations, she benefits from being noticed, being flattered, being valued – for whatever reason – and this is what she craves to continue. The tragedy of the tale – and of life – is that it cannot.

Her husband is rather dull, and problems arise early in the marital relationship. Charles' devotion persists but Emma is bored by its predictability. Later her partners begin to tire of her or, for other reasons, move away. Her looks eventually start to fade. Less attractive, Emma's behaviour aimed at beguiling and holding on to her suitors grows desperate and therefore increasingly offputting. This brings about what she dreads most: isolation. In the tale's tragic finale Emma takes poison and dies.

Madame Bovary perfectly portrays the heady beginnings, the ensuing suffering and regrettable end of a person doomed by something beyond her control – in this case the early loss of maternal love, advice, example, restraint and support. The book's continuing success attests to its accuracy. Good parenting is important. A deceased or absent parent or, equally, an emotionally cold one (who is therefore effectively absent and unable to respond to more than the child's basic physical needs for survival) or, even worse, two absent parents – these are unfortunate circumstances. The resulting conditions are capable of severely handicapping a person's life unless compensated for by effective parental substitution, when the grandparents step in, for example, or a kindly, generous and well-disposed step-parent.

Similarly, developing a warm relationship in childhood or later with a compassionate and merciful parent-like God, 'our father in heaven', 'a father-mother who gives birth to unity, vibrating life into form in each new instant' and, 'a parent of the universe, from [whose] deep interior comes the next wave of shining life' (see p. 52), will protect and nurture us in all the ways necessary that our human – therefore, like us, fallible – natural parents could not provide.

Changing trajectory

Diagram 2 (p. 73) also shows how relatively abrupt changes in trajectory occur whenever 'something happens'. Changes can occur in either direction at any stage, although they usually follow the natural trends, increasing

the split between everyday ego and spiritual self in the first half of the
arc of life, decreasing it in the second.

Consider how a child, raised with a simple belief in God and in Jesus
who is capable of healing miracles, may have that faith weakened by an
introduction to the principles of science at a school where an emphatically secular environment prevails. Further imagine that the child's adored
parent develops and later dies of a painful and debilitating disease, and
that no healing miracle occurs despite intense prayer.

It seems likely that the challenge to that child's belief system will be severe.
Innocence is tarnished by experience. Such spiritual awareness as the
child possesses becomes dulled and is easily ignored, overwhelmed as the
everyday ego shifts to a higher trajectory, towards more material concerns.

Nevertheless, as the bottom line shows, the spiritual self is not extinguished. It remains an influence, accounting for the important possibility
of later reintegration. Imagine now, for example, that the same child
experiences – months or years later – a comforting vision or dream in
which the image of the dead parent communicates that he or she is
well, at peace and free of pain.

This is not unrealistic. Both Thomas Merton[18] and Barack Obama[19]
have recorded powerful and meaningful dreams or visions about their
dead fathers. In both cases they recall the episode being followed by
a bout of crying, this catharsis being followed by the release of some
kind of psychological block and by a gradual but permanent change in
the direction of their lives and ambitions. Whenever the dissonance is
substantially reduced in this way a person's developmental trajectory
is spontaneously lowered. A readiness to pay attention to one's inner
spiritual awareness is rekindled, with consequences in terms of a change
in attitudes and values, general demeanour, patterns of speech and behaviour. Thomas Merton's particularly instructive story will be explored at
greater length in Chapter 7.

Stages of spiritual development

The earlier brief account of Carl Jung's psychology points to patterns of
psychological development: from the conscious–unconscious combination

of 'ego' and 'shadow' towards a more mature 'self' that is increasingly attuned to the 'collective unconscious'. Other pioneers of developmental psychology include Jean Piaget, Erik Erikson and Lawrence Kohlberg,[20] the last three particularly relevant because of their influence on a Christian professor from North Carolina, James Fowler. The son of a minister, Fowler studied divinity, went on to teach the subject at Harvard University and was later appointed Professor of Theology at Emory University in Atlanta, retiring from the post in 2005. He was also an excellent academic psychologist.

Fowler explained the focus of his working life by recalling that he had been taught theology as an adult 'as though he had never been through childhood'. This seemed profoundly misguided. He objected that it ignored that powerful images of God and other spiritual experiences had occurred to him before he was five. The conviction spurred him on throughout his academic career to develop a way of understanding people's lifelong development of faith. It had formerly been the custom for psychologists and theologians to concentrate on people's intellectual beliefs. Fowler felt it important to go further and include the whole of human experience. This led him to develop a theory based on three sets of already well-established ideas – of Piaget, Erikson and Kohlberg – before putting it to rigorous experimental test.

Fowler's contribution – the delineation of six stages of faith development – has not yet been sufficiently appreciated. There are problems with it admittedly, including that his major study was based on a relatively small sample size (359 people), with a wide age range (under 6 to over 61 years) and a strong bias towards both Christian participants[21] and white Americans;[22] but there was no bias in terms of gender.[23]

Fowler's findings support a general trend that age brings maturity but also suggest that this is not always or necessarily the case. Of the 249 adults in the survey (over 21 years old), the majority were either at Stages 3 ('conformist') or 4 ('individual') or between the two. Only 11 per cent had progressed beyond Stage 4 to Stages 5 (integration) and 6 ('universal'). The data therefore seem to support Richard Rohr's assertion that although everybody gets older, not everybody begins the important second half of life's pilgrimage or makes it very far. In the coming chapters we will try to explain this.

The age of the participants in Fowler's study is relatively less important because spiritual maturity depends only partly on age. Religious and racial bias may also be less important because, despite differences of religious language and interpretation, there does seem to be an acceptable degree of universality, both worldwide and through history, concerning human spiritual experiences. Anthropologists generally, and Jung's work in particular, reveal essential similarities in this regard. There is plenty of evidence that people have comparable spiritual experiences, whatever their faith, religious or non-religious cultural background.

Fowler's term 'faith' compares satisfactorily with the term 'spirituality' used in this book. He describes it as a universal feature of human living and dying, recognizably similar everywhere despite the remarkable variety of forms and contents of religious practices and belief. In all major religious traditions, he writes, 'faith involves an alignment of the will, a resting of the heart, in accordance with a vision of transcendent value and power, one's ultimate concern'. Faith, he says, 'is an orientation of the total person, giving purpose and goal to one's hopes and strivings, thoughts and actions'.[24]

In the light of these comments there can be no doubt that people's attention to their faith, to the spiritual dimension of their lives (or their neglect of it), will be a major influence on their psychology – on their emotions as well as on their thoughts, words and actions. The full title of Fowler's book, *Stages of Faith: The Psychology of Human Development and the Quest for Meaning*, reveals his strong emphasis that a person's spirituality involves finding a robust sense of meaning and purpose in life. Depending on the level of spiritual development attained, the nature and degree of such influence will vary with time throughout a person's life.

A final drawback of Fowler's scheme is its obscure nomenclature. It may not immediately be clear, for example, what he means by 'intuitive-projective' faith or 'mythic-literal' faith. To make matters clearer, and because Fowler's ideas are reinterpreted and developed here, it seems best to rename the stages. They will therefore (as in Diagram 2 on p. 73) be referred to in sequence as the 'egocentric', 'conditioning', 'conformist', 'individual', 'integration' and 'universal' stages. These will form the focus of discussion in the following chapters.

It is important to heed, as Fowler insisted, that the six stages are not to be understood as an achievement scale. They are not to be used to evaluate the worth of people. Neither are they valid as educational or therapeutic goals towards which to hurry or pressurize people. They are best thought of as descriptive guidelines for people on a journey of personal development, eventually to be undertaken in full but at no particular pace.

A scientific revolution

Fowler was the first to admit that the results presented in his book were in rough form; also that while the preliminary evidence revealed the pattern he had predicted, it was not yet sufficient either to confirm or deny his developmental theory. He was content to display such evidence as was available in the hope of inviting thought and further comment as well as further research. His framework has stood the test of time as a basis and departure point for further speculation and investigation.

As an early bridge between psychology and spirituality, Fowler's work is unparalleled. The attempt to explain people to themselves and each other as embodied beings developing throughout life within a spiritual dimension is of immense value. This is especially so because spirituality is deeply personal and therefore essentially subjective. It is difficult for a person to report spiritual experiences accurately and it is difficult for another person to interpret such a description with objectivity in a way that is meaningful and does it justice. Any well-considered account of such experiences, and the way they develop through life, is therefore useful.

In acknowledging the degree of subjectivity involved, any interpreter of the links between psychology and spirituality must equally consider his or her own spiritual life. Reza Arasteh, for example, once wrote: 'The subject of research projects is partly related to the character of the researcher.'[25] Unless the investigator of human spirituality has reached an advanced stage of maturity, he implies, that person is unlikely to feel any incentive for researching the topic or even be fully capable of comprehending it.

It is necessary, then, for those of us reading Fowler and other works on the subject to reflect carefully on our own experiences to see if we can relate positively to them. In other words to ask, 'Does this ring true?' This resonance is important. If the account of spiritual development in stages that follows rings true with good numbers of readers, a consensus will build – a consensus that gradually increases both the truthfulness (validity) and the usefulness (value) of the diagram and its description, a new and more detailed map detailing life's spiritual journey.

This is revolutionary science: liberating research participants, turning the human objects of study into creative and intuitive observers of their own lives and minds, free to experiment with new ideas and search out new experiences. In this way everybody has the opportunity to learn and grow, especially when our wisdom is pooled. As St Paul said: 'We have gifts that differ according to the grace given to us' (Romans 12.6).

To interpret and understand human spirituality afresh in a profitable way will take the engaged participation of many people, spiritually united – as with maturity we are bound to become – within the mind of Christ. Like Hero and Claudio, Beatrice and Benedick, the irresistible force of love is at work in our lives. However high the trajectory and however great the dissonance at the zenith, the arc will bend downward during life's second half. As the direction reverses, the split between everyday ego and spiritual self diminishes. Accordingly the false gap closes between each of us, between each other, creation and the sacred unity that is God.

Notes

1 William James (1982).
2 James (1982), p. 31.
3 James (1982), p. 2.
4 James (1982), pp. 485–6.
5 Pierre Teilhard de Chardin (1964).

6 Teilhard de Chardin, with Julian Huxley (1955).
7 Teilhard de Chardin's life and work are admirably summarized in Amir Aczel (2007).
8 For the source of quotes in this section see websites (Teilhard de Chardin).
9 See, for example, Frieda Fordham (1953).
10 Carl Jung (1933).
11 This principle is central to the Taoist tradition, where the sacred whole is formed from dynamic interplay between the complementary attributes of light and dark, Yin and Yang (see Chapter 9).
12 Diagram adapted from Larry Culliford (2011), p. 160, with permission from Jessica Kingsley.
13 Alexander von Humboldt, 1769–1859.
14 Donald Winnicott, paediatrician and psychoanalyst, 1896–1971.
15 Winnicott, quoted in Victor Schermer (2003), p. 115.
16 A. Reza Arasteh (1975).
17 Gustave Flaubert (1950), p. 47.
18 Thomas Merton (1948 and 1998), p. 123.
19 Barack Obama (2008), pp. 128–9.
20 The works of Piaget, Erikson and Kohlberg are summarized in Culliford (2011), pp. 83–9.
21 The sample included: 45 per cent Protestant Christian; 36.5 per cent Roman Catholic; 11.2 per cent Jewish; 3.6 per cent Orthodox Christian; only 3.6 per cent from other religions.
22 Only 2.2 per cent were non-white.
23 There were 180 males and 179 females in the study.
24 Quotes from James Fowler (1981), p. 14.
25 Arasteh (1975), p. 14.

5

Childhood spirituality

Suffering little children

And they brought young children to him, that he should touch
them: and his disciples rebuked those that brought them. But when
Jesus saw it, he was much displeased, and said unto them, Suffer
the little children to come unto me, and forbid them not: for of
such is the kingdom of God. Verily I say unto you, Whosoever shall
not receive the kingdom of God as a little child, he shall not enter
therein. And he took them up in his arms, put his hands upon
them, and blessed them.   (Mark 10.13–16 KJV)

My preference is for this, the King James Version of the story, because
it uses the word 'suffer', which means here 'to allow' rather than 'to be
in pain or distress'. As outlined in Chapter 3, allowing ourselves to
experience rather than suppress pain – especially emotional pain –
enables the healing process. Within tolerable limits we need to really feel
our pain because, as we observe it, so we become increasingly detached
from it. This is how we grow.

The incident in which Jesus blesses young children is reported in
similar terms by three of the four evangelists (see also Matthew 19.13–15;
Luke 18.15–17). It must therefore be a key passage of Christian Scripture, worthy of close attention. The first thing to note is a paradox.
Jesus' words seem contradictory to those of St Paul quoted in
Chapter 1: 'when I became an adult, I put an end to childish ways'
(1 Corinthians 13.11). Paul is apparently decrying the mentality of
childhood, but that is the point. Jesus is not talking about the intellect;

he is referring rather to the inherent, intuitive, spiritual sensibility of children.

This notion fits well with Donald Winnicott's idea, introduced in the previous chapter, that each of us starts out with a 'pristine ego'. This cannot remain untarnished for long, however, because little children do suffer. The newly born infant soon faces challenges for survival. Daily necessities for optimal development include shelter, warmth, sustenance and hygiene. Important requirements too are comfort and affection. The pristine ego is therefore rapidly provoked into a dissonant split. The guitar string – as we might again imagine it – oscillates as the anxiety-susceptible 'everyday ego' is plucked repeatedly in early life by, for example, cold, hunger or soiling. Similarly, relaxing sometimes, restored to being the still and more serene 'spiritual self', the same taut string reverts to the baseline where it vibrates gently, almost imperceptibly, in a slow rhythm along the calm, deep, penetrating, to our ears soundless wavelength of a living universe: the kingdom of God.

That which is becoming the everyday ego starts oscillating at birth – or earlier, in the womb. Both physical pain and emotional suffering therefore start with the onset of physical existence. Consciousness and memory, however, do not usually start until later. There are rare people who seem to remember being born and there are others in contrast who claim no memories of childhood before the age of five or six or even later. Whenever it may happen during early life, little new people eventually come to recognize themselves as a separate beings, as somehow separate from whatever is going on around them. This important milestone denotes entry to the first stage of spiritual development.

The child initially experiences a rather blurry and shifting reality of both external and internal sensations. Some are pleasurable, some painful and some neutral. The first-stage ego is at the centre of his or her limited but expanding world, hence the name of this 'egocentric' stage.

Faced with different sensations, babies experience rudimentary desire and dislike from the outset. Whether male or female they develop attachments to comforting and pleasurable experiences, aversions to uncomfortable and painful ones. There is often a mid-zone to be sought and dualist extremes to be avoided: being too hot or too cold; feeling empty (hungry) or overfed (satiated, bursting); understimulated (risking loneliness and boredom) or overstimulated (risking distractibility and restlessness), for example. Naturally, very young children depend on their parents to provide what they need and prefer and to protect them from what is unpleasant and harmful.

Maternal love

In the first letter of John we read the clearest, most succinct statement of Christian understanding, wisdom and belief: 'God is love' (1 John 4.16).

One of the purest examples of love, like that of the Christian mother-father God, is the unconditional love of a mother for her infant child – a bond of selfless devotion that, in ideal circumstances, arises spontaneously with the pregnancy, with the birth or soon after. This is natural love that happens, rather than involving a conscious choice. It finds an echo too in the love of a father for his newborn daughter or son.

In the best-case situation we are conceived in and born into loving relationships. Utterly dependent on our parents to provide for and protect us, long before we can recognize, much less accurately articulate our needs and desires, they must interpret our signals of distress and satisfaction – our cries, screams and tears, our sighs, gurgles and smiles. Their aim is vigilantly to note, and then dampen, the discordant oscillations of the guitar string, returning us towards the baseline – to provide what we require and remove what is upsetting; to restore tranquillity, joy and contentment. This is nurturing at its best.

When things go well for us as small children we grow increasingly to trust our environment and the parents who create and provide it. The seeds are sown for the development of a secure sense of self-worth; protection against feelings of anxiety, doubt, shame and inadequacy later in life; protection at the next level against anger associated with dislike of circumstances that appear to threaten our egocentric self-importance. In other words love – parental love, a mirror of God's love – is vital for healthy emotional growth and development. When it is limited, conditional and inconsistent or apparently absent, compensatory sources – such as grandparents – may supply sufficient high-quality nurturing; otherwise the dissonant split between everyday ego and spiritual self is likely to be substantial. Happily, it can be reversed.

Note that good parenting emphatically does not involve the persistent removal of a child's discomfort and pandering to all of his or her whims. This is impossible, but even if it were achievable it would not serve children well. From the earliest days we will not routinely get what we need or avoid situations that are unpleasant. We cannot always have what we desire or avoid what we dislike. Good nurturing therefore includes some experience of physical pain, psychological and emotional suffering. Good parenting does involve ensuring, where possible, that these are within tolerable limits. In other words the pain and suffering should not be too intense or prolonged. In this case a child able to experience and tolerate physical discomfort and emotional distress until the period of suffering passes will develop strong and lasting qualities of confidence, endurance, resilience, courage and optimism.

Parental loving attentiveness ensures that small children return frequently to baseline feelings of joyful calm and contentment. There is seldom much need for excessive anxiety: parents can have faith that nature – God's natural laws – help too. Parental instincts and intuition come into play from the outset. Sleep too is exceptionally restorative; and the process of emotional healing and growth is, as previously described, a natural bio-psychological one.

Holy Baptism

'I baptize you in the name of the Father, and of the Son, and of the Holy Spirit.' As a child develops a sense of separateness from mother, father, siblings and surroundings, it helps that close family members see and interact with that child as a separate individual. In consequence, the new baby needs a personal name to go with the family name he or she already shares.

When Christian parents seek baptism for their children within a few weeks of birth it is partly for this reason: to give them one or more Christian names. To be christened, though, is more than to receive a name. The title 'Christ' means to be the 'anointed one', and so to be 'christened' also means to be ritually anointed into the family of God. The service of Holy Baptism invokes the Holy Trinity, the word 'Holy' reminding all concerned of the sacred unity of divine creation 'from which' – rather than 'into which' – we are born and to which we shall each one day return.

Some people would say that all children are blessed with divine origin; that baptism simply marks an acknowledgement of the child's true nature, preordained and present from a timeless beginning. A second view holds that baptism somehow transforms a child and that there are therefore two kinds of children and people in the world: baptized and unbaptized. This is a dualist concept, with all the attendant risks of disharmony and conflict and arguably therefore less wise and mature than the first, unitary way of interpreting the baptism ritual – as symbolic.

The symbols of the baptism service are oil, water and candlelight. Like King Saul at the hands of the Prophet Samuel (1 Samuel 10.1), to be anointed with oil suggests being granted the status of royalty, becoming thus an heir to the kingdom of heaven. The use of water symbolizes cleansing and return to purity; an acknowledgement that birth inevitably brings trial and temptation, a split between living reality and the blameless ideal of sinless perfection. In terms of psychology, Holy Baptism marks the inevitability of dissonance between the everyday ego and the spiritual self: a gap that may widen but may also later be bridged and finally closed, with God's help and blessing through the guiding influence of the Holy Spirit.

Once cleansed, the light of a candle signifies the pure energy of the divine, the Holy Breath, the Holy Wind, the Holy Spirit, burning brightly from within. This is the essence of the blessed and ritually surrendered child, illuminating the world with purity, innocence and truth, with calm, joy and contentment, a reflection of the living Christ, a beacon of love shining out into the world.

God's help and blessing are important but the baptism service makes clear that the parents and godparents also have important roles to play, setting examples in terms of Christian values, morality and conduct, and ensuring that the child has the benefit of a Christian education. These, with other members of the extended family, are among the central figures in the young person's life. Their adult attitudes, expectations and intentions towards the child will contribute significantly towards the upbringing of those for whom they have accepted a share of responsibility. Members of the local church community, a number of them quite likely present and participating in the baptism service, will also be offering their examples, prayers, practical assistance and emotional support to child, parents and family henceforward. This will be the major difference between a child who has undergone baptism and one who has not: a positive adjustment to the social environment within which the child is to grow.

The child's upbringing will also be affected by the wider social and cultural environment in which the family find themselves. The prevailing attitudes, expectations and intentions of people from the local, regional, national and global communities are unlikely, in a multicultural world, to be fully consistent with those of the family and church.

These factors are all of particular relevance and importance as the child gains the capacity for increasing independence – through mobility, through speech and other forms of communication, including, eventually, by starting school and learning to read and write. Learning will be unstructured, informal and intuitive as well as structured, formal and set by official institutions. As education proceeds, so will each child be moving forward into the second developmental stage of 'conditioning'.

Conditioning

We each have our unique and personal genetic fingerprint. Even genetically identical twins have subtle differences, one necessarily being born first and the other second, for example. This represents an early example of the many shifting and unpredictable environmental factors that have such a big and wide-ranging influence on our lives alongside our genetic inheritance.

Depending on how you see and experience the matter, we are each from the outset subject to chance or fate, to luck or destiny. Christians say as a matter of faith that whatever happens is God's will. Few people live their lives through, though, without that faith being tested.

'To what degree,' we might ask, 'can a school-age child be said to have a specifically Christian faith?' A better question, which has been formally researched by psychologists, is 'To what extent does a school-age child have any kind of inherent spiritual sensibility?' This would fit well with the idea of a persistent spiritual self, in constant silent communication with the Holy Spirit and in dissonant tension with the everyday ego.

The everyday ego is the conscious 'me' that most people experience most of the time. It is the personal self that interacts with mother, father, siblings, the wider family and social group at community, cultural, national and global levels throughout life. It is through this that children build up their attachments and aversions; their preferences, likes and dislikes, regarding first sensations (in infancy) then people, places, objects, activities, ideas, values, ideologies and all manner of things, real and/or imagined.

It is the everyday ego that is subject to conditioning, learning from parents, family, teachers and others, especially those 'with authority'. Children learn too from books, television and computers, also through other technical means and methods. They learn much too from their peers. The majority of children have strong tendencies towards pleasing others and away from upsetting people. They readily adapt to and adopt the ideals and social conventions that prevail. Some children are more willingly directed than others, easier to mould. Is there a countervailing spiritual influence at work too? General observations, backed by research evidence, strongly suggest that there is.

Feeling unlovable

A child has only to receive 'good enough' parenting to stand a fine chance of living life along a relatively low trajectory of spiritual development. Where care received is seriously lacking or inconsistent – perhaps because of poor parenting received by one or both parents or through other detrimental circumstances such as poverty and other forms of deprivation – there is a significant possibility of the child living on a much higher trajectory.

The risk here is of what psychologists call low self-esteem, in other words of a deep-seated sense of being unloved and, by implication, unlovable. In such situations we have a natural tendency to compensate, to try to fill the apparently bottomless needy hole for affection and for feeling valued. This is when, as adults, we are at risk of trying to fill the unfillable void with power, wealth and status, for example, or by turning to potentially self-destructive, often addictive behaviour involving gambling, sex, alcohol, nicotine and other stimulant and sedative drugs.

These activities, closely bound up with society's commercial economy and the supremacy of worldly over spiritual values, remain socially sanctioned and in extremely common use. When we are motivated by deep-seated feelings of insignificance and inadequacy we seldom recognize the full extent of our antisocial and self-destructive behaviour. Neither do we realize the spiritual nature of what we are so tragically ignoring and missing. When a change of fortune or circumstances does force awareness upon us we may seek to change our habits and improve our lives. However, without rediscovering some kind of spiritual connection we will find it hard to achieve.

To think of yourself as humanly unlovable means feeling unloved by God too – a situation in which there is the strongest temptation to reject God and disallow any notion of a divine or spiritual reality. Perhaps this is what happened to Veronica (see Chapter 4), who had never believed in God, idolizing Lady Luck instead. Finally cured of her gambling addiction, she felt grateful and 'Somehow blessed'. Love, the love of her family, made the difference.

That a spiritual rather than worldly deficiency is involved in addiction behaviour is supported by the success of the Twelve Steps method for many addictive conditions. First pioneered by Alcoholics Anonymous (AA), Steps 3, 7 and 11, for example, involve making, 'A decision to turn our will and lives over to the care of God *as we understand Him*'; 'Asking Him humbly to remove our shortcomings'; and 'Seeking through prayer and meditation to improve our conscious contact with God, praying only for knowledge of His will for us and the power to carry that out.'[1]

The phrase 'As we understand Him' can be interpreted very broadly, not necessarily from a Christian perspective. It is certain, though, that some form of spiritual assistance and intervention is being invoked. The other phrase used by AA appears in Step 2: 'We come to believe that *a Power greater than ourselves* could restore us to sanity.'[2] AA guidance elsewhere also insists on the benefits of spiritual experience.[3]

What about the medium-trajectory life, the middle path? It is a challenging thought, particularly for Christians, that even well-meaning parenting can result in problems. It is natural to want happiness for your child, both now and in the future. It is equally natural and blameless to hold to certain priorities and values, to a range of ambitions, expectations and intentions – hopes and fears – based on what you think your child's happiness might depend on, how you think it could best be achieved and how unhappiness might best be avoided.

Much of this is unplanned and unconscious, governed largely by attachments and aversions in one's own life. A person who had only rudimentary schooling, for example, might work hard to ensure that his or her children received a more comprehensive education. Someone who grew up in relative poverty might, in compensation, emphasize a need for financial success. Religious people, including Christians, may naturally wish to stress religious adherence. Those who are not religious may be similarly disposed to promote a robustly secular world view.

There will usually be differences in ambitions and expectations depending on whether the child is a girl or boy. One parent's way of trying to promote happiness may differ significantly from that of the other. Grandparents may reflect different values, hopes and fears too; and eventually the child will encounter increasingly contrary attitudes and opinions outside the home. Some of these will take the form of social imperatives, accompanied by the possibility of sanctions, penalties and discrimination if one does not appear to conform.

These are all factors in the process of 'conditioning' which, in the commonest scenario, leads children between the extremes along a medium trajectory of development. The dissonant split between the everyday ego and the spiritual self grows during this stage. The wisest of parents will ensure that this split is minimized, but such wisdom is unusual, its rarity linked to a powerful secular-scientific cultural bias, as a result of which the inner worlds of children are barely recognized. Their spiritual lives are not therefore sufficiently respected and seldom adequately validated. The advice of Brendan Hyde, an Australian academic and religious educator, is that the spiritual awareness of children needs to be discovered, acknowledged and nurtured if they are to grow into rounded people who are cognitively, emotionally, socially and spiritually developed and healthy.[4]

Children as teachers

There is a growing fascination with the spiritual but it has not yet overturned the high degree of suspicion and secrecy concerning the subject in Western culture, especially in the minds of those unable to see spirituality except as irrevocably linked to inflexible religious dogma or irrational superstition.

Children are very aware of this taboo within society, quickly recognizing what is acceptable to speak about and what to avoid. This makes it all the more important for parents and others to develop and demonstrate the capacity to observe and listen to children sympathetically and to set examples as mature spiritual persons, for example by telling stories reflecting their own spiritual experiences and by making some effort to remember and recover their lost skills of spiritual awareness. This will necessarily be hard for those who have not been paying attention to the spiritual dimension of their own lives. In such a situation, unlikely as it may at first seem, even the youngest of children can help. The trick is to allow them – to suffer them – to be our teachers. If we let them, children make good spiritual guides.

The miracle of rain and other stories

Reza Arasteh, a psychology professor at Tehran, Princeton and George Washington Universities who died in 1992, suggested that the prevailing wisdom whereby 'in every adult there is a child who is responsible for certain aspects of [his or her] behavior' is incomplete. Missing is the complementary idea that 'in every child is a potentially mature [person] who should be given a chance to unfold.'[5]

One autumn day in London I noticed a small crowd of mothers and young children clustered outside the doorway of some kind of pre-school. One mother accompanying her daughter was deep in conversation with another woman, possibly a teacher, as the small girl went inside. What caught my particular attention, though, was the mother's other child, a boy of about six, waiting for his mother to take him to another school nearby. It had started to rain, and this boy stood with his back to everyone else holding his hands extended upwards. His concentration was intense as he studied the raindrops landing and conjoining to form small puddles in the cups of his palms. Oblivious to everything else, he seemed transfixed by the miracle of rain. The boy seemed somehow alert to his seamless connection, through the droplets landing on his skin, with the rain-filled sky and thus with the greater cosmos, the universal whole. 'Aha!' I thought. 'He is having a spiritual moment.' This was a brief instance of spiritual insight for me too.

One of the first people to take a professional interest in childhood spirituality was the American child psychiatrist Robert Coles, who undertook a large-scale study over many years, reporting on numerous conversations with children.[6] Coles considered it a mistake to give priority to children's intellectual abilities, as previous investigators had always done. He insisted on listening to what each child said without laying his own interpretation on his or her narratives. As a result he began thinking of spiritual awareness as a universal human attribute. In support of the idea he reported conversations with children from different religious and cultural backgrounds. Here are three of them:

> **Habib** was a twelve-year-old Muslim boy who felt a strong personal connection to God, to Allah. When he heard the call to prayer he would stop everything and say to Allah, 'I am only this one boy, but I believe in you.' Habib also felt that he had a special relationship with the wind, describing his conviction that Allah, 'Hears prayers and answers them through the wind.'[7]

Natalie was a young Hopi Indian girl. Central to the belief system of the Hopi community of North America is the concept of close connections with their ancestors. Natalie explained to Coles how, in her thoughts, she often met with her ancestors, who would give her a blanket, hold her and point to the sky, saying there were more ancestors living up there. She said the ancestors often visit and whisper to the elderly people in the community, who then pass on the wisdom of these conversations to the children.[8]

Ilona was an eleven-year-old Jewish girl who spoke of her Jewish faith and her closeness to God. She had travelled overseas with her father and said how, on a plane, she felt nearer to God, 'Because you can see the world, a lot more than when you're on land, and you can realize how big the whole universe is.' She made it clear that it was important for her to pause and reflect on God from time to time, 'Because it's the big picture that counts, and if you forget that, you get lost in going from one place to another, because you don't think of what you should be doing for God.'[9]

All researchers in the field echo the point that no religion has a monopoly on spiritual sensibility and experience. This may alarm some Christians, especially those who see Holy Baptism and the words of John's Gospel – 'No one comes to the Father except through me' (John 14.6) – as indicating only one path to salvation. A broader interpretation is possible, however, one that seems more in keeping with the overall gospel message.

The Holy Spirit knows no boundaries. The true nature of God is love, and love is universal. Love breeds tolerance, acceptance and affection rather than opposition and conflict. These observations render exclusive thinking redundant. It seems unwise for anyone to start reckoning who might and who might not be saved. Partisan theologies and ideologies are therefore a mark of spiritual immaturity. As will become clearer in the next chapter, this is a position from which to move on.

Two big questions arise when trying to find out about the spiritual experiences of children: 'What constitutes a spiritual experience?' and 'How might a child communicate about his or her experiences?'

Daniel Scott, a Canadian research psychologist, avoided these problems by obtaining from a group of adults written accounts of spiritual experiences recalled from their childhoods. Introducing his results, Scott wrote: 'To hear spiritual stories requires an attitude of acceptance. Part of my work has been to create conditions of openness and respect in which the telling of spiritual narratives is acceptable and possible.'[10] He records being impressed by the persistence and potency of the recollections, significant memories often credited with life-changing power. He also noted how often the accounts had long been kept secret.[11]

Scott allowed the adults themselves to make the decision about what was a spiritual experience, and to describe it in their own words.[12] One woman, Helen, recalled her reaction to the death of her grandmother when she was eight. Her parents were not religious, and children were barred from the funeral. Helen was disturbed until, with her brother, she went into nearby woods and created a little memorial marker 'for Grandma'. She would visit the site regularly, saying she found 'times of reverence' there. Always, during these times, she said, 'I felt still and quiet and calm.'[13]

Another woman, Penny, was six when she almost drowned in a motel swimming pool. She recalled getting ready to die, saying a series of goodbyes in her mind, and was praying when she saw an old man watching from nearby – a man who was not physically present. Penny realized she was 'not ready to leave'. She refused to die, whereupon she was rescued. The benefit to her thereafter, she said, came from having had 'a glimpse into the knowledge that there is some greater "spiritual being" looking out for us as we tread through our physical lives'.[14]

Joyce, who later in life became a clergywoman, told Scott that when she was three her seven-year-old brother took her outside one night to see a full moon. She remembered being completely astonished by its utter beauty and the glittering light. Her brother explained to her about the relationship between the earth, moon and sun. As a result Joyce felt a strong sense of connection with these three great orbs in space. Later, and throughout her life, she felt that she had been given a precious gift which, in her own words, 'had fed, warmed and amazed' her ever since.[15]

Another of Scott's subjects, Kay, remembered that when she was twelve she 'discovered forgiveness' and 'felt a weight being lifted off my shoulders that I didn't realize was there'. She said that she knew it to be absolutely true that 'God is love'.[16]

These fascinating stories may be biased by adult recollection and interpretation. A comprehensive study of actual school-age children was conducted by David Hay and his research assistant Rebecca Nye. The theoretical background, the conduct of the research and the authors' further reflections and conclusions are summarized in their book *The Spirit of the Child*, originally published in 1998.[17]

Hay and Nye looked at 18 children in the six to seven age range, and 20 children aged ten to eleven, all chosen at random from classes in state primary schools in Nottingham and Birmingham. Of these 38 about three-quarters (28) had no active religious affiliation, being described as from 'lapsed or secular Christian families'. Of the remaining ten children, four were from Muslim, four from Anglican and two from Roman Catholic families.

Nye attended school assemblies and worked as a helper to become familiar to the children. She then arranged up to three 30-minute tape-recorded conversations with each child. Hay, echoing Scott, explains how sensitively the interviews had to be conducted, saying that the skills required have close affinities with spiritual awareness. Nye describes being a 'human instrument' during both the interview and analysis phases of the research, becoming highly focused while remaining detached and non-intrusive, in a contemplative, almost meditative, frame of mind.

In commenting on the research material, Nye admits that while it was moving and impressive to encounter the quality of such material in children so young, there was at first no obvious rationale for labelling

it 'spirituality'. She said her intuition that these passages were representative of children's spirituality had to be justified in another way.[19] In due
course she and Hay were able to identify a common thread: the core
category of spiritual awareness that they decided to call 'relational consciousness', establishing two main aspects for it, as follows:[19]

1 While speaking about their spiritual experiences, children demonstrated
  'An unusual level of consciousness or perceptiveness, relative to other
  passages of conversation spoken by that child'.
2 The conversation concerning spiritual experience was expressed most
  frequently in terms of four types of relationship:
  (i)   to things
  (ii) to other people
  (iii) to the child himself or herself
  (iv) to God or some power greater than himself or herself.

A distinctly reflective type of consciousness is involved. Each child also
demonstrated some degree of awareness that what he or she experienced
was remarkable. The sense of being objectively aware of himself or
herself as 'subject' seemed particularly important. According to Nye it
was often this apparently 'objective' insight into his or her 'subjective'
response that fostered in the child a new dimension of understanding,
meaning and experience.

Hay and Nye found, like Coles, that some children's spirituality
is strongly informed and flavoured by the faith context of the family
and culture to which they belong. Nevertheless they usually also retain
a personal element – what Nye calls a 'signature' – in terms of spiritual
expression. Six-year-old Ruth, for example, is described as having a
profound sense of wonder and delight. Happy and articulate, Ruth said
that attending Anglican Sunday School was boring, but she also imagined
heaven as:

  A mist of perfume, with gold walls, and a rainbow stretched over
  God's throne ... With a smell like you get when you wake up on
  a dull winter morning ... And then when you go to sleep, and
  you wake up, the birds are chirping, and the last drops of snow

are melting away, and the treetops, shimmering in the breeze, and it's a spring morning ... It's not a season at all, not really, because it's just a day in delight, every day.[20]

Nye adds that Ruth resembled many of her peers in other respects, for instance in struggling with ideas about death and the afterlife. She showed some deference to parental world-view ideas but these were decidedly subordinate to her unique and individual spirituality at this stage.[21]

Six-year-old John, another of Nye's research subjects, also describes 'seeing' God in a very personal way:

With my mind and with my eyes. Sometimes I feel that ... I am in a place with God in heaven and I'm talking to him ... And there's room for us all in God. He's ... God's ... well, he is in all of us ... He's in everything that's around us. He's that microphone. He's that book. He's even ... He's sticks. He's paint. He's everything around us ... inside our heart ... heaven.[22]

Asked how he came to hold his Christian beliefs, John replied:

I worked about it and I received ... one day ... I was with my Mum and I begged her ... um ... for me to go um ... some church. And we did it and ... I prayed ... and after that praying ... I knew that good was on my side. And I heard him in my mind say this: 'I am with you. Every step you go. The Lord is with you. May sins be forgiven.'[23]

Later John also described an encounter with the Holy Spirit, looking like a ball of fire; but his mother rejected his account. He seems outwardly to have accepted her authority but added to Nye afterwards, 'I often felt the Holy Spirit in me.'

More types of children's spiritual experience

Many children, like the boy in the rain and Joyce with the full moon, experience a connection to the spiritual dimension through a sense of awe and wonder. A number of further different, often overlapping, types of children's spiritual experience have been described by researchers in the field.

Unusual sensory experiences

Some children have sensory experiences not available to adults. Brendan Hyde describes nine-year-old Lisa who was able to see auras, coloured lights seeming to shine around people.[24] These various sensibilities may be more common than is usually recognized and accepted.

Turning to prayer

Scott describes the experiences of Doug (ten at the time) and Ben (six) who both, as adults, recalled turning to prayer during times of crisis. Doug remembered such an occasion when 'I went to my room, lay on my bed, and prayed to God like I had never prayed before.'[25]

Dreams and premonitions

In a small-scale study, Kate Adams found that many children dream about God or have dreams with strong religious or spiritual meaning.[26] More than one-third of the children in Hay and Nye's study described their spiritual experiences by reference to dreams. Bob, for example, expressed a sense of ultimate mystery and meaning that he described as feeling like 'Pictures going through my head, like dreams or something . . . They all seem to fit together like a big puzzle . . . Like one dream in all, telling me things.'[27]

Adams does not reveal the content of the children's dreams in her study, but Scott gives an extended account of Rita, an Indo-Canadian woman who was ten when she went on vacation with her grandparents. There she had a series of scary dreams after 'playing fairies' with another girl, Maria, and refused to continue their games together. Later Maria was taken to hospital with neck and back injuries, having fallen in the forest while out playing the 'fairy game' alone. Rita's grandmother said nothing and 'constructed a ring of silence' around Rita's dreams and their implicit warnings. Rita continued to have a fear of her pre-monition dreams. As an adult, however, what stayed with her most was 'Not being heard as a child.'[28]

Meaning and morality

A number of authors suggest that spirituality is important in childhood as a basis for finding enduring meaning, purpose and connectedness throughout life.[29] Timothy, for example, was a four-year-old with a painful recurrent condition. Once, in the hospital, he was drawing pictures with intense concentration when his father asked about one of them. It showed a sick child in bed with another person beside him offering help. Timothy said the helper was himself, adding that when he became well again he would like to help other children in hospital because he knew what it was like to be sick. He told his father that the reason he was ill involved giving him the opportunity to think of ways of helping others.[30]

Timothy had been able to find a positive sense of meaning in his suffering, through recognizing the suffering of others and experiencing a desire to be of service. This is clearly an example of moral behaviour as connected with spiritual experience.

Afterlife and other philosophical questions

A number of researchers have remarked on children's curiosity and fascination with death and questions about a possible afterlife. Hyde has written about a young boy, Jake, who wonders if his recently dead, beloved pet dog Scamper's spirit is somehow alive in one of the pups newly born in a house nearby.[31] Hyde suggests that some aspects of children's spirituality are helpful when losses and other forms of adversity are encountered – a further indication of one of this book's main themes, namely the highly significant relationship between loss and spiritual development.

Some children are reported as having direct experience of people who have died. For example, Adams, Hyde and Woolley describe a woman, Jean, asking her six-year-old son Paul where he has been. She is surprised when he replies: 'I was sitting on the stairs talking to Grandma.' Paul's grandmother had died some months before.[32]

According to Hyde, children ask adults about death and what might lie beyond as a way of weaving threads of meaning and to connect with those who have died. They often link this enquiry with other deep, philosophical questions that help them explore their meaning and purpose in life. Three-year-old Jane, for example, was paying close attention during a family meal as her mother spoke of a time when Jane's brother – six years older than Jane – got stuck up a tree at the age of five. Jane, captivated, asks: 'Where was I when this happened?' Her mother explained that she had not yet been born. 'Yes, I know,' answered Jane, persisting, 'but *where was I*?'

Hyde describes Jane's sense of wonder and curiosity as having been aroused by the story. He reports that she clearly had an inkling of an eternal connection to something greater than herself.

Because of their curiosity, Hart describes children as 'natural philosophers', often seeking to know why the human race exists, whether there is life before physical birth or after death, why people suffer, why war and poverty exist and whether or not there is a God.[33] Many, he says, are able to develop a positive identity and sense of purpose through awareness of being part of something far greater than themselves. Echoing Hay and Nye's conclusions, Hart says that the questions children raise, and the experiences they have, strongly relate to their relationship with self, others, the world and sometimes also to a 'transcendent other' or God.[34]

Inner struggles

Another of Rebecca Nye's subjects was ten-year-old Tim who – like his family – rejected any form of religious affiliation. Despite this he spoke spontaneously on themes broadly linked to religious matters, such as animal reincarnation, polytheism, afterlife, morality and free will. Here is an excerpt from his interview:

> I sometimes think about if there is one God and there is ... everybody, well ... most people believe in one God and um ... there's um ... different people believe in different gods. Which God's real? Um ... I just can't figure that out.

The distinctive characteristic that coloured Tim's discussions, according to Nye, was a sense of inner struggle. His allusions to the spiritual were framed as conflicting hypotheses. This framework of discomfort and struggle also characterized his sense of wonder, awe, meaning and mystery.

Tim appears to have engaged in two particular spiritual dilemmas without resolving them: 'Is there a single true God?' and 'How can we cope with the mystery of infinity?' Nye remarks that his sense of inspiration was clear, but frustrated and struggling rather than joyful. Tim was also concerned about a similar problem regarding the efficacy or otherwise of prayer, saying that it was annoying trying to think about because he could not find the answer. He said he worried that his brain was going to get scrambled.[35]

Tim thought of spirituality as, 'A feeling of being emotionally moved', and told Rebecca Nye about 'a lot' of experiences when younger of something like God's guiding, an influence shaping his life. His spirituality was clearly marked at this stage in his life, though, by an insistence on wrestling mentally and thinking things through for himself, despite the emotional pain of frustration. He received no guidance from his family or elsewhere.

Hay and Nye do not speculate further on Tim's struggle, except to suggest that it represents a 'darker side' of spirituality. It is problematic from a rational, left-brain point of view; but this – while admittedly perplexing and uncomfortable – need not be viewed negatively: it could lead to a very positive resolution. This is precisely why Zen Buddhist teachers give their pupils insoluble riddles (called *koans*) on which to meditate. The eventual breakthrough involves the dissolution of dualist thinking. When the attributes of both right and left hemispheres of the brain are combined in harmony, a remarkable new insight – full appreciation of the unitary nature of existence – is revealed. We will return to this valuable point in Chapter 9.

Fading spirituality

Research has shown that almost all young children experience the spiritual dimension of life, and they do so in unique and personal ways, according to their particular 'signature', which may be influenced by their religious background but remains unique and idiosyncratic. But as children grow older, past puberty into the teenage years, all researchers agree that 'something happens'. Awareness and expression of the spiritual dimension in their lives fade away.

As in the cases of John and Rita, children are often strongly discouraged from discussing their spiritual experiences and frequently disbelieved or ignored. Many children fear that revealing their spiritual encounters will result in others misunderstanding, ridiculing and dismissing them. In addition, growing older we usually forget – and may be embarrassed by thoughts of – our (as adults) less acceptable childhood experiences. Few can tolerate being considered different, mentally unbalanced or weird.

Scott says that children know intuitively who has the capacity to respond supportively to significant spiritual experiences in their lives, listening to them without judgement. He recommends such an attitude of acceptance, particularly as it may then reveal how common children's spiritual experiences actually are.[36]

Hay and Nye report the inhibiting effect of the wider contemporary culture in the UK, according to which children are encouraged to suppress and abandon any tendency towards spirituality or religiousness and adopt a predominantly secular world view. Science and the 'evidence-based' approach to which children are eventually introduced in school, coupled with a kind of rampant secular, materialist consumerism in Western society, militate strongly against whatever vestiges of spiritual sensibility remain within the hearts and minds of young people, despite any countervailing religious education and experience that might be available.

The apparently insoluble paradoxes and conundrums of spirituality – as experienced by Tim – might become too exhausting or may seem too familiar and boring for continued struggle. They are therefore abandoned, like a crossword puzzle that proves entirely too difficult. Perhaps it is a response to opposing cultural factors. Either way, by the teen years, spiritual awareness has largely withered and in many cases vanished from sight. It cannot be fully extinguished, however. It continues lying not dead but dormant within the unquenchable spiritual self, while the everyday ego proceeds from 'conditioning' into the 'conformist' stage.

In Jung's terms, spiritual sensibility remains in the personal unconscious, a more positive part of the repressed 'shadow', awaiting reintegration.

Meaning-of-life priorities

'The spiritual dimension of human experience is the realm where the universal and the deeply personal meet.'[37] Spirituality therefore involves particularly the search for a sense of meaning and purpose in life, equally for a sense of belonging and self-worth. In infancy the meaning-of-life priorities are concerned mainly with safety, security, survival and comfort; with seeking to fulfil – or have others provide for – our natural likes and dislikes. During the second, 'conditioning' stage, our meaning-of-life priorities involve learning what we need to learn – through the instruction, precepts and the examples of others – about the world in general and especially about traditions, rules, conventions, beliefs and practices. This includes faith traditions and religious beliefs and practices.

Christians reading this chapter might feel that there has been insufficient emphasis on a more Christ-orientated version of childhood spirituality. Note, however, that there is a testament to the enormous value of a sensitive Christian education later.[38] Children raised in a Christian milieu will want to satisfy their curiosity and will absorb eagerly the Christian culture, traditions, beliefs and practices that surround them, but cannot be expected to do so unquestioningly. Education and indoctrination are not the same.

Howard Worsley has described in detail a research project he conducted involving people telling seven Bible stories (from a catalogue of 21) to their children and recording the ensuing conversations.[39] Children's responses differ frequently from their parents' expectations. Some children will be easy to mould into a kind of formula of Christian orthodoxy regarding biblical history, prayers, practices and beliefs; but there is a risk of them developing just a Christian 'persona' or mask rather than engaging wholeheartedly in a spiritual relationship with Christ and the Holy Trinity. Other children, attracted by secular considerations, will be much harder to convince. In between, a better outcome would be for children

to retain a strong sense of their innate, signature spirituality while enrich
ing and adapting it through a sensitive religious education. This is the
challenge for parents, teachers and religious leaders to acknowledge,
accept, and somehow try to surmount.

Transition and getting stuck

Whereas we all tend to carry some traits from the 'egocentric' stage into
adulthood, it is relatively rare for a person to remain fully fixed at this
first stage of spiritual development. Nevertheless the consequences are
worth thinking through because they can be fearsomely destructive.

People who retain a strong degree of egocentricity into and past
biological adolescence will selfishly insist on having their needs and
wishes met and on being kept free from feeling either want or discomfort. Such power-hungry people often develop into irascible bullies or
charming despots, sometimes a combination of these, coercing others –
for whom they have little individual regard – to do their bidding, using
both fear and magnetic allure. Tyrannical psychopaths, autocrats, dictators
and religious cult leaders are often formed in this way, blind and deaf
to the needs and wishes of others except where they can be twisted,
manipulated for the self-appointed one's own selfish ambitions.

The transition from egocentricity to the 'conditioning' stage happens
naturally, in most cases, as a child grows in size and ability. In a secure,
nurturing family environment there will be few problems. However,
for some children the transition period is highly problematic because it
involves a dawning awareness that we are no longer at the centre of an
environment dedicated to our well-being. Even before we can walk and
talk we may experience a strong sense of risk at being left alone, left
out and unable to fend adequately for ourselves.

Persisting feelings of anxiety and vulnerability put us at risk of remaining overlong in Stage 2, dependent on others. In this situation we might
easily become highly malleable, with limited strength of personal will
and ambition. Naturally we would then remain low in any social hierarchy, seeking strong, clear and relatively inflexible direction from above.
Tyrants and other strong leaders need loyal and unquestioning followers

and are attractive to relatively timid people stuck, like this, in the 'conformist' stage. Often fanatical in obedience to those they tend to idolize, for the comforting security and reflected glory it affords, such spiritually immature people readily volunteer to become dutiful minions.

Destruction on a global scale can be explained, at least in part, by this unfortunate combination: the egocentric leader, stuck largely in the 'egocentric' stage, and a multitude of servile or (paradoxically) self-important followers, likewise stuck in the 'conformist' stage. Brutal dictator-led, totalitarian regimes of the twentieth century and fundamentalist religious movements throughout history, extending into present times (together responsible for millions of deaths, uttermost cruelty, injustice and deprivation), stem arguably from this dynamic of immature personal and spiritual development and from a profound neglect of spiritual truths.

According to Neil Douglas-Klotz, in Semitic languages the word for 'good' primarily means 'ripe' or 'mature' and the word for 'corrupt' or 'evil' primarily means 'unripe' or 'immature'.[40] For this reason everyone's continuing spiritual education and development – bringing the best out of people as the wiser alternative to coercive indoctrination – is therefore everyone's business. When people are stuck they need help. However, before we can help others, we need to make progress ourselves.

Notes

1 *Alcoholics Anonymous* (2001), p. 59; italics in original.
2 *Alcoholics Anonymous* (2009), p. 59; italics added.
3 See, for example, *Alcoholics Anonymous*, pp. 567–8.
4 Brendan Hyde (2008), p. 20.
5 A. Reza Arasteh (1975), p. 13.
6 Robert Coles (1990).
7 Coles (1990), p. 199.
8 From Coles (1990), reported in Kate Adams, Brendan Hyde and Richard Woolley (2008), p. 67.
9 Coles (1990), p. 255.
10 Daniel Scott (2004), p. 69.
11 Scott (2004), p. 68.

12 Scott (2004), pp. 67–8.
13 Scott (2004), p. 70.
14 Scott (2004), pp. 72–3.
15 Scott (2004), p. 75.
16 Scott (2004), p. 69.
17 David Hay and Rebecca Nye (2006). Hay wrote eight chapters, Nye the other two.
18 Hay and Nye (2006), p. 105.
19 Hay and Nye (2006), p. 109.
20 Hay and Nye (2006), p. 50.
21 Hay and Nye (2006), pp. 94–5.
22 Hay and Nye (2006), p. 102.
23 Hay and Nye (2006), p. 100.
24 Hyde (2008), pp. 14–15.
25 Scott (2004), pp. 68–9.
26 Kate Adams (2001).
27 Hay and Nye (2006), p. 111.
28 Scott (2004), pp. 71–2.
29 Hyde (2008), p. 19.
30 Story adapted from Adams, Hyde and Woolley (2008), p. 88.
31 Hyde (2008), p. 14.
32 Adams, Hyde and Woolley (2008), p. 63.
33 Tobin Hart (2003), p. 91.
34 Adams, Hyde and Woolley (2008), p. 66.
35 Hay and Nye (2006), p. 96.
36 Scott (2004), p. 78.
37 Culliford (2007b), p. 19.
38 See Afterword: My Christian journey.
39 Howard Worsley (2009).
40 Neil Douglas-Klotz (1999), p. 1.

6

Adolescent religion

———◆———

Tribal origins

We can learn much about personal development, especially the next 'conformist' stage, by examining indigenous people and aspects of tribal living.

I met Mrs Woodcock, the widow of an English anthropologist, in 1981. Her husband had studied Australian Aboriginal people and, with the full co-operation of tribal elders, she had helped him investigate female initiation ceremonies, participating in several of these powerful mysteries. As a result she had developed lasting clairvoyant powers. She told me that she normally kept silent about this but had a particular reason for mentioning it, saying, 'I have a strong image of you as a baby being cradled on an older man's knee. The two of you are playing with a gold watch chain.' She asked if I knew who the man was, but I had no idea. When I asked my grandmother, back in England some weeks later, she immediately said, 'That was your Grandpa! He never did get a watch for that chain.'

My grandfather had died a couple of years earlier, leaving me a riddle to solve with his final words.[1] It was comforting to hear about this vision of intimacy between us over a gold chain, symbol of pure, radiant and everlasting connection.

Apart from the personal significance attached to Mrs Woodcock's astonishing, mystical ability, I realized that indigenous people seem to retain, as a normal part of their culture, powers that today we call 'paranormal'. Their intimate affinity with nature, and with the landscape on which they depend, hallows everything, making it sacred. They mythologize animals and places. Tribal people, through the ages and throughout the world, hold to a similarly religious connection between people, life, land and creator. Here is how the psychologist and author Steve Taylor puts it:

> Primal peoples respect nature because they see it as the manifestation of Spirit. Since they see themselves as manifestations of Spirit, too, they feel a sense of kinship and connection with nature, a sense of sharing identity with it ... Primal peoples see themselves as custodians of the land, looking after it on behalf of the Great Spirit.[2]

Quoting this passage, the Roman Catholic priest and social psychologist Diarmuid O'Murchu says that for indigenous peoples, 'Everything throughout the cosmos is essentially related. Energy – the basis of matter – is "spiritual power". The "Great Spirit" is an empowering breath, a creative energy, a unitive being, the forerunner of all.'[3]

O'Murchu added that indigenous people do not so much worship the Great Spirit as co-create with it. Their ethics and morality are about relating rightly with nature and creation. The prayerful aspect of their religion is about expressing Spirit rather than addressing God.

There are still many tribal people in the world living, more or less, in their traditional fashion. Bruce Parry has written about 15 tribes in four different continents with which he spent time while making a television series.[4] Some, like the Sanema of the Orinoco Basin in Venezuela, were first studied when still relatively isolated and untouched by modern culture and technology. For them the spirit world encompasses everything in their environment: trees, rocks, water, animals – everything. And not all their spirits are benevolent. Similarly the Adi people, subsistence farmers living in the foothills of the Himalayas, hold that spirits can cause illness and must be placated with offerings and incantations.

Tribes like these have experienced little change for many generations, perhaps thousands of years. Their culture is one of stability. They do not experience time as resolutely linear, like clock-time (*kronos* in Greek). The cyclical and rhythmic nature of time forms another important aspect of the tribe's spirituality. This is more like appointed time, God's time (*kairos* in Greek). The year goes by according to seasons and the months according to the lunar cycle. Weeks may be marked by a day kept special and sacred, the equivalent of the Sabbath for rest and ritual, a day set aside for reflection and recuperation, a day of healing and of preparation for immediate and longer-term challenges. Each day is marked and divided by light and dark, by the relentless passages of sun and moon across the sky.

> For everything there is a season, and a time for every matter
> under heaven:
> a time to be born, and a time to die;
> a time to plant, and a time to pluck up what is planted;
> a time to kill, and a time to heal;
> a time to break down, and a time to build up;
> a time to weep, and a time to laugh;
> a time to mourn, and a time to dance;
> a time to throw away stones, and a time to gather stones
> together;
> a time to embrace, and a time to refrain from embracing;
> a time to seek, and a time to lose;
> a time to keep, and a time to throw away;
> a time to tear, and a time to sew;
> a time to keep silence, and a time to speak;
> a time to love, and a time to hate;
> a time for war, and a time for peace.   (Ecclesiastes 3.1–8)

It is little wonder that, throughout mankind's history, sun and moon both have been objects of worship in many cultures. Even today the Adi people honour a sun-moon deity, which they acknowledge as the visible manifestation of the Supreme Power of the universe.[5]

For a child in such a tribal culture, with no exposure to alternatives, the 'conditioning' stage merges into conformity at adolescence. Male rites of initiation signify that transition after puberty, when the youths are sufficiently strong. The secret and esoteric nature of these rituals – which may involve trials of strength and courage, plus the use of alcohol and/or hallucinogens to bring on altered states of consciousness – no doubt assist transformation. 'Something happens' to help turn boy into man.

The change from girl into woman after puberty is similarly marked by rites and ritual. The crucial alteration involves the onset of the menstrual cycle with its inevitable link to the passage of the moon and the capacity for reproduction. Important knowledge and skills are passed on at this time.

Among these tribes, in a relatively unchanging environment, there is little need and little scope for independent thinking or behaviour. Any substantial form of deviancy could, in any case, threaten the stability and well-being of the tribe. Its success depends on conformity among its members, developing a powerful shared sense of identity. Accordingly they tend not to experience themselves and each other so much as separate individuals, but as corporate parts of the whole, members of one tribal body.

This sets a limit on personal development among indigenous peoples. Only when significant environmental changes arrive do they need to adapt and develop. Unfortunately this is often through intrusively destructive encounters with outside agencies, with people from a different culture bound by their own self-seeking agendas.

Interventions from outside, contact with more complex and developed civilizations, often prove highly toxic. The Aborigines of Australia were widely persecuted, for example, and wiped out completely from the island of Tasmania. The Inca of Peru and other First Nations people of North and South America are also among those extensive, previously viable tribal communities around the world that have been decimated by clashes with what began as European culture. Smaller groups survived longer in isolation but experienced the same threats to survival and challenges to adapt.

The physical and biological challenges included loss of territory, changes to the ecological environment, interbreeding and the introduction of deadly diseases. Psychological threats from the destructive changes resulted in bewilderment, anxiety, anger, shame and sorrow. In addition there were challenges affecting the tribes' social dimension: by introducing different – especially monetary – values; by reducing a sense of connection between past and future; by decreasing cohesiveness – such as when the young are enticed away by the seductive promises of a different culture.

Above all there is usually irreparable damage to the spiritual health and integrity of these tribes. Their life-giving spiritual connection with the landscape is brutally interrupted. Their belief systems and mythologies, their rituals and superstitions, their 'paranormal' abilities – alien and unacceptable to Western culture and religion – are widely suppressed.

Primal people were considered primitive, as if there was nothing they could teach us. Their religions seem strange and ignorant, replete with idol worship, superstition and unhealthy practices involving blood sacrifices and the use of potent, hallucinogenic intoxicants. When these once proud peoples seemed quickly to degenerate, to fade away in numbers (if not completely erased by disease and genocide), to be reduced to poverty, unemployment and widespread addiction to alcohol, gambling and other self-destructive activities, it seemed to confirm to Western newcomers the unworthiness of the native people's former ways. This now seems astonishingly careless and short-sighted.

From the perspective of spiritual development the problem involves primal people having no previous experience of adapting to change. According to the scheme of this book, having reached conformity there was no easy way forward for them into an 'individual' stage, or therefore through this into reintegration and full spiritual maturity. They were already as spiritually mature as their society required.

In lands colonized by Europeans and European culture the tribal people needed help. Arguably their best hope came from mature Christianity, from enlightened missionaries carrying the gospel of love, from the likes of David Livingstone and Albert Schweitzer and from people living out redemptive Christian values. Even these brought difficulties; and they were in a minority. The indigenous people fared much worse when rapacious and godless pioneers and plunderers, people with more mercenary values, preceded more tolerant and compassionate settlers.

It is important to note that the challenge to adapt affected both sides. Among both established residents and intrusive newcomers, the most rigid – in terms of beliefs, myths, traditions and practices – fared the worst. Mutual respect, a desire to seek out compatible aspects of the differing cultures and a willingness to share both commodities and ideals, held the key to successful intermingling and integration; but even in the most favourable circumstances there were difficulties. In some parts of the world these remain a cause of much suffering.

Conforming – into a comfort zone

Returning the discussion to people growing up in contemporary Western culture, there is no timetable involved in moving from one stage to the next. Progress is usually gradual. Three things, happening at roughly the same time, contribute to children's development: physical growth, sexual maturity and the capacity for abstract thinking. This is the start of adolescence.

In James Fowler's sample, 16 per cent of 13- to 20-year-olds remained below the 'conformist' stage (see Diagram 2). Even when physically developed, those with relatively weak egos cling longer to strong authority figures and the social imperatives of Stage 2. Half the teenagers were at the 'conformist' Stage 3. Only 5 per cent had reached the 'individual' Stage 4, leaving 29 per cent between the two.

According to this scheme most people today – teenagers and adults – are still 'spiritually adolescent'. Among Fowler's adult group (over 21 years), only 11 per cent had progressed beyond the 'individual' stage. The majority remained at Stages 3 or 4, or between them, confirming that relatively few among us have yet embarked on the 'journey into the second half of our lives'. In the remainder of this chapter we will therefore concentrate on the 'conformist' and 'individual' Stages 3 and 4, and the transition between them.

The difference between the earlier 'conditioning' Stage 2 and 'conformist' Stage 3 involves the degree to which the emerging faculties of choice and decision-making remain under the influence or control of parent figures and the social group. In Stage 3 a rudimentary degree of independence operates, and with it an early sense of the person taking responsibility for his or her thoughts, words and behaviour. Most, however, choose to subordinate their will to that of the social majority.

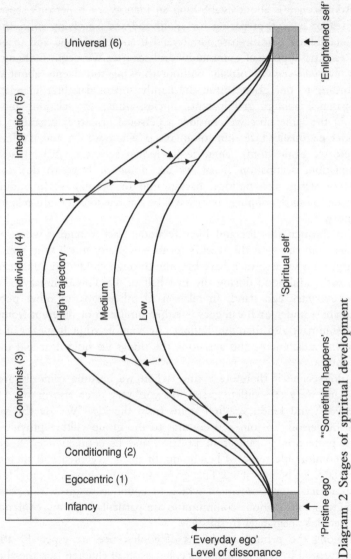

Diagram 2 Stages of spiritual development

Adolescence is about establishing an identity: each person's sense of himself or herself, preparing for adulthood and 'surviving successfully' by establishing a home-base, family and friends, livelihood and so on – the essential aspects of community and security. We begin building up our 'everyday ego' – usually without thinking too deeply about it – according to our place within the family: son or daughter, in relation to parents, siblings, grandparents, uncles, aunts, step-relations and so on. At the same time we consider a personal inventory regarding our gender, nationality, race, skin colour, place (where we live and, if relevant, where we came from), language (including accent or dialect), sexual orientation, occupation (what we are doing or hope to do), social class or status, also political background or persuasion. In addition, integral to our developing identity will be our religious (or non-religious) identity.

Go through this list and identify under each category where you belong, and this – in the world's terms – is pretty much who you are. This is who we will each have become through childhood, adolescence and early adulthood during the first half of life. This summary of our own everyday ego stands in relation to other egos, to other people who are – under each category – either similar to or different from us. The summary also therefore defines our comfort zone. It speaks of our evolving attachments and aversions: the things we hold dear and those we shun.

Adolescence is therefore a time when we become critically aware of – and wary of – differences. 'I like you' very often also means 'I am like you'; and kindness often stems from the idea 'We are the same *kind* of person.' To join and commit to the group culture provides us with protection from fear of isolation and its consequences. It gives us a comfortable sense of belonging, of being accepted and therefore acceptable, of being valued. This gives our life meaning and provides us with a social environment in which to continue to grow as a person. Religions and religious communities are particularly strong contenders for people's allegiances in this way.

Among the primary problems of adolescence are especially those characterized by fear and ignorance. Just as small children lack the ability to provide food, shelter and other physical necessities for themselves, so typical young teenagers may lack adequate knowledge and experience to think and behave entirely independently for the best. Whether they admit it or not (and whether their parents fully appreciate it or not), they are under threat from both emotional and intellectual imperfections and immaturity. Over this, available to the 'spiritual self', ready with corrective advice, Christians say, the Holy Spirit keeps silent watch.

Isolation carries danger, giving rise to fears of loneliness and feelings of personal inadequacy, of helplessness, hopelessness and worthlessness – strong risk factors for anxiety, depression and other psychological problems.[6] Suboptimal exposure to what a young person needs or desires – in the way of stimulation, education, instruction, role models and general worldly experience – also leads to ignorance in terms of both knowledge and wisdom, of both vital information and advice on how best to behave.

Isolation must therefore be avoided, and to conform makes excellent sense. However, there may be a cost. At the same time as we experience the drive to belong we also experience an opposing drive: to experience oneself as independent-minded, as a separate person. Accordingly we want to think, speak and act on our own initiative, feeling capable of making decisions and taking responsibility for ourselves.

For this reason adolescence is a time of trial and error, of experimentation in terms of appearance, friendships, interests, values and ideas. Depending on how adventurous you are, there may be an element of rebellion; but even this will be characterized by a tendency to conform. Young people frequently form groups – including virtual groups on the internet and social media – and do things together. They feel comfortable following trends – in clothes and music, for example – and keeping in step with their peers, however at odds they may seem to be with the parent generation. This remains a kind of conformist behaviour.

Religion's big mistakes

Within a powerfully secular culture, strongly influenced by the methods and findings of science, by a widespread reliance on technology and by ubiquitous seductive commercial enticements, there is considerable risk of teenagers rejecting the religion of their parents' and grandparents' culture, never to reconsider deeply this vital aspect of their lives.

Some people, indeed, come to define their religious identities in negative terms: 'I am not religious'; 'I do not believe in God'. Only if this is adopted narrowly and as a final position, though, need it be considered seriously problematic. This may not yet represent true independence of thinking and behaviour. It may be the positive start of something, an honest move forward in terms of spiritual development in the direction of the 'individual' stage.

It is a mistake when churches and religious leaders fail to understand this. Many people have doubts about and leave their parent religion for the best reasons, in the search for a wider, bigger, grander truth than they have encountered so far. The big mistakes of religious institutions, of some religious leaders and followers, then, include:

1 being too rigid;
2 exercising exclusivity;
3 claiming superiority over others.

These errors compound and are often associated with another: overly literal or idiosyncratic interpretation of Scripture; missing and therefore neglecting the all-important intuitive, imaginative inferences and possibilities. Such mistakes are particularly counterproductive in terms of genuine, lasting appeal when claims are backed by threats of a God more harsh and vengeful than loving and merciful. Many are critical, accordingly, that churches fail blithely to hold on to the devotion of people, young or old, who see through some of the apparent inconsistencies of Christianity, who cannot square miracles with science, who find in an expanded form of Darwin's evolutionary theory sufficient explanation for altruism and moral psychology, who reject the need for a creator or any so-called 'supernatural' phenomena and who argue that a multiplicity of religions – and divisions within those religions – indicate the implausibility of each.

There may also be another neglected group: those who have never felt sufficiently loved or valued to believe that anyone would sacrifice a life for them, as Christian teaching says of Jesus, much less do so through the shaming process of public arrest and trial and the extremely painful and humiliating processes of torture and crucifixion. This congregation, aimless and among the neediest of God's flock for his love, requires particularly wise and compassionate attention.

Richard Rohr says that the institutions of Christianity, the churches and associated organizations, 'are almost entirely configured to encourage, support, reward, and validate the tasks of the first half of life'.[7] This is not in itself a mistake. Christian churches and organizations are bountiful treasure houses of living spiritual history, wisdom, traditions and beliefs, saintly example, sacramental practices, sacred music and prayers, perfectly sufficient for the full and proper education of Christians from baptism onward. They perform a valuable service. But clearly, in Rohr's eyes, there remains an enormous omission: churches do not do enough to promote spiritual enquiry and development. They do not at present provide the leadership, rationale, role models, environment, encouragement or means for life's more holistic second half.

The problems of rigidity

As we pass through the 'conformist' stage, holding to our comfort zone, we seek stability and security. Quite naturally we seek certainty and are thus strongly inclined to use rational logic – dualist, either/or, left-brain thinking – to achieve and maintain that. Seeking to avoid uncomfortable feelings of anxiety, bewilderment and doubt, we hold all the more tightly to our opinions, beliefs and convictions and ally ourselves strenuously with those of similar views. Equally, we oppose and reject those who appear markedly different.

An us/them attitude and corresponding practice develops, which then underpins the big mistakes and tragedies of every religion. Christianity, sadly, is no exception. Whenever attachment to the tenets[8] of Christianity becomes rigid and inflexible, and where claims of superiority are made, the preconditions of division and conflict are met. Dualist, either/or, right/wrong thinking is by nature exclusive. Partisan groups inevitably come into being. Competition, based on differences, predominates over co-operation, based upon what is shared.

Church history supports this assertion. Christianity fragmented first into Western Roman Catholic and Eastern Byzantine Orthodox parties. The Protestant movement later split the Roman Church at the Reformation in the early sixteenth century.[9] Today there are many further subdivisions, Anglicans, Methodists, Baptists and Quakers among them. How is the intelligent, inquisitive adolescent to choose and decide?

The time has passed for any group to claim privileged knowledge or exclusive access to the divine. This is a real challenge for people still at the 'conformist' stage. Holding to Christianity – or any religion – gives a person a comforting sense of safety, of being prized and protected, not only through life but after life, forwards into eternity. This is a lot for the self-protective everyday ego to give up, but it must if the whole person is to develop, because the picture is one-sided, incomplete and therefore false.

The Amish experience

We can learn about the risks of rigidity from a respectful examination of an exclusive Christian group. The Amish people today live in communities mainly around Pennsylvania and in Canada, having gone to North America from Switzerland and South Germany in the early eighteenth century, following a religious split in the parent Protestant Mennonite church. They are, in many ways, highly successful. Well-known for their plain attire and simple lifestyle, they hold an aversion to modern technology, preferring to use horse-drawn rather than motorized vehicles, for example, and disallowing televisions and telephones in their homes. Outsiders are not permitted to join, and the Amish people maintain a firm separation from mainstream society based upon a strict interpretation of a passage of New Testament Scripture: 'you are a chosen race, a royal priesthood, a holy nation, God's own people' (1 Peter 2.9). This gives them a powerful sense of identity, their certainty about it providing members of their communities with a potent and authoritative buffer against the risk of meaninglessness.

The young are conditioned through limited exposure to external cultural influences, and by adulthood the Amish are overwhelmingly conformist. Their leaders do seem to appreciate that during adolescence some behaviour testing imposed limits is natural, so a degree of leniency is applied until teenagers or young adults make a personal commitment to uphold the rules, whereupon they undergo ritual baptism. After that, no challenges to the traditions, beliefs or rules are tolerated.

It is no doubt possible to make personal spiritual progress within the constraints of such a theologically and practically restrictive environment but the impediment to individuality is powerful. To ensure conformity among the stricter, so-called Old Order Amish, for example, their Bible, written in an antique form of German that people no longer speak or understand, cannot – according to their rules – be translated into English. Neither is any English translation permitted to be acquired or read by members of the community. Scripture can only therefore be interpreted by the Elders and this, according to a BBC television documentary,[10] was the first rule broken by two Amish men, Ephraim and Jesse, who joined regularly with others from the wider Amish community to study the Bible in English and sing English-language hymns. After refusing to repent publicly and change their ways, both men were excommunicated. They are both now shunned by the community, members of which are no longer allowed to associate with them in any way. This includes their own parents and other relatives, who would themselves be excommunicated otherwise.

Neither man wanted to leave the community. Both were still attempting, with their wives and children, to continue to live near the parent community and broadly according to Amish culture, while practising what they considered a more liberal, enlightened and authentic form of Christianity. Their dissent from the order was based on a deep and powerful sense of personal conviction. It had become apparent to the men, from reading the Bible and reflecting on its message, that many of the strict rules of the Amish were not, as they had consistently been told, based on Holy Scripture. Some rules appeared particularly arbitrary and unnecessary, and the authority of the leaders of the community grew correspondingly weaker and questionable in their minds.

Explaining that his excommunication was not based on reading the Bible, rather on disobedience to rigidly enforced instructions, one of the two men said on camera, 'I was not supposed to challenge. I was just supposed to mindlessly agree and listen to what they say . . . Well, I cannot do that.' Failure to abide by any rule or instruction from church officials would, he added, have had the same effect. Their misdemeanour counted the same as would any crime of theft, for example, or even murder.

Ephraim and Jesse were not alone. A number of other families were similarly outcast but remained in touch with the wider community, trying to live by their Christian principles on the outside. As the documentary ended, the future for the two men and their immediate families remained unclear; however, their religious faith and personal conviction regarding their conduct was definitely holding firm.

An astonishing group of migrant survivors, with much in common with indigenous tribal people in terms of group loyalty and identity, the Amish know themselves to be under threat from external influences. Their staunch exclusivity does not lead to open conflict, however, first because contact with non-Amish people is kept to a minimum; second because they are deeply pacifist by both inclination and practice; and third because their diligence and integrity has earned them the respect of their American and Canadian neighbours.

We do not know how many members leave the Old Order Amish or, like Ephraim and Jesse, have been excommunicated, but it is not enough currently to rock the stability of the group, which is growing in size. There does not appear to be any great impetus for the group as a whole to change. There are powerful motives, though, for some individuals within it to risk and suffer exclusion and the associated emotional suffering involved. As the documentary made clear, the anguish is often immense.

Ephraim and Jesse were profoundly affected by a combination of biblical insights and the knowledge that these had been corrupted and concealed by their Elders. They had discovered an important aspect of their own ignorance, knowing in their souls that something vital was missing. These Amish men not only wanted but needed to seek and find a more complete truth. Partial or distorted versions could no longer suffice. They had embarked towards the 'individual' stage but remained yet in orbit around the parent group, reluctant to break ties of family as well as of culture.

No one can do the spiritual work of another

Staying in touch with the parent group like this represents an example of fixation within Stage 3 to 4 transition, a situation that can endure for a long time, depending on many factors and circumstances. In other cases reluctance to move into full independence arises from the desire to return and educate members of the parent community, to stay back and try altering the character of the whole group. It is not impossible for this to happen but in most cases a kind of ambivalent struggle ensues without resolution.

> He came to his home town and began to teach the people in their synagogue, so that they were astounded and said ... 'Is this not the carpenter's son? Is not his mother called Mary?' ... And they took offence at him. But Jesus said to them, 'Prophets are not without honour except in their own country and in their own house.' And he did not do many deeds of power there, because of their unbelief. (Matthew 13.54–58)

In order to progress we must each think, consider and reflect deeply for ourselves. We must draw our own conclusions and act accordingly. No one can do the spiritual work of another. Neither can we force our new beliefs, opinions, attitudes or values on anyone else. That would be to make the same mistake as those who remain at Stage 3; to make the same mistake as those who insist on conformity by dismissing new ideas; to follow the same strategy as those prepared to use strong coercive tactics to maintain the status quo. In the end we must loosen our most cherished attachments and move on, risking and accepting isolation. This is properly to enter Stage 4.

> Do not think that I have come to bring peace to the earth; I have not come to bring peace, but a sword. For I have come to set a

man against his father, and a daughter against her mother, and a daughter-in-law against her mother-in-law; and one's foes will be members of ones own household. Whoever loves father or mother more than me is not worthy of me; and whoever loves son or daughter more than me is not worthy of me; and whoever does not take up the cross and follow me is not worthy of me. Those who find their life will lose it, and those who lose their life for my sake will find it.   (Matthew 10.34–39)

This is among the most difficult of Christ's teachings because we are used to associating love with the caring bonds between family members. But the story of Ephraim and Jesse exemplifies the pitting of sons against fathers and the splitting of families. At the 'conformist' stage we are not ready for this; entering the 'individual' stage we begin to see and experience what it means. All our ties and attachments – to people, places, activities (including religious activities), values (including the near-sighted value of loyalty) and beliefs (including religious beliefs) – must be reconsidered. This, for a Christian, means engaging with and taking up Jesus' cross. This is the work at the start of the second half of life as we seek to discover – each of us, one by one – who we truly are.

Until then a false 'persona' or mask has been shielding us from a deeper and more blessed reality, from our true spiritual self. At some deep level each one of us already knows this. Our immortal soul retains a profound and seamless connection to the sacred whole, to the divine, by which in turn God, the Holy Spirit, knows and has always known us. This is not a question of belief, right or wrong. It is a matter of personal experience, the knowledge of God by epiphany, through incontrovertible encounter and by irrevocable intuition. Entering the 'individual' stage, we may have inklings but will not yet with conviction have fully reached this understanding. This is not the end-point of our journey.

The psychology of transition

From the perspective of psychology, except for those on a low spiritual trajectory the dissonance between false everyday ego and true spiritual self increases during Stage 3 until – as with the two Amish men – it becomes unbearable. Denial and falsehood can no longer be sustained.

Our emotions are more truthful than our confused thoughts in this, and come at last to overpower our attachment to comfort, security and the blind desire – come what may – to belong. Anxiety and bewilderment percolating repeatedly through into consciousness offer a warning that we have been going off track. Doubt – about our conditioning, about what we have been taught, about what we think and believe, about how to behave, about our attitudes and values – rises up now to save us, propelling us into enquiry, into independence of mind, into thinking essential philosophical and spiritual matters through for ourselves and stimulating us to seek guidance, whether online, from books, from wise teachers, mentors and gurus or from all of these sources.

Doubt, duly considered, helps us break with conformity and can force us where we need to go, into the individual stage. But this is not inevitable – doubt can be ignored and overridden. In the conformist stage, much of the time when our most cherished beliefs are challenged we retreat and simply resort to denial. This is our defence when any threat to personal integrity, to our sense of who we are, grows too great. Pressed further, we commonly respond with anger – a sign that we are resisting some kind of threatening loss. Anger, of course, in turn fuels discord and discrimination, aggressive words and destructive, alienating behaviour.

Those who disagree with and challenge us become enemies; and we are far from ready yet to love our enemies, as Christ would have us do. We remain caught up in left-brain style thinking, lacking the capacity for empathic fellow feeling, seeing our opponents as offensive impersonal objects to be either ignored or eradicated. This is the great tragedy of immaturity: intolerance based on persistent, self-seeking one-sidedness. 'I'm right; you're wrong,' we always insist, to which our equally limited opponents reply, 'No, we're right; you're wrong.' And so it continues – fruitlessly, harmfully, until one or the other is destroyed or forced to back down!

In *Romeo and Juliet* Shakespeare gives us a moving account of the bitter destructiveness of highly defensive/aggressive clan-like allegiance and feuding, where the rival Montague and Capulet families are pitted venomously against one another. As the genius playwright poetically reveals, such entrenched opposition can lead only to enmity, insult, exclusion, aggression, death and bereavement. Love is conditional here: only sanctioned between followers of the same clan. True love, crossing boundaries, is spurned, unacceptable, and must either be hidden or trampled on and debased. Finally, in Shakespeare's hands even the highest form of innocent love leads to a tragic finale. Grief-stricken, Romeo dies first, then Juliet follows him: they disappear into both death and immortality.

At the time, passing through the conformist stage, group loyalty seems to us natural and praiseworthy. Religious loyalty and patriotism remain cherished ideals for many. But whether on a large scale or in a more local, parochial sense, these types of loyalty have painfully destructive consequences. The additional participation of those less discerning and easily led people, still holding back in the conditioning stage, provides the material for armies and the occasion for serious and bitter conflict, with little hope of resolution except through the maturation of those concerned. Territorial disputes, clan feuds, class war, civil war, revolutions, so-called Holy Crusades and Jihads all depend on such circumstances, on right/wrong, us/them, intolerant, immature, 'fundamentalist' thinking.

There are of course more mature ways of behaving. Looking back later, growing wiser, we can see that wars and other conflicts – including wars of words, written and spoken – are less about religious matters, for example, than about territory, power and the control of people.[11] In our own lives, with maturity we may also come to see our earlier intransigent decrees and insistent behaviour towards others as unfair and unrealistic. With an increasing facility for appreciating other people's points of view we learn to give way gracefully in the interests of restoring harmony. Even when continuing to disagree we eventually come to see how much can be gained for everyone by hearkening to Jesus' advice: 'Do not resist an evildoer. But if anyone strikes you on the right cheek, turn the other also' (Matthew 5.39).

Another way of saying it is, 'If you find yourself with the choice between being right and being kind, always choose kindness.' With the adoption of such enlightened ideas there is hope. According to the natural laws and processes described earlier, maturity is achieved by letting go over matters of strong opinion and belief. The process involves the everyday ego accepting and tolerating increasing degrees of doubt and uncertainty. It may be that holding firm to a belief, being sure that it is correct, makes us feel strong and proudly 'in the right'; but this is a trap, binding us to falsehood, to an incomplete rather than whole and mature vision of reality. As Christians we are tasked with seeking that mature vision because to 'find a life' in falsehood, as our Lord has said (Matthew 10.39), is surely also to lose it.

In seeking greater truth it is certainly profitable to reflect on our emotions. The 'traffic lights' story about Peter from Chapter 3 demonstrates how reflecting on anger, when it arises, can be helpful. It often allows us to discover where we might be holding on too tightly to something. If we can then see how counterproductive and destructive this is (how hurt people – especially those close to us – become as a result of our arrogance and insensitivity), through remorse and the accompanying emotions of shame, guilt and sadness, we can grow. In fact this is mainly how we do grow as people: by loosening our attachments, letting go of our aversions and making friends with our enemies, learning to see things from their point of view. This too accords well with the Christian vision of maturity: for only by 'losing your life' – by giving up our false ego-identity, removing our mask, transforming our rigid persona into a true and spontaneously reflective face – will we eventually 'find life'. This is the only way for each of us to discover our authentic and trustworthy spiritual self.

The dangers of liberal alternatives

Relatively few people are raised in so inflexible a tradition as the Amish. It is more common to experience a comparatively liberal form of Christian religious upbringing – too liberal, in some cases, to find anything sufficiently consistent with which to conform. This presents a different kind of problem. It is hard to make a leap forward if the ground beneath you is not sufficiently firm.

Speculate, for a moment, on the fate of Ephraim and Jesse's children, being raised neither fully within nor outside the Amish community. Their future is much less well defined. They will have more options than their cousins still in the community, and will necessarily have to think things through, drawing conclusions and making decisions for themselves. Although difficult, from the perspective of independent-minded maturity, this seems like a healthier situation to be in.

Weak moral guidance, though, associated with a less than robust religious education, might lead teenagers towards delinquency in the absence of any other (non-religious) ethical training or discipline, especially when coupled with other negative or antisocial influences. Temptations abound, and with them the risk of losing oneself in excesses of acquisitive, intoxicated and/or sexualized activity, with the consequent risk of addictive patterns of behaviour.

Such young people, attempting to conform with others outside society's mainstream, may associate with other potential miscreants, who are often older and unscrupulous. Such a young person, feeling undervalued, will go through a self-destructive 'conformist' period, conforming to regrettable antisocial patterns of thought, speech and behaviour. However, hope remains. The same factors might equally, depending on the person's innate temperament and other external factors, promote independence of mind. Given adequate investment of spiritual capital – love, tolerance, compassion and guidance, for example – these developing adults may yet emerge with courage, inner strength and a sense of optimism, more powerfully capable of self-reliance in the following 'individual' stage. As many already do, Christians and Christian organizations have an excellent opportunity to be among those external factors and contribute sensitively here.

The individual stage – responsibility and the threat of isolation

Leaving the comfort zone of conformity behind, the fourth 'individual' stage of spiritual development is difficult for nearly everyone. Each person's passage into and through it will be unique, such that valid generalizations are not so reliable. There may be an initial, compensatory search for a new group to join, for new companionship and self-validation in a different, broader, more self-determined comfort zone. If this route is not taken – or does not bring satisfaction but only further compromise – the second pathway often involves a painful period of isolation, loneliness and uncertainty, a kind of 'exile of the soul'. However brief or long, this is a necessary prerequisite for entry into the next 'integration' stage. Death precedes resurrection. We need breaking apart before we can grow back together.

A common story might be that of a person raised within a liberal or medium-strict Christian tradition who, as a teenager, grows bored with repetition and stops attending services, reading Scripture or engaging in regular prayer, deciding to reject a Christian identity and pursue other priorities. Like such a person, we may consider it more important to concentrate on furthering our education, find employment and establish an income, find a life partner, acquire a home then build and educate a family. These become principally worldly pursuits in our life. Spiritual awareness has diminished and spiritual needs – the tug on the everyday ego from the spiritual self – are readily deferred or ignored.

The prevailing secular, consumerist culture in the West does, however, sanction some spiritual influence and activity; and there are growing numbers of people who consider themselves 'spiritual but not religious'. They are to be found among those who still have their children baptized in church and get married there, who attend services at the great festivals of Christmas and Easter, visit cathedrals and other sacred places and who enjoy sacred music.

In a less religious but no less spiritual context, people come together en masse to share both painful and uplifting emotions: at a royal wedding, Jubilee or funeral, for example, when the remains of service personnel killed in the line of duty are repatriated, at the Olympics and other emotive sporting events, at music festivals, when some man-made or natural disaster occurs or in protest against some form of apparent public injustice. People still make the sign of the Christian cross – by 'crossing fingers' – when appealing for good fortune, and invoke the same true cross of the crucifixion whenever they 'touch wood'.

The links between religion and politics, between Christianity and the state, long and often problematic, remain important. The distinction between tourist and pilgrim is also often blurred, reflecting a kind of 'spiritual adolescence'. Cathedrals charge entry fees while secular buildings – both new and converted, like the Dome built for the Millennium and the Tate Modern art gallery – have cathedral-like qualities. Other nominally secular buildings – including the British Library, great sporting arenas like Wembley and the Olympic Park stadia, the Globe and Stratford theatres (venues devoted to Shakespeare and his plays) – fulfil people's need to come together in spirit.[12] Green-belt land, the great national parks, bird sanctuaries, botanical gardens, arboreta and National Trust properties are reserved and maintained largely commerce-free for people to enjoy the landscape and engage meaningfully with nature. These all bear witness to the innate spirituality – the spirit of wholeness – of humankind.

During adolescence, while preferring 'people like us', we also discover the attraction of opposites, the most important and powerful of which is that between women and men, men and women. Adolescent love, when we first experience it, tends to be complicated by a powerful biological, hormonal, sexual element and by strong ties of possession. It is in this way conditional, falling short – however wonderful and heavenly it seems at the time – of the more spiritually mature, selfless and unconditional love it may grow into. We find someone precious, become attached and strive to hold on, risking jealous anxiety at the possibility of separation and loss, quick to anger, recrimination and self-blame when this seems to be happening, deeply sorrowful when a genuine affair of love seems to have reached an end. This is very painful; yet many of us grow through such experiences, moderating our possessive needs and adjusting our expectations to take greater account of those of the other person in future relationships. To echo a theme from earlier chapters, loss is, in this way, beneficial.

Those successful in love and in forming a partnership, especially when the couple is blessed with children, may find this small nuclear group sufficient within which to conform, setting their own rules, guidelines and values – without necessarily thinking about them very deeply – and living essentially for each other. Work is for personal satisfaction, status and mainly monetary reward – to pay the household bills and for spending on material benefits and luxuries – rather than to offer service to others. In this way many people find an acceptable level of comfort in joining the great public at large while retaining some definition of self as separate and competitive. This inevitably turns other people into rivals: in love; for work; over purchases and possessions reflecting status; as fans in 'fanatical' support of a favourite team, rock group or whatever. 'For where your treasure is, there your heart will be also' (Matthew 6.21).

This is, then, only a partial move forwards into the independent-mindedness of the 'individual' stage because an element of self-seeking remains. With the continuing possibility, therefore, of threat and loss, predispositions to both anxiety and anger persist, depending on con-tinuing attachments and aversions based on differences: personal, national, political, cultural – and religious.

Whatever new group we may align ourselves with will eventually prove to have similar problems to those left behind. It might be too rigid, exclusive and therefore partisan; or it may be too liberal and weak, lacking in discipline, consistency and coherence.

We are still thinking primarily for ourselves in this stage, setting our own goals and achieving our aims as far as we can; but eventually – either gradually or suddenly – we grow aware that something vital is yet missing. We may have achieved a degree of worldly success in terms of family, wealth and security, also public esteem and status, but it does not seem sufficient. Our self-seeking ambitions and our criticisms of others – rivals, helpers deemed to have fallen short, people with dif-ferent values and standards – may have damaged relationships along the way, leaving us feeling isolated, alone and vulnerable. If we are to progress, we need to encounter further situations in which 'something happens'. As we reach towards the depths of the 'individual' stage and accompany-ing isolation, we require reconnection to the spiritual dimension to assist us in reappraising our lives, turning us around in another, more fruitful direction.

Notes

1 See Afterword: My Christian journey.
2 Steve Taylor (2009).
3 Diarmuid O'Murchu said this while leading a day of reflection on 'Indigenous Spirituality' at St John's Seminary, Wonersh, Surrey, on 25 October 2014, at which I was present. See also Diarmuid O'Murchu (2012).
4 Bruce Parry with Mark McCrum (2008).
5 Parry and McCrum (2008), p. 45.
6 Paranoia, involving delusions of persecution, for example, is often coupled with grandiosity, a defence against strong feelings of insignificance. 'I am so great', the powerful person reasons, 'that people envy and want to destroy me.' The reality – of being ordinary or even inferior – is too threatening of personal integrity for that person to accept.
7 Richard Rohr (2012), p. xvii.
8 Literally, from the Latin, *held* doctrine: 'That to which Christianity *holds*'.
9 The Anglican Church, for example, was established through an English king, Henry VIII, asserting his individual will over national conformism and political obedience to the Pope in Rome.
10 *Trouble in Amish Paradise*, directed by Andrew Tait, produced by Ludo Graham; BBC2, screened on 18 February 2009.
11 See, for example, Karen Armstrong (2014).
12 In one Sussex town, adding immensely to community feeling and solidarity, new buildings in the past 20 years include: a community centre with an auditorium and additional space for local groups and society meetings; a leisure centre with a swimming pool, two gymnasia and squash courts; also a museum and a library.

7

Turnaround

Ambivalence

In contemporary secular culture, retaining the identity of a Christian through the 'individual' stage can be difficult. For one thing, the defection of our peers away from religion represents a challenge and a temptation to do likewise. Retreat into conformity – tying oneself more tightly to one's Church in terms of doctrine, practices and community – might seem the better solution. Nevertheless for those responding to the drive to think, speak and act independently, neither defection nor blinkered adherence to a prescribed form of Christian religion will suffice. Isolation, doubt and uncertainty unavoidably beckon.

Another hindrance is the powerful hold of the 'everyday ego'. Even the most ardent Christian finds his or her will and desire pitted sometimes against apparently unfavourable circumstances, and against the will of God. Even those who would be faithful and obedient find themselves in a struggle. Thomas Merton, for example, after nearly six years in the monastery, wrote:

> By this time I should have been delivered of any problems about my true identity . . . But then there was this double, this writer who had followed me into the cloister. He is still on my track. He rides my shoulders . . . I cannot lose him. He still wears the name of Thomas Merton . . . He is supposed to be dead. But he stands and meets me in the doorway of all my prayers, and follows me into church. He kneels with me behind the pillar, the Judas, and talks to me all the time in my ear. He is a business man. He is full

of ideas ... I can't get rid of him ... Nobody seems to understand that one of us has got to die.[1]

Progressing through the individual stage, Christians will develop an increasingly personal relationship with the father God and his son Jesus. There is a strong tradition for many people also to call upon the Divine Feminine, on the Holy Mother, St Mary the Virgin. Communication includes the repetition of formal prayers but there will be important times of silent conversation, contemplation and communion.

We talk to God in our minds, ask for things to happen, for other things not to happen, praise and thank him. In the uncertainty of the individual stage what we seek most from God is reassurance and guidance, by asking questions like: 'Am I in the right place, with the right people, doing the right things? Where am I meant to be? What is my true vocation in life?' If our prayers do not seem to be answered; when the only answer is prolonged silence, we are at risk of feeling neglected. 'He does not care,' we might conclude; or, worse, 'He is not really there.' Perhaps then, in bitterness or boredom, we stop asking. The true nature of our relationship with the divine now is ambivalence: we are being drawn in two directions at once.

When Jesus said to the rich young man seeking eternal life: 'go, sell your possessions, and give the money to the poor' (Matthew 19.21), the youth rejected this idea and turned away, grieving. If we similarly dislike the direction God invites us to follow, the self-denial and self-sacrifice he asks of us, might we not also feel negative, perhaps growing angry with God? If we do not yet understand that self-denial and self-sacrifice are rather 'ego-denial' and 'ego-sacrifice', giving us a golden opportunity to find our true selves, we may think to bargain with him, to ask for more time, or hope for an easier passage through this phase of our lives. The struggle for an agreeable compromise might go on for a long time as we try to make God fit our terms rather than submit to his. Eventually for some the effort – and God's apparent intransigence – grows too much; we turn our back on him rather than let go of our desires, grieve our losses, surrender control and so mature into greater obedience and faith. This is the choice we face at this critical stage of development.

Some people make progress – rather than wrestling in their minds with an external God – by developing the capacity for internalizing the ongoing problem, which becomes more like a struggle between two sides of their own nature: the false, lower everyday ego of the flesh and the true, higher spiritual self of the soul. It is hard to overstate the tenacity of this ego. In 1963, 15 years after writing about 'the double who had followed me into the cloister', a wiser but still troubled Merton explained: 'There is a false self that has to be taken off...There is still much to change before I will really be living in the truth.'

The quote is from a letter to the theologian Jacques Maritain,[2] and appears in *The Thomas Merton Encyclopedia*[3] under the heading 'Truth', where the authors add Merton's idea that:

> Buried within the true self is who we really are. The true self knows its Source in the God who is Truth, and in so doing recognizes its unity with others whom it meets 'on a common ground of spiritual Truth'. Fidelity to Truth means fidelity to 'the light that is in us from God'.

Seek the truth and discover your most authentic self. Merton's advice reveals how best to overcome our ambivalence.

Secularism's big mistake

Elsewhere, in a contrast that extends his thesis, Merton wrote:

> Despair is the absolute extreme of self-love. It is reached when a man deliberately turns his back on all help from anyone else in order to taste the rotten luxury of knowing himself (or herself) to be lost...But a man (or woman) who is truly humble cannot despair, because in the humble man (person) there is no longer any such thing as self-pity.[4]

Here is another choice: to accept or reject help from the Holy Spirit and from her instruments: other people, our spiritual guides. Humility can be counted among the most important of religious values, alongside others like honesty, trust, kindness, tolerance, patience, perseverance, discernment, courage, compassion, wisdom, beauty and hope. These compare with the 'fruit of the Spirit' according to St Paul (see Galatians 5.22). To highlight and promote them does not mean that worldly values are intrinsically worthless or bad. The idea of self-improvement with the aim of achieving worldly success, including fame and financial success, is praiseworthy in many instances. However, problems arise – for the individual and for society – when selfish, material and commercial values overtake spiritual values. This is secularism's big mistake. In the reverse situation, with mature, spiritual values predominating, everything tends to happen more smoothly, less destructively, and for everyone's benefit.

In whatever way anyone's unique journey has been unfolding, the individual stage involves particularly discovering and developing ourselves as independent and responsible observer-participants in our own life story; people with choices to consider and make. This means comprehensive reappraisal of our assumptions and values and the relinquishing of former attachments, while coping with and adjusting to the resulting uncertainty and relative isolation. For Christians it means developing our personal relationship with God, playing out an inner dialogue of ambivalence concerning the pull of the flesh versus integrity of the soul.

The individual stage continues as long as worldly ambitions and values hold sway. As the pendulum swings towards maturity, as spiritual awareness is somehow rekindled, we grow ready at last for a homecoming experience, for the 'integration' Stage 5.

Contemplation

During the teen years it is increasingly common for people to move away from home to college or university, where they encounter people whose conditioning experiences are likely to have been similar, in some ways but different – often markedly different – in others. This is how many of us are first exposed to new ideas, traditions, opinions, lifestyles, customs and beliefs; also to new religions.

The challenge to conformity with our parent group culture is thus expanded when we travel, first within our own country and especially

when we go abroad. Higher education also contributes to further knowledge and broader experience; naturally, therefore, we begin to assimilate
all these factors with our conditioning, with our habitual ways of thinking
and being. A combination of challenge and opportunity is extended for
those students who take time out before university specifically to travel.

Taking a short holiday abroad allows just a snapshot to contrast and
compare differences – favourably and unfavourably – with what we are
used to. We discover whether we like or dislike foreign climates, scenery,
food, customs and the people we meet, without having to think too
deeply about it. We will, after all, be returning home soon. Taking months
or a year and spending longer in a particular country – not isolated in
a tourist hotel in a resort but actually living and working in a foreign
environment, necessarily adopting new ways of thinking, communicating
(perhaps in another language) and operating – we are likely to consider
these matters more deeply, to concentrate on behaving appropriately and
fitting in while also contributing what we can from our own background
and education to the benefit of our hosts and host country.

This process of concentrating on something, thinking and reflecting
deeply about it, is a form of 'contemplation'. Contemplation is a practice
that simultaneously increases awareness of both our environment and ourselves. As such it enables us to clarify our place within the environment,
in the place and community we inhabit. Contemplation, then, leads
naturally to personal growth. Thomas Merton considered contemplation
as at the pinnacle of human endeavour:

> Contemplation is the highest expression of man's intellectual and
> spiritual life. It is that life itself, fully awake, fully active, fully aware
> that it is alive. It is spiritual wonder. It is spontaneous awe at the
> sacredness of life, of being.[5]

Merton here correctly identifies both spiritual and intellectual components. The year out before starting higher education is often called a
'gap' year. This is a happy coincidence, because some sort of awareness
gap – a break in our habitual patterns of consciousness – is all it takes
to propel us forward. 'Something happens', even if only in a minor
way (because such steps are irreversible and cumulative), and such a

shift in mental activity will be accompanied by biological changes in the brain. Spiritual growth requires greater than usual involvement of the more emotional and imaginative right hemisphere, while activity in the more intellectual left hemisphere continues but is comparatively weaker.

For a person living along a low trajectory of spiritual development, with a tendency to pay more attention to similarities than differences, contemplation of new and foreign experiences may not seem especially remarkable or challenging. For those on higher trajectories, in contrast – those with a stronger level of dissonance between the everyday ego and the spiritual self – contemplation can lead to moments of self-awareness of such magnitude as to bring about an abrupt and major shift in balance between the two. Seeds may be sown, leading – slowly or abruptly – to a marked revision of lifestyle, aims, ambitions and values.

Steve Taylor, a researcher in transpersonal psychology at Liverpool John Moores University, interviewed over 30 people with experience of major positive psychological change for his book *Out of the Darkness*.[6] He concluded that there are three possible types of experience resulting from what he calls 'spiritual alchemy':

1 temporary awakening experiences
2 gradual but permanent change
3 sudden, dramatic transformations.

Thomas Merton – one of only seven people named by James Fowler as having reached Stage 6, the final stage in his scheme of spiritual development[7] – had experience of all three.

The example of Thomas Merton

Merton was an exceptional person who kept a remarkably complete, revealing and articulate record of his inner life and spiritual journey.[8] Born in France in 1915, he was educated partly in that country and in England. He lost his mother tragically early. She died of stomach cancer aged 34 when he was six, so it was particularly unfortunate when his father also succumbed (to a brain tumour at the age of 43) three days after Merton turned 16. Merton completed his studies at Oakham School in Rutland two years later, and then had a gap period of several months before starting at Clare College, Cambridge, during which he took a vacation in Rome.

From a broadly Christian parental background he had been educated in a form of Protestant Christianity at Oakham and previously at the Lycée in Montauban, France, but was not especially religiously inclined or active. In Rome, however, he visited several churches and was vividly impressed by the many Christian mosaics he inspected there, vibrant images that, in his words, 'Told me more than I had ever known of the doctrine of a God of infinite power, wisdom and love Who had yet become Man.'[9]

Merton had for some time been deeply unsure and unhappy within himself and, while in Rome, had a brief but powerful vision of his father that resulted in a strong sense of shame. He was, as he later wrote, 'overwhelmed with a sudden and profound insight into the misery and corruption of my own soul'. At that moment his desire for freedom from all the worldly matters holding him in a kind of addictive slavery broke through and he began to pray, 'with my intellect and my imagination ... out of the very roots of my life and of my being ... to the God I had never known ... to help me get free.'[10] Momentarily, having previously felt incomplete and corrupted, Merton felt whole. Apparently his left brain (intellect) and right brain (imagination) were in this instance working together.

Merton started reading the Bible and praying in churches. His final ten days or so in Rome, he said, were 'full of joy'. This was apparently a temporary experience, yet important seeds had been sown. Nevertheless he experienced a significant relapse into temptation after starting at Cambridge later in the year. There followed a period distinguished by academic failure and by what Merton himself called 'riotous living'.[11] He lost his scholarship at the end of the academic year, whereupon his guardian insisted that he must leave Cambridge.

During that summer of 1934, under a cloud, Merton moved to New York, where his mother's parents lived, enrolling the following

January at Columbia University to continue his studies. It was not until 16 November 1938, when Merton was almost 24, that those Roman seeds began bearing fruit. By then he had come to accept his destiny as a Christian, and was baptized into the Roman Catholic faith.[12]

After the spiritual wake-up call in Rome, things had clearly been happening gradually within the soul of Thomas Merton; then 'something happened' to him again. In April 1940 he was travelling alone in pre-revolution Cuba on another pilgrimage-type vacation. Attending mass in church one Sunday he felt uplifted by the strong, clear singing of a crowd of schoolchildren and their vibrant response at the start of a prayer; then:

> Something went off inside me like a thunderclap ... I knew with the most absolute and unquestionable certainty that before me ... directly present to some apprehension or other of mine, which was above that of the senses, was ... God in all His essence, all His power, God in the flesh and God in Himself ... The unshake-able certainty, the clear and immediate knowledge that heaven was right in front of me, struck me like a thunderbolt and went through me like a flash of lightning and seemed to lift me up off the earth.[13]

After this, being less than utterly committed to the Christian life was no longer an option. Soon after, on 10 December 1941, Merton entered the Abbey of Our Lady of Gethsemani in Kentucky and became a Cistercian monk.[14] He received the religious name 'Brother Louis' on formally entering the novitiate in February 1942. As a monk he was encouraged to write by his Abbot and in 1948 the best-selling account of his religious journey to date, *The Seven Storey Mountain*,[15] was published. The following year Merton was ordained a Roman Catholic priest, becoming in turn 'Father Louis'.

In worldly terms Merton was a success; in spiritual terms too, many would say; but his doubts persisted. As his journals show, he continued to worry about whether he was in the right place, doing the right thing. He was concerned about being cut off and estranged from people in the world. The tension within him seems to have grown until 'something happened' to him yet again. In March 1958 Merton had to go to Louisville on monastery business, to arrange the printing of a leaflet. As he described the event:

> In the center of the shopping district, I was suddenly overwhelmed with the realization that I loved all those people, that they were mine and I theirs, that we could not be alien to one another even though we were total strangers. It was like waking from a dream of separation, of spurious self-isolation in a special world, the world of renunciation and supposed holiness.[16]

If the effects of earlier epiphanies had weakened, this new insight provided a great spur to Merton, who wrote at this time of his wariness of the 'constant, habitual passivity' of being a monk, and of a 'new and constant struggle in my interior life'.[17] To address this struggle he felt called to spend more of his time in contemplation, completely alone. He sought the opportunity to become a religious hermit and was eventually able to fulfil his purpose, moving into a hermitage in the grounds of the Abbey in August 1965.

From the late 1950s Merton's writings became more socially relevant and critical, speaking out against race hatred, for example, and with powerful warnings regarding the world of technology, mass media and big business. Particularly mindful of the sixth commandment, 'Thou shalt not kill' (Exodus 20.13 KJV), and our Lord's second great commandment, to 'love your neighbour as yourself' (Matthew 22.39), Merton came out strenuously in favour of peace, against war in general and specifically against US nuclear capability, the arms race and his country's involvement in the Vietnam war.[18] After the bombing of Haiphong in April 1967, for example, he wrote witheringly in his journal about the financial gains associated with an economy geared to war as the prime motivation for continuing the destruction:

> The V.N. war has made this country richer than it ever was before. It is keeping the economy up, preventing a recession … The brutal truth is that the people of America by and large have *no real objection* even to a war with China as long as things go on

as they are here now . . . I am living in an immoral, blind, even in some sense criminal society which is hypocritical, bloated, self-righteous, and unable to see its true condition – by and large people are 'nice' as long as they are not disturbed in their comfortable and complacent lives. They cannot see the price of their 'respectability'. And I am part of it and I don't know what to do about it.[19]

Turnaround

Merton's inner spiritual journey was not yet over, but these three 'epiphanies' – in Rome, Cuba and Louisville – reveal how for some people the Holy Spirit bursts through and breaks apart aspects of the persona, the brittle mask of the habitual everyday ego, the identity we construct from tightly held attachments and aversions, the false person we think we are. Each such breakthrough reveals in us a gap, an empty space, a void, a silence, which only the divine essence can fill. In addition, simultaneously we may be blessed with the miraculous revelation that we, through the agency of the spiritual self, are linked seamlessly to God and the sacred unity of creation – and thereby to each other – and that we have always been.

For this is the essential insight of the integration stage: that the group to which we ultimately belong is no partisan subgroup of people – whether defined by family, gender, race, religion, politics or anything else – but the entirety of diverse humanity. As an old proverb says: 'Everyone's blood is red; everyone's tears are salty.'

Once the overriding knowledge of universal kinship takes over within us – deeply and wholeheartedly rather than just superficially and intellectually – there can be no going back. Our compassionate nature is increasingly revealed to us and to the world. Our lives no longer have meaning unless dedicated to finding the wisdom to live accordingly, governed by selfless love.

When the Holy Spirit takes hold, when 'something happens' to bring us to this remarkable insight, we have reached the great turnaround. We have become committed 'seekers after truth'. Propelled onward from the isolation of the individual stage into the integration stage, we have at last fully entered Richard Rohr's 'second half of life'. Ambivalences revert into wholehearted appreciation and affection. We embark upon a mighty homecoming; the collapse back of the dissonant self-seeking ego towards the sanctity of the soul.

As St Paul approached Damascus, 'suddenly a light from heaven flashed around him' and he was blinded (Acts 9.3–8). Three days later, at God's bidding, Ananias went and laid his hands on him: 'And immediately something like scales fell from his eyes, and his sight was restored' (Acts 9.17–18). For many the conversion experience is similar (like the lifting of a veil or scales falling from our eyes), characterized by immediacy, vibrancy, vitality, energy and power – 'like a thunderbolt', as Thomas Merton said.

Biologically speaking, the description speaks of an altered state of consciousness followed by an immense resurgence of the right hemisphere; the master regaining control over his errant emissary. Such events are not only mind-blowing but transformative. When they happen a permanent shift is achieved and we find ourselves protectively enveloped by a magnificent spiritual comfort zone. The experience of thorough personal renewal feels to many like being 'born again'; and such a rebirth – into the pristine state of the pre-infancy ego – brings Christians to renewed communication and communion with the almighty and the infinite, to the start of a newly reverential and loving relationship with God and with Christ. This is the true meaning of 'conversion'. Rather than any kind of superficial switch in allegiance from another path to nominal Christianity, it is a deep-seated transformation from spiritual ignorance into wisdom.

With the change our partial beliefs and religious doubts are transformed into absolute faith. After this all questioning is of oneself rather than God; of our willingness and ability to surrender our earthbound will in obedience and submission to the divine. That is the remaining work of the integration stage as we approach closer towards full spiritual maturity. Non-Christians, connected in their own way to the sacred unity of being, may find themselves travelling a similar path.

Post traumatic growth

The pioneering Persian psychologist Reza Arasteh wrote about people working towards, as he put it, 'final personality integration', which – as he makes clear[20] – is equivalent to achieving full spiritual maturity. Arasteh studied the lives of both exceptional historical figures (notably Goethe,[21] the German poet and philosopher, and Rūmī,[22] the Sufi love-poet and spiritual leader from Konya in present-day Turkey) and of less remarkable people (including 'Kamal', a 32-year-old Turk born into a middle-class family in a small town in Anatolia). Kamal fits the pattern of a person – like a student on a lengthily extended gap-year – who through education and extensive travel, immersed in both Eastern and Western cultural value-systems and faith traditions, had become engaged in concerted self-exploration. By the time he met Arasteh, having become confused by secularism and by the diversity of religions and values he encountered, he needed help. With wise therapeutic assistance Kamal was able to redefine his life's aims, eventually becoming, as Arasteh remarks, 'not a man related to place and time, but to production, activity and creative behaviour'.[23]

Arasteh described the critical turnaround in people on the road to final integration as linked to the awakening of what he called, 'existential awareness', a concept similar to the term 'relational consciousness' used by David Hay and Rebecca Nye (see Chapter 5), similar also to the notions of 'holistic vision' and equally of 'spiritual awareness'. This turnaround is what we are deliberately making 'much ado' about here.[24] According to Arasteh a number of factors can provide a shock to instigate existential awareness and therefore spiritual awakening. Among these he lists:

1 being in a situation in which power, wealth and fame lose their security value;
2 continuous struggle against social and mental obstacles, paradoxes and discrepancies;
3 a traumatic experience, such as loss of a loved one.

These are all situations involving threat and loss, capable of triggering the whole spectrum of painful emotions described earlier in Chapter 3:

anxiety, bewilderment, doubt, anger, shame, guilt and sadness. They spark, in other words, the process of bereavement, of letting go of attachment (lysis) and release of emotional energy (catharsis), followed by healing and growth.

It should not surprise us, then, that in *Out of the Darkness* Taylor describes people as benefiting from what he calls 'post-traumatic growth' and 'suffering-induced transformational experiences' (SITEs).[25] There is considerable research about this, covering people who have suffered life events such as serious illnesses, house fires, military combat and becoming refugees, as well as bereavement. Positive and lasting changes reported include: new inner fortitude and courage; the discovery of new abilities and skills; greater self-confidence and faith in the outcome of life's problems; improved appreciation of life generally (especially of the 'little things' previously taken for granted); the awakening of compassion for the plight of others; and increased comfort with intimacy, together with deeper, more satisfying relationships. One of the commonest changes described is a more philosophical or spiritual attitude to life and a 'deeper level of awareness'.[26] These are among the fruits of the integration stage.

Taylor appropriately calls his interview subjects 'shifters'. Some were public figures (like Dr Gill Hicks, survivor of the 7/7 London Tube terrorist bombings, and spiritual writer and teacher Eckhart Tolle), but most were otherwise unknown. Few thought of themselves as religious or particularly spiritual before their shift but all had in common the contributory experience of intense and/or prolonged psychological turmoil and suffering. One woman described by Taylor, for example, suddenly abandoned by the father of her two-year-old daughter, feeling betrayed and a terrible sense of loss, cried herself eventually to sleep one night after seriously contemplating suicide. When she awoke her torment had been replaced by a profound sense of peace and well-being. The loss had brought her to an emotional catharsis, the result of which was a healthy change of attitude. She slept again, and awoke in the morning 'feeling more positive and resilient'.[27]

Power, wealth and fame are no protection against illness or mental ill-health, both of which offer the opportunity for deep personal reflection and may even demand it. A number of Taylor's subjects' spiritual experiences occurred in the context of disease. One had myalgic encephalitis (ME), for example, another was hospitalized for weeks with a hip fracture, and more than one woman in the sample had breast cancer. Their stories are heartening.

One of the cancer sufferers, after her shift experience, became a poet. Trying to explain the changes of perception that led to this, and the shift in attitude afterwards, she said:

> When I'm out in the countryside and I see animals, I feel that I *really* see them. It's difficult to describe, but it's like there's an extra dimension ... I really want to use my time productively ... I wasn't doing that before. I know that time is really precious and that before I wasted it by not really being myself ... The old me tried to avoid being by myself ... But now I'm quite happy to do nothing on my own.

Taylor writes about this businesswoman – who had by then sold her company – as having 'a new sense of values and a sense of the preciousness of life'.[28] There is an interesting paradox involved here: being happy doing nothing while not wanting to waste any time. The shift involves contentment with 'being' rather than 'doing'. About time spent doing nothing this shifter said, nevertheless, that she felt really fulfilled.

Another cancer survivor, who initially became depressed and felt defeated following the diagnosis, said similarly:

> I've had a weird but wonderful journey, hitting rock bottom and going back up again ... It's been very liberating, and led to a massive change in my values ... I used to be really ambitious ... Now I feel as if I'm rejecting material things ... I have a really strong connection with nature, feeling part of it for the first time ever ... Now I live very much in the present ... And that helps me to enjoy things for what they are ... And because I'm more present with other people, I'm connecting with them more. They've responded to the change in me ... So my relationships have definitely improved.

This woman's account continued:

> I'm very much aware that I used to live a very ego-based kind of life and I feel that through being aware of it, I can drop it. Now I see myself as part of a whole. I see my life in a universal context, whereas before I didn't think beyond my own desires. If this is what all these traumas have led to, then I guess I'm very lucky I've emerged from the experience a rather different, more 'evolved' spiritual person.[29]

Another example from Steve Taylor concerns a 20-year-old who described to him how, during a lengthy episode of depression, she had picked up a marble and started playing with it, whereupon the familiar world melted away, a mystical vision of beauty and perfection suddenly in its place.

> I saw reality as simply this perfect oneness ... Everything felt just right. The marble seemed a reflection of the universe. All my 'problems' and suffering seemed meaningless, ridiculous ... There was a feeling of acceptance and oneness. It was a moment of enlightenment.[30]

These are not unusual stories. In my life as a doctor and psychiatrist I have heard many people, after a period of significant adversity and distress, say that although they would not want to suffer similarly again they are glad to have done so. Why? Because the painful experience had given them pause, caused them to think and reconsider, to contemplate their existence; and this had taught them something vital about themselves. They had discovered a set of true values and learned more about the central meaning and purpose of their lives.

Someone I interviewed and encouraged to share her experiences, Nikki Slade, a talented singer, musician and now therapist,[31] went through an unpleasant episode about 20 years ago of what appeared to be severe mental illness, a manic episode complicated by problems of excessive alcohol and drug use. Rather than being ultimately destructive, however, it was for her no less than a spiritual breakthrough. Describing the search for her true, spiritual self, Nikki wrote: 'I believe

I wanted to know who I was in essence since I could first speak in infancy. Nothing could satiate my hunger more than the awakening of my inner divinity.'[32]

After coming fully to terms with her experiences during the episode, a process which took her more than a decade, she added:

> Upon this mighty awakening, I could no longer doubt that there is an infinite loving presence in this universe and it lives inside me and in all sentient beings, waiting to be beckoned ... I now embrace life on life's terms, enjoying its apparent paradoxes and sudden changes. No matter how rough life becomes, I can never forget the peace of my own 'inner self'.[33]

The homecoming journey

One of Steve Taylor's examples, after years of turmoil, uncertainty and distress, had a high intensity spiritual awakening, during which:

> The void rolled out completely, the world disappeared and my consciousness expanded into an infinite timeless consciousness which was me, although everyone else at the same time ... I knew what had happened was the pure truth, beyond any question ... Everything shone with a light ... A massive energy pervaded my body, which I couldn't seem to contain.[34]

Taylor's point was that this person did not understand the experience and found it difficult to process. Never sufficiently exposed to Christianity or any other religion, she knew almost nothing about spiritual traditions or practices. It follows that a Christian education, together with a life of prayer and worship, can provide an excellent context in which to make sense of the kind of breakthrough spiritual experiences or 'epiphanies' described here. For this reason many people with limited formal religious training turn to explore Christianity after a spiritual awakening, expanding their knowledge and experience accordingly. There is an obvious opportunity for churches here, taken up by those which already run 'beginners' and 'back to faith' courses.

At one time a Christian who experienced the Holy Spirit in his or her life – especially when young – might have felt called to the religious life, making vows of poverty and obedience to God and his Church, accepting a life of celibacy too in a monastery or a convent. Others, both men and – when permitted – women, may seek ordination as deacons and priests, living not cloistered lives but out in the world, preaching the gospel of Christ.

People taking up a religious vocation are, however, in a minority. For others a calling to the service of others will make them health-care professionals or teachers, or have them bring Christian principles and values to whatever other occupation seems to them right and promising. This is by no means an easy task when secular organizations – including those in charge of health care and education – are controlled by economic and political priorities. Religious organizations come powerfully under such pressures too.

Each of us must navigate our way through the terrain of contrasting and contradictory forces, worldly and spiritual, but matters are clearer by the time we have entered the integration stage when the struggle, which once seemed to be between ourselves and external powers, is now increasingly internal: 'Do not be conformed to this world, but be transformed by the renewing of your minds, so that you may discern what is the will of God – what is good and acceptable and perfect' (Romans 12.2). If we reflect honestly on Paul's advice, the *only* way we can hope to change things in the world is by starting where we are, interiorly, with our own hearts and minds.

Reintegration begins when a person recognizes and starts living by the idea that the group he or she must fully acknowledge membership of includes everyone, the entirety of humanity. From the point of view of psychology, whatever our starting point, whatever trajectory we are on, however great or small the dissonance between everyday ego and spiritual self has become, once reawakened there is subsequently a corresponding relaxation of inner tension and the onset of a welcome feeling of homecoming.

During the integration stage there is a permanent switch in motiva-tional dominance from that of the false/incomplete everyday ego, which continues to assert itself but with diminishing strength, towards the true/whole spiritual self. Holistic or spiritual values such as honesty, kindness, generosity, patience, humility and so on – values with universal appeal, values that foster well-meaning co-operation – start to govern within us over more worldly, material values such as wealth, power, luxury and fame, which have only partisan appeal and a tendency rather to promote competition and conflict.

The integration stage involves the playing out in a person's life – in the direction of universality, wisdom, love and compassion – the clash between two sets of values: worldly and spiritual, and the thoughts, emotions and actions they engender. The self-centred, habitual everyday ego is experienced as material, embodied flesh and blood. In contrast the spiritual self, all-encompassing and having no fixed location, renders ego boundaries increasingly permeable. Although essentially inward-looking, it is experienced paradoxically as outwardly focused, expansive, seamlessly connected to others, to nature, to the timeless and the infinite. Our inner spirit, we discover, is creative and intuitive; capable of acquiring incontrovertible knowledge without necessarily leaving us able to explain how we know what we know.

New priorities

The new priorities for us at this stage, therefore, involve discovering – or rediscovering – the spark of the divine Spirit that is kindling within us. This is what St Paul calls 'having the mind of Christ' (1 Corinthians 2.16). This superior mentality then allows and encourages us to reappraise contemplatively our values and behaviour from a universal perspective, bringing our lives increasingly into line with the highest altruistic ideals. In this noble endeavour, as well as Christianity, many turn towards the teachings and practices of other world religions, just as those of other religions expand their understanding by turning towards Christianity. The contemporary Buddhist teacher and writer Adyashanti, for example, has written: 'It was through Christianity that I started to understand what Zen was all about.'[35] Thomas Merton simplified further the nature of the spiritual journey:

For me to be a saint means to be myself. Therefore the problem of sanctity and salvation is in fact the problem of finding out who I am and of discovering my true self ... The secret of my identity is hidden in the love and mercy of God.[36]

After his ordination Merton participated in or celebrated the Holy Eucharist every day of his life, even when away from the monastery. His testimony confirms that no rejection of Christianity need be involved by exploring other faith traditions, only its enrichment. The right hemisphere's activity allows us to consider *both* this *and* that, remember, rather than being obliged – as the left hemisphere would dictate – to choose *either* this *or* that: 'For there is no distinction between Jew and Greek; the same Lord is Lord of all and is generous to all who call on him' (Romans 10.12).

Here, for example, is Thomas Merton writing about the great centre-piece of Hindu Scripture, the *Bhagavad Gita*, the 'Song of God':[37]

The Gita sees that the basic problem of man is the endemic refusal to live by a will other than his own. For in striving to live entirely by his own individual will, instead of becoming free, man is enslaved by forces even more delusory than his own transient fancies ... It is in surrendering a false and illusory liberty on the superficial level that man unites himself with the inner ground of reality and free-dom in himself which is the will of God, of Krishna, of providence, of Tao. These concepts do not all exactly coincide, but they have much in common. The Gita, like the Gospels, teaches us to live in awareness of an inner truth that exceeds the grasp of our thought and cannot be subject to our own control.[38]

Eastern faiths pay more attention to the fruits of unitary, holistic thinking and experience than Western traditions, where a more dualist orientation predominates. Merton's deep interest in Hinduism, Buddhism, Taoism, Judaism and Sufism[39] is well documented.[40] It began before his baptism, with meeting a Hindu monk, Bramachari Mahanambrata, in New York in June 1938,[41] continued after his Louisville epiphany through correspond-ence begun in 1959 with the Zen scholar D. T. Suzuki (who Merton flew to meet in New York city in 1964 on one of his rare occasions of absence from the Abbey), through many letters to friends, writers, other religious scholars and devotees throughout the world,[42] and through meetings with those drawn to visit him in Kentucky, until his journey to Asia in 1968 for a series of interfaith conferences and meetings with spiritual leaders (including the Dalai Lama), as recorded in his final *Asian Journal*.[43]

The Dalai Lama, the spiritual leader of Tibetan Buddhists, speaking at a three-day seminar organized by the World Community for Christian Meditation at Middlesex University near London in 1994, spoke of the 'profound spirituality and love' in the eyes of Thomas Merton, during their three meetings between 4 and 8 November 1968.[44] This was shortly before Merton's death in Thailand on 10 December, exactly 27 years to the day after he entered the monastery. He was 53, and died by accidental electrocution from a faulty fan. In reciprocation, Merton wrote about the Dalai Lama in his journal as follows: 'I felt we had become very good friends ... I feel a great respect and fondness for him as a person and believe, too, that there is a real spiritual bond between us.'[45]

This seems to be a key aspect of mature Christianity: knowledge and the faith that love, respect and the bonding of spirit between people have the power to transcend religious differences. In the next chapters we will also look at how teachings and especially spiritual practices from different world religions can amplify those of Christianity, aiding our approach to spiritual maturity, ushering us one by one through a golden gateway into the final 'universal' Stage 6.

Notes

1 Thomas Merton (1948 and 1998), pp. 448–9.

2 First published in Thomas Merton (1993), p. 39.

3 William Shannon, Christine Bochen and Patrick O'Connell (2002), p. 496.

4 Merton (1962), p. 180.

5 Merton (1962), p. 1.

6 Steve Taylor (2011).

7 The remaining six were: Mahatma Ghandi; Mother Teresa of Calcutta; Martin Luther King Jr.; Dag Hammarskjöld; Dietrich Bonhoeffer; Abraham Heschel.

8 Merton's journals have been published in seven volumes, plus an eighth compilation volume: Thomas Merton (1990). A prolific writer, he also wrote over 50 other books, including books of poetry – see websites (Thomas Merton).

9 Merton (1948 and 1998), p. 121.

10 Merton (1948 and 1998), p. 123.

11 Notably drinking and womanizing. In later life Merton admitted fathering a child as a result of a brief sexual encounter at this time. The mother and child are said to have died in the London Blitz during the Second World War.

12 In Corpus Christi Church on W 121st Street, Manhattan, by Fr Joseph Moore.

13 Merton (1990), p. 36.

14 OCSO: Order of the Cistercians of Strict Observance, known as Trappists. The Order, based on the sixth-century Rule of St Benedict (St Benedict, 1998), was founded at Citeaux in France in 1098. By 1153, under the leadership of St Bernard of Clairvaux, more than 300 Cistercian houses of men and women had been established. When Merton joined, the Cistercians were still a silent order, communicating with each other only when essential, and then only by sign language. The rule of silence was relaxed in the 1960s.

15 Merton (1948 and 1998). The book's name is takes from the seven-circled mountain of Dante's *Purgatorio*.

16 Merton (1966), p. 140.

17 Quotes from Merton's journal of 2 and 5 May 1958 in Merton (1990), p. 162.

18 Merton's social criticism became problematic for the Roman Catholic Church. In 1962, bowing to political pressure, the Abbot General of the Cistercian Order forbade him from publishing anything further on war and peace. The book he completed in April 1962 was not published for 42 years: Thomas Merton (2004). It remains highly relevant today.

19 Merton (1997), pp. 224–5 (entry for 26 April 1967).

20 A. Reza Arasteh (1975).

21 Johann Wolfgang von Goethe, 1749–1832.

22 Jalāl ad-Dīn Muhammad Rūmī, 1207–73.

23 Arasteh (1975), pp. 217–23.

24 In Mahayana Buddhism, teachers also emphasize the importance of a turn-around involving the development of 'awakening mind' (*bodhicitta*). After this a person is recognized as a *Bodhisattva*, a being who devotes his or her life to achieving Buddhahood – full spiritual maturity – for the sake of all other sentient beings.

25 Taylor (2011).

26 Taylor (2011), p. 19.

27 Taylor (2011), pp. 3–4.

28 Taylor (2011), p. 30.

29 Taylor (2011), pp. 34–6.

30 Taylor (2011), pp. 7–8.

31 See websites (Nikki Slade).

32 See Nikki Slade (2004), pp. 167–90.

33 Slade (2004), pp. 179–80.

34 Taylor (2011), p. 9.

35 Adyashanti (2014), p. 8.

36 Merton (1962), pp. 31, 35.

37 For a recommended English translation see Swami Prabhavananda and Christopher Isherwood (1987).

38 Merton (1973), pp. 348–53.

39 A mystical distillation of Islam, historically associated with the poet Rūmī.

40 Louisville, Kentucky publishers Fons Vitae have published a series of books under the general editorship of Jonathan Montaldo and Gray Henry, including: *Merton and Sufism* (1999); *Merton and Judaism* (2003); *Merton and Buddhism* (2007); *Merton and the Tao* (2014). An addition to the series, *Merton and Hinduism*, is due for publication later.

41 See Merton (1948 and 1998), pp. 213–17. Merton remembers especially Bramachari's advice to read not Hindu but Christian mystical books, like St Augustine's *Confessions* and Thomas à Kempis' *The Imitation of Christ*.

42 Merton (1985, 1989, 1993).

43 Merton (1973).

44 H. H. the Dalai Lama (1996), p. 39.

45 Merton (1973), p. 125.

8

Mature faith

Universality

From the psychological perspective, the final 'universal' stage of spiritual development involves eventual and full reunification of the 'everyday ego' with the 'spiritual self'. Shakespeare, in *Much Ado About Nothing*, reunited Hero and Claudio happily together. Neither could Beatrice and Benedick be kept apart. Similarly the everyday ego, in tune with the worldly dimensions of human experience (physical, biological, psychological and social), must inevitably merge with the pristine spiritual self eventually. As the spiritual journey approaches its conclusion, such a person – 'perfect' now, in the sense of whole and complete – is permanently, seamlessly, holistically in tune with the spiritual dimension. The guitar string, no longer plucked and strummed repeatedly by worldly concerns, eventually stills and falls silent.

The universal stage is characterized by the unforced, intuitive emergence and expression of loving kindness, wisdom, compassion and creativity. Flashes of insight may occur in earlier stages, and be a factor in promoting spiritual development; by Stage 6, though, the condition is increasingly permanent. The spiritual self has become dominant, with little reversion to the everyday ego. Life is more about *being* (natural, spontaneous, in the moment) than about either *having* (possessions, status and so on) or *doing* (achieving, seeking results). In consequence, renunciation – letting go of former attachments and aversions – is easier. Ideas and beliefs are no longer seen and held one-sidedly.

Fully spiritually mature, enlightened people are unlikely to feel bias or take sides, and therefore make natural mediators in disputes. They become natural teachers of wisdom, of how to be and behave for the best; and they become social and emotional healers, calmly cooling the temperature of heated situations. These attributes bring benefits to the people in their local communities and to those further afield in both place and time.

Whether recognized publically or not, whether known to us or not, we all gain from such spontaneously generous, warm-hearted and wise people. They may seem rare. James Fowler only found one person who had reached Stage 6 in his study-sample of 359; but this rate of 0.3 per cent, if extrapolated, would translate into over 200,000 people in the UK, over 950,000 in the USA and over 20 million in a worldwide population of over 7 billion. The figures are not reliable: there may be fewer or there may be more. Either way, though, the beneficial influence of this cohort will be significant and can be counted on to outweigh, through purity of motive, effects measured in terms of numbers alone.

The psychologist Reza Arasteh – whom Thomas Merton befriended, and with whom he corresponded in the 1960s[1] – gave us a helpful summary when he wrote of ten factors that singly or together promote the attainment of 'final integration'. This goal, he says, is open to those who have:

1 experienced the social self (everyday ego) as fragmented or incomplete;
2 become aware that reason does not provide trust and certainty;
3 doubted their personal hierarchy of values by coming in contact with another set of values;
4 found religion and culture as a means of further self-realization;
5 received a genuine vocation leading to a disciplined examination of their inner selves;
6 attained final integration through constant struggle, resistance, and concerted effort;
7 progressed slowly, perhaps due to scientific and other worldly accomplishments, after which they found time (for contemplation) to give meaning to their existence;
8 found that they were by nature sensitive (compassionate) enough to apprehend humanity's situation in a few tragic signs;

9 had grown up in a creative environment;
10 tasted life in companionship and were awakened by the death of the beloved.[2]

Arasteh describes people reaching this goal as having become 'subjectively objective', with all their formerly conflicting drives now merged into one force, directing itself towards unification with a similar non-local, spiritual force in other people and nature.[3] Their intuitions are accompanied by reliable feelings of satisfaction and certainty. In addition to the fruits of 'creation, discovery and invention', Arasteh states that the internal results of attaining this stage are: 'happiness and total awareness'.[4]

This last point needs clarification because a form of suffering does continue. Through compassionate fellow feeling, in the company of those in distress, there is often direct empathic transmission of painful emotions. The spiritually mature person, in other words, feels not his or her own but the other person's pain. The difference is that he or she is capable of neutralizing or absorbing it to some degree, dampening down its intensity or taking it away altogether. This is how the emotional healing of others works and why such people are so valuable, both within their community and to the world at large.

In the universal stage, then, life's *intrinsic* meaning is revealed, understood and accepted. Being rather than doing or achieving is given priority. This results in living in the moment, without fear of further loss; without fear even of death.

The paradox of darkness

For those among us who have not yet attained the more advanced stages of spiritual development, there are many harsh realities to accept. What God or the universe sends in the way of natural disaster, man-made calamity, human cruelty, illness, ageing and other causes of intensely painful threat, worry, loss and suffering often seems regrettable, unnecessary and hard to understand. 'Why should it be?' we cry out – 'And why me?'

There is no greater threat – and no greater certainty either – than the eventuality one day of our own death. The everyday ego, gripping tenaciously to its own existence, seeks to deny and avoid this, to avoid even mention of it. Strangely, though, contemplation of our own death and the end of everything can bring us to a better understanding of these painful matters, to enlightenment, wisdom and peace. It can give us the paradoxical experience of feeling fully alive. During the First World War, in April 1917, on approaching the battle of Arras, Siegfried Sassoon wrote in his memoirs, 'For me, the idea of death made everything seem vivid and valuable.'[5]

The oft-avoided subject of death introduces important and valuable reflections on the finality of material existence for us all. The physical, biological, psychological and social dimensions are interdependent and somehow collapse at the end of a person's life. Brain and body assume lifelessness and begin to decay, releasing the residue of energy and physical matter back to the universe for recycling. Social records, memorials, books, photographs, recordings and the memories of others still alive maintain something of each of us when we are gone; but on deep reflection we are forced to admit that these too are ultimately limited and finite. To think otherwise is vanity.

The question of the continued existence after death of a *personal* spiritual self of some kind is much debated, both informally socially and more formally theologically. Some people have reported experience of confused and unhappy spirits or 'entities' that remain morbidly attached to people or places and require 'deliverance', involving permission, encouragement and guidance about rejoining the infinite.[6] Such possibilities appear to support Christian teaching and tradition that, after death, human souls find their way to 'heaven', 'purgatory' or 'hell'. From a mature perspective, these are powerfully descriptive words but better taken as poetic metaphors of joyful, middling and miserable afterlife eventualities than as actual places with physical co-ordinates somewhere in the cosmos wherein very pleasant, restorative or very unpleasant things happen to 'people' no longer alive, depending on their thoughts, beliefs, words and conduct during life.

Einstein's insights and equations have revealed that time and space are co-dependent. To appreciate space–time we need to be alive within a body and occupying space, a particular location on earth. After death the person who was alive no longer occupies space and can no longer therefore be realistically considered as inhabiting time. Indeed the term 'after death' has no possible meaning except as a metaphor. Our essence, our souls, such as they may be considered (by ourselves while alive and by others when we have died), must be said to have rejoined the great, infinite, eternal, timelessness of the whole, that sacred unity from which our physical selves once emerged.

'Awareness of the presence of the dead' was one of the two rather darker types of spiritual experience used in the BBC 2000 *Soul of Britain* survey.[7] About a quarter of the survey population reported having it; and some subjects, paradoxically, found it beneficial. It was often experienced during the immediate period of bereavement and was frequently comforting.

The other experience, 'Awareness of an evil presence', also reported by 25 per cent of people, was more often disturbing, accompanied by feelings of misery or dread; but this was not always so. One woman told David Hay that, when 13, after seeing a photograph of dead, emaciated concentration camp victims piled high awaiting burial, some dark insistence, as she put it, 'took the opportunity to pound my brain from the inside for 12 hours'. Afterwards she was left with the unshakeable idea that she should set out to become a doctor, which she did.[8]

The case of Etty Hillesum

Greater suffering could hardly be imagined than that of Jews and others as a result of Nazi persecution in the first half of the twentieth century. However, great and prolonged adversity offers considerable opportunity for spiritual growth. The proximity of death can help us deal profitably with both our worldly affairs and, especially, our spiritual concerns.

Born in January 1914, Etty Hillesum was from a Dutch Jewish family, living in Amsterdam at the time of the Nazi invasion in May 1940. Over a period of about 30 months, her life was completely transformed, as her astonishingly revealing personal diaries and letters record. These valuable documents were eventually published almost 40 years after her death.[9] She did not become a baptized Christian but she did read about and encounter the living Jesus of the Gospels. From relative spiritual immaturity, burdened by inhibitions and a sense of shame, she set out to improve herself through spiritual exercises, reading Scripture, poetry and philosophy, meditating, reflecting and praying.

Etty was sent to the concentration camp Westerbork in Eastern Holland. She knew her life would be short. Eventually, as her letters about love and about harmony between good and bad attest, she achieved a completely holistic vision, exemplifying the supreme wisdom of spiritual maturity. In July 1942, for example, she wrote, 'I know now that life and death make a meaningful whole.'[10] One of her starkest and most revealing observations comes from a letter dated 8 June 1943:

> The sky is full of birds, the purple lupins stand up so regally and peacefully, two little old women have sat down for a chat, the sun is shining on my face – and right before our eyes, mass murder ... The whole thing is simply beyond comprehension.[11]

Expressing a view beyond dualism, her words and ideas frequently take on a truly mystical quality, as in this extract from the following month:

> Everywhere things are both very good and very bad at the same time. The two are in balance, everywhere and always. I never have the feeling that I have got to make the best of things; everything *is* fine just as it is. Every situation, however miserable, is complete in itself and contains the good as well as the bad.[12]

By now Etty was dwelling firmly and freely within an invincible spiritual comfort zone. Sadly, she was taken from the camp by the weekly train transport the following month. A letter about her from a friend, a witness to her departure, confirms her remarkable spirit:

> when the time came she, too, was ready and waiting ... She stepped onto the platform ... Talking gaily, smiling, a kind word for everyone she met on the way, full of sparkling humour, perhaps just a touch of sadness, but every inch the Etty you all know so well ... with

what grace she and her family left! ... After her departure I spoke to a little Russian woman and various other protégés of hers. And the way they felt about her leaving speaks volumes for the love and devotion she had given to them all.[13]

At the age of 29, Etty Hillesum died in Auschwitz, murdered by the Nazis on 30 November 1943.[14]

Heaven and hell

Questions about the afterlife, heaven, purgatory and hell remain problematic but become less so when considered in terms of spiritual development – in terms, for example, of Richard Rohr's two halves of life, particularly if we introduce a third, 'transition' phase between them.

During the first half, when the focus of our lives involves 'surviving successfully' (establishing an identity, home-base, family and friends, livelihood, regular pastimes and so on), we establish patterns of thought and behaviour depending on an array of attachments and aversions. At such a time we have a lot to lose. The prospect of our own death and that of those we love is almost unimaginable, hellish. We are not ready for it. We tend to deny and suppress the idea, and so risk cutting ourselves off from something, from that vital part of ourselves connected to the whole. Uncoupled by our ignorance or obstinacy, our souls become as if detached from the Holy Spirit, from Christ and from the Father, from God. This is indeed an image of hell for a Christian, the feeling of being cut off from creator, saviour and guide.

During the transition phase, though, we begin to reawaken, to recognize again with growing humility what we experienced less coherently in childhood: our connection to the sacred whole, to the universe and to each other. The dominance of the everyday ego recedes. The promptings of the spiritual self begin taking over, ushering in a period of remorse and repentance, of corrective atonement, therefore a kind of purgatory.[15] This is reflected, for example, in the Twelve Steps advocated by Alcoholics Anonymous: after turning our will and our life over to the care of God in Step 3, further advice involves:

- making a searching and fearless moral inventory of ourselves (Step 4);
- admitting the exact nature of our wrongs (Step 5);
- humbly asking God to remove our shortcomings (Step 7);
- making a list of all the people we have harmed (Step 8);
- making direct amends to such people, wherever possible (Step 9).

Support for the idea of a period of penitence comes from people who have reported, on return from a so-called near-death experience, having undergone a transformative rapid life-review in which they have relived occasions when they acted harmfully towards others, but this time *from the perspective of the other person*.[16] Feeling the pain they have inflicted on others has, they say, an indelibly corrective effect. Presumably if they had behaved well, correspondingly favourable experiences confirming them in goodness might also apply.

These experiences accompany only momentarily the biological processes of nearly dying (or, in some cases, of being under anaesthetic), and do not necessarily indicate what happens when life is completely extinct. They do ring true psychologically, though, and seem to add weight to the importance *in life* of purification and reconnection with the sanctity of the universe. One way or another, the changeover period from the first to the second half of life involves letting go of harm-inducing former attachments and aversions. By changing our habits of mind, speech and behaviour towards greater consideration for others, we also discover the truth behind the universal principle of 'reciprocity' according to which, as St Paul wrote, 'you reap whatever you sow' (Galatians 6.7).

Buddhist teaching about karma may also help us understand this point. It concerns the so-called law of cause and effect, according to which acts of kindness, compassion and generosity are rewarded with good fortune. Unselfish thoughts and altruistic intentions, whether they manifestly bear fruit or not, also result in benefit. Conversely selfish, inconsiderate, cruel and destructive thoughts, intentions, words and actions result – sooner or later – in misfortune.

These matters, however, are not entirely simple because Buddhism recognizes a distinction between worldly and spiritual fortune and prizes the idea of adversity as an opportunity for growth. As a result, karmic fortune cannot easily be predicted. Something apparently beneficial in a material or worldly sense might be followed by an eventually negative outcome in a spiritual sense. A person who wins a large gambling bet is unlikely to give up gambling, for example, remaining trapped in destructive behaviour. Similarly, when something apparently bad happens from the ego's perspective, the outcome for the soul could still be very positive. Someone who loses a highly paid job may suffer at first but find much greater satisfaction in a new, less well-paid occupation, devoted to caring for the sick, disabled or elderly, for example, freeing time too perhaps to enjoy making use of God-given artistic and other talents.

The underlying, soul-prompted reason for many people's vocations similarly involves immersion in the suffering of others – in hospitals and mental hospitals, for example, through social work or other forms of humanitarian service. There is nothing like close and prolonged encounters with the problems and pain of others for revealing and divesting us of our egocentric ideas about the world and false personal pretensions about ourselves.

Spiritual growth depends on learning from folly, from ignorance, from our lack of wisdom, from inattention to the indwelling spiritual self. The universal principle of reciprocity and the Buddhist law of karma are both similar in effect to the will of a loving God. Understand and accept this, interpret it spiritually, and we come to realize the truth of the testing but infinitely valuable idea that: 'Whatever God sends is for the best.'

The life, death and resurrection of Jesus

When facing the challenges of pain and suffering, memories of putting self first and harming others, the prospect of death and the possibility of despair, there is enormous advantage for a Christian – and anyone who has heard and reflected deeply on the gospel story – through knowledge of the life, teachings, example, death and resurrection of Jesus Christ.

As recorded in the Gospels, Jesus tells us what we need to do, how we must behave towards one another, towards God and creation. He

lives out a human life, seamlessly connected – despite worldly temptation – to the sacred unity of the universe. He is a divine being, the Son
of God, in whom everyday ego and spiritual self are utterly united. He
is thus totally and lovingly committed to the welfare – the spiritual
welfare – of all, even to the point of complete humiliation and self-
sacrifice on the cross.

It is not enough to 'know about' Jesus, though, to acquire simply
factual knowledge (using the left hemisphere of the brain). We must
'know' Jesus as a person (using our right hemispheres), as a loving
brother, too, living in our hearts. Imagine yourself, then, as a shepherd
called by angels to witness Jesus' birth in a stable (Luke 2.8–20); as a
leper, healed by him of your sores and of being outcast from society
(Mark 1.40–44); as blind and given your sight (Matthew 20.29–34); as
deaf and hearing once more (Mark 7.32–35); as the young daughter of
Jairus, restored to life, waking with Jesus by your side; then as Jairus or
as his wife, the young girl's mother (Mark 5.22–24, 35–43). Imagine
yourself now in the crowd as Jesus rides a donkey in triumphal entry
to Jerusalem (Matthew 21.1–11); and in another crowd a few days later,
yelling for the Roman authorities to put him to death (Luke 23.13–25).
Imagine yourself as Peter in the Garden of Gethsemane when a large
armed crowd arrives to arrest Jesus (Matthew 26.47–56); or as Jesus'
mother, Mary, standing at the foot of the cross while he suffers and dies
(John 19.25–27). What thoughts arise and, particularly, what emotions
are conjured up by recreating for yourself these different situations, linked
by the life of one man?

There are lessons to be learned from this kind of 'creative imagination',
from our thoughts and feelings as we engage in this sort of exercise.
Such is the case even for those who doubt the historical accuracy of
the events. The greater truth within them is nevertheless revealed: that
we are loved, and loved unconditionally. As we come to realize – to
make real for ourselves – that Jesus loves us, whoever we are, whatever
we have done or left undone, so feelings of amazement, wonder, gratitude, peace and joy will arise, for Jesus' love brings renewal, redemption,
forgiveness and direction to our souls. As he said when healing the
paralysed man, 'your sins are forgiven' (Mark 2.5); and, on the cross,

'Father, forgive them' (Luke 23.34). Not knowing in our heart that he forgives us is based on lack of spiritual knowledge and experience, on a misunderstanding of our fundamentally divine nature, of who we all truly are.

Jesus' words and actions at the Last Supper have provided Christians with the central sacrament of the Eucharist. An Anglican service sheet describes it in a prayer as follows:

> Lord, you are holy indeed, the source of all holiness;
> grant that by the power of your Holy Spirit,
> and according to your holy will,
> these gifts of bread and wine
> may be to us the body and blood of our Lord Jesus Christ;
>
> who, in the same night that he was betrayed,
> took bread and gave you thanks;
> he broke it and gave it to his disciples, saying:
> Take, eat; this is my body which is given for you;
> do this in remembrance of me.
>
> In the same way, after supper
> he took the cup and gave you thanks;
> he gave it to them, saying:
> Drink this, all of you;
> this is my blood of the new covenant,
> which is shed for you and for many for the forgiveness of sins.
> Do this, as often as you drink it,
> in remembrance of me.[17]

Here is an extraordinarily powerful opportunity for 'creative imagination', for putting ourselves into the scene and imagining what it would be like. Jesus foretells his immediate death and asks us to keep his memory. It is formalized in Christian church services but we can bring Christ's betrayal, death and resurrection to life in our hearts and minds *whenever* we eat bread or drink wine. How often, for example, do you make toast, order pizza, or simply eat a sandwich? Every time we do this offers an opportunity to remember, to offer a brief prayer of thanks and so make a personal spiritual connection to the realm of the divine.

Jesus Christ is alive in the Holy Spirit, which blessed agency so often brings us guidance in the voice and sayings of Jesus and through reminding us of his selfless example. If we seek and allow it, Jesus can be as alive and glorious to us inwardly in this way as he was when he appeared outwardly to his followers in the days after his torture and death. If our Christian lives are to have meaning, then we must bring him alive.

Psychologically speaking, Jesus' death and resurrection were not therefore one-time events. They may be recreated regularly in our hearts and minds as we grow in wisdom and compassion, as our vision grows increasingly clear and as we thereby mature in spirit and in love. This is the essence of his 'coming again' to assist us through the homecoming stages of our journey. It is not necessary to think of his return taking place in some apocalyptic future. The Revelation of John can be interpreted as another tremendous metaphor, a representation of the cataclysmic change of heart and mind wrought by direct perception and connection with an all-powerful, loving God, such as Paul too experienced on the road to Damascus. Within space–time only the present exists for us, instant by instant. We can only be reunited with our God here and now. We do not know the moment of our approaching death and we have been warned against delaying our search for such an encounter: 'Behold, the bridegroom cometh' (Matthew 25.6 KJV). Well embarked upon the journey, we are all pilgrims now.

Heavenly joy

Etty Hillesum's story demonstrates that spiritual growth often involves encounters with great hardship. The transition phase may prove particularly testing; but as we journey further into the second half of life, freedom from attachment not only releases us from the accompanying painful emotions but also ensures the emergence of their complementary counterparts. As desire for things (and for things to be different) fades, contentment with what is (and with the way things are) remains.

We find it easier to go with the flow. Also as doubt, anxiety and bewilder-ment depart, so confidence, tranquillity and clarity of mind take their place. 'For now we see in a mirror, dimly, but then we will see face to face. Now I know only in part; then I will know fully, even as I have been fully known' (1 Corinthians 13.12).

Renewed clarity is an important concomitant of spiritual growth, allowing new insights and wisdom to emerge. Anger and shame even-tually disperse too, revealing satisfying feelings of acceptance and of meekness coupled with robust self-esteem. Cleansed of the transgressions of attachment, of putting world before spirit, shame and guilt subside and – feeling now somehow redeemed and forgiven – we are renewed with feelings of worthiness, innocence and purity, extending through ourselves to and throughout creation. In the absence of sadness, what remains is lasting, heavenly joy.

This is the reward of the saints, mystics and sages, the many who have gone before and those living among us now. It is also why teachers like Thomas Merton and Richard Rohr echo Jesus and urge us each onward to fulfil our destiny and contribute to humankind's spiritual evolution. There is in the final analysis no alternative, however daunting this seems. Our lives have no other ultimate purpose, no other genuine source of meaning than to discover and live according to the divine being within. We need not worry that to fulfil the task may take a long time, a lifetime, for there is nothing else of equal importance to be done. Living in the immediacy of the present moment removes all risk of possible boredom.

On 2 December 1968 Thomas Merton visited a sacred Buddhist site in Sri Lanka, an ancient ruined city called Polonnaruwa, and had there an epiphany of completion. He was unaware that he was only eight days away from death. Approaching the three immense and beautiful Buddha figures, carved from marble-like rock, he was taken with the silence of their extraordinary faces and their great, subtle smiles, which he saw as: 'Filled with every possibility, questioning nothing, knowing everything, rejecting nothing.'

Deeply aware of the statues' perfect design, of the monumental bodies thoroughly blended into the rocky landscape in surroundings of trees

and shrubbery, with wet sand and grass underfoot, 'something happened'!
A day or two later Merton wrote that he had been:

> suddenly, almost forcibly, jerked clean out of the habitual, half-
> tied vision of things, and an inner clearness, as if exploding from
> the rocks themselves, became evident and obvious ... All problems
> are resolved and everything is clear, simply because what matters
> is clear ... Surely my Asian pilgrimage has become clear and puri-
> fied itself. I mean, I know and have seen what I was obscurely
> looking for.[18]

Merton's death, so soon after he wrote this, has removed the possibility
of any further explanation from him of what he meant; but surely, in
its place, there is an appeal from him for us to look too – however
obscurely – for the same inner clarity, the same wisdom, the same peace,
the same joy; to seek like him that which is beyond question, beyond
refutation, the 'something that happens', the absolute, in the knowledge
that the Holy Spirit is no false myth but a true and transcendent reality waiting patiently, lovingly, to be found.

This is the journey we are all already embarked together upon.
Guidance, rather than at our fingertips, is already in our hearts. 'Do not
be afraid,' as God said to Abraham, the father of Judaism, Christianity
and Islam, 'I am your shield; your reward shall be very great' (Genesis
15.1). Rejecting fear we shall be calm, confident, content and joyful, at
peace within ourselves and with our neighbours. This is the aim, intention, goal and reward of the pilgrimage that is human life.

Pilgrimage

A pilgrimage is an adventurous undertaking, an exploration of self and
a journey towards faith as much as to a sacred object or place.

> For in their hearts doth Nature stir them so,
> Then people long on pilgrimage to go.[19]

Geoffrey Chaucer wrote *Canterbury Tales* in the late fourteenth century.
The stories tell of a group of 30 pilgrims travelling together to the

memorial tomb of St Thomas Becket. Times have changed but people still long to visit sacred places, near and far. Those who do not clearly understand why are nevertheless answering a dimly perceived call: their 'spiritual selves' seeking to be reawakened and re-energized. A similar motivation applies in the case of many who take a gap year in their studies or who simply wish to travel and encounter new people, new places and new ideas; to see the world without necessarily having any other specific goal in mind.

According to Phil Cousineau, a pilgrimage begins with a sense of longing followed by a call – like a call of destiny – that cannot be denied or further deferred. Next comes a period of preparation, after recognition of the need – if we are to benefit fully from the experience – to reduce the clutter in our lives, to let go of our attachments or at least learn to hold on to them less tightly. Then, our lives simplified, when we are ready enough, comes departure.

The journey itself – travelling the pilgrim's way – traditionally involves a number of things: the routine and discipline of travel; getting used to hardship; taking care of daily necessities (food, drink, sanitation and a place to rest at day's end). In particular it means meeting, becoming companionable with and learning from fellow travellers on the journey; making 'spiritual friends'. Clashes of personality and conditioning frequently occur, so this aspect can already prove quite a challenge.

Cousineau advises that before the anticipated goal is reached, pilgrims must go through what he calls the 'labyrinth', a mythical metaphor for a challenging passage that has the power to transform us. It is a psychological struggle rather than an actual physical maze to be negotiated. Describing it in poetic terms, Cousineau quotes Joseph Campbell, the renowned and influential twentieth-century American interpreter of mythology:

> We do not have to risk adventure alone, for the heroes of all time have gone before us. The labyrinth is thoroughly known. We have only to follow the thread of the hero path, and where we had thought to find an abomination, we shall find a god. And where we had thought to slay another, we shall slay ourselves. Where we

had thought to travel outward, we will come to the centre of our own existence. And where we had thought to be alone, we will be with all the world.[20]

Eventually the pilgrim arrives at the tomb of the martyr or wherever else we have decided upon as our sacred goal; but arrival is not the final point of the journey. We must yet go back to the beginning, to return home. Cousineau reminds us about 'bringing home the boon'. How can we recall what we have seen and experienced on the journey, the important things we have learned? 'How will you remember to remember when you return home?' writes Cousineau, suggesting by way of reply that we do well to take time to *re-imagine* the pilgrimage from start to finish, paying special attention to the 'sacred rhythms' of the journey, to remembered 'small joys' and 'humble experiences' along the way, while also repeatedly thinking about who has been bestowing these gifts.[21]

'Who keeps us safe, going in the right direction? What is the source of our blessings?' These, similarly, are the types of question worth keeping in mind throughout life, according to the spiritual writer and peace activist Jim Forest. In his book *The Road to Emmaus: Pilgrimage as a Way of Life*, Jim quotes his friend, Thomas Merton:

> I believe my vocation is essentially that of a pilgrim and an exile in life, that I have no proper place in the world, but that for that reason I am in some sense to be the friend and brother of people everywhere, especially those who are exiles and pilgrims like myself.[22]

This represents the highest ideal of Christian maturity. But how do we get there? We each have a unique starting point and there are many paths, but there are also similarities, as we shall see. To consider the role of worship in contributing to personal spiritual growth will make a good start.

Notes

1 Merton thought 'final personality integration' was a description of what monasteries should help monks to achieve. See Thomas Merton (1968), republished for a wider readership in Thomas Merton (1971).

2 A. Reza Arasteh (1975), pp. 262–3.

3 Arasteh (1975), p. 57.

4 Arasteh (1975), p. 36.

5 Siegfried Sassoon (1930), p. 132.

6 See, for example, websites (Spirit Release Foundation).

7 David Hay (2006), p. 11.

8 Hay (2006), p. 22.

9 Etty Hillesum (1999).

10 Hillesum (1999), p. 203.

11 Hillesum (1999), p. 332.

12 Hillesum (1999), p. 391.

13 Hillesum (1999), letter from Jopie Vleeschhouwer, pp. 426–30.

14 For more on Etty Hillesum see Culliford (2011), pp. 180–90.

15 'Purgation' (from Latin), and 'catharsis' (from Greek), both mean cleansing or purification.

16 See, for example, Peter Fenwick and Elizabeth Fenwick (1995) and Pim van Lommel (2010).

17 *Common Worship: Services and Prayers for the Church of England*, Principal Services, Holy Communion, Eucharistic Prayers for Use with Order One, Eucharistic Prayer B, London: Church House Publishing, 2000, p. 189. See also Matthew 26.26–29; Mark 14.22–24; Luke 22.14–20.

18 The two quotes are from Merton (1973), pp. 233–6.

19 Geoffrey Chaucer's *Canterbury Tales*, from the 'General prologue'.

20 Joseph Campbell, quoted in Phil Cousineau (1998), p. 127.

21 Cousineau (1998), pp. 213–14.

22 From Jim Forest (2007), p. 169. The quote is from Merton's letter dated 4 April 1962 to Abdul Aziz, also reproduced in Thomas Merton (1985), p. 52.

9

Towards spiritual maturity

Worship

The word 'worship' is a contraction of 'worth-ship'. To worship is therefore to acknowledge the absolute value of something or someone. Everybody, at least occasionally, worships the divine, infinite, eternal, sacred unity that is God. This spontaneous and immediate kind of worship takes place informally, either silently or with a single exclamation – Wow! Aha! or Aah! Breathtaking, it takes us by surprise in those moments when our hearts and minds are dramatically captivated and filled with awe, wonder, joy, love, gratitude and the urge to praise.

People come deliberately together more formally in congregations, as worshippers in churches and assemblies, using traditional prescribed services that are based on reading Scripture, singing psalms and hymns, listening to homilies and sermons and saying prayers. If we ask, 'What is the purpose of church services?' many will say that in addition to worship they are about education (in terms of Christian history and tradition), about encouraging loyalty and obedience (in terms of Christian doctrine) and about preaching moral and ethical codes of behaviour. There is a strong emphasis on Jesus being the good shepherd showing the way to people like us as his – often wayward – flock of sheep.

The more mature Christian, accepting moral guidance under the direct influence of the Holy Spirit, might answer differently; that the purpose of church services and the role of religious leaders is less about this kind of preaching, more about awakening and kindling within us experience of the spiritual dimension, of the sublime and holy mystery of existence.

This means Christian teachers bringing alive the Jesus story, revealing above all the transcendent presence it evokes.

The Gospel of John testifies especially to this mystical interpretation, speaking of Jesus as 'The true light, which enlightens everyone'.

> He was in the world, and the world came into being through him; yet the world did not know him ... And the Word became flesh and lived among us, and we have seen his glory, the glory as of a father's only son, full of grace and truth.   (John 1.9–14)

John highlights Jesus as a creative principle in the universe, as the breath or 'spirit' animating all life. His divinity evokes our own. Within us, in other words, is that 'little point of nothingness', something untouched by the material world, by space–time, something transcendent of everything that happens, something constant to be relied on through all the tragic and painful episodes of adversity in our lives.

Thomas Merton, a living example of Richard Rohr's ideal, a man who spent the first half of his life in the world and the second half as a monk,[1] said much the same, as follows:

> Life is this simple: we are living in a world that is absolutely transparent and the divine is shining through it all the time. This is not just a nice story or fable, it is true.
>
> This is something we are not able to see; but if we abandon ourselves to him, forget ourselves, we see it sometimes ... that God manifests himself everywhere, in everything: in people, and in things, and in nature, and in events; so that it becomes very obvious that he is everywhere and we cannot be without him.[2]

We need help, then, to 'forget ourselves', to 'abandon ourselves to God', to experience transcendent, spiritual reality alongside everyday perception; and everything in Christian worship and the Christian way of life – if we read it with both intelligence and imagination – points in that direction.

In order to explore this approach in a Christian context and so communicate meaningfully and consistently with the divine principle, a number of networks and communities characterized by monastic

ideals have emerged in recent times. One example is the Northumbria
Community, a dispersed network of Christians whose 'Mother House' –
Nether Springs – lies in peaceful and beautiful countryside near Morpeth.
According to their website:

> The Community's founders discovered a way of life centred in *Availa-*
> *bility* to God and others, and *Vulnerability*, being teachable and accept-
> ing accountability to others. In discovering the history and heritage
> of Celtic Northumbria, the strong links to the saints and scholars
> of Ireland, the wisdom tradition of the Desert Fathers, and the 'mixed
> life' of the Franciscans, there was a blending of cell and coracle, of
> monastery and mission, from which the language and ethos of the
> Community was born and is sustained.[3]

Central to the life of the community is the daily office: morning,
midday, evening prayer and compline. The regular cycle of daily prayers,
based on the Community's own Celtic liturgy,[4] constitutes the essential
rhythm of life around which other activities take their proper place.
Twice weekly there is also Holy Communion, held in the atmospheric
candlelit 'Lean-to Chapel', on the edge of the woods, distant from the
main building. There are permanent residents but Nether Springs also
functions as a retreat centre for visitors.

The spiritually connected way of life of a community like this avoids
the big mistakes made by some churches and church people as a consequence of ignoring, forgetting or in other ways losing touch with their
spiritual roots. 'Just as the branch cannot bear fruit by itself unless it
abides in the vine, neither can you unless you abide in me. I am the
vine, you are the branches' (John 15.4–5).

Distance from divine inspiration leads to weakness and uncertainty.
This position is often countered by assertive compensatory repetition of
favoured scriptural texts, rules and commandments. The unfortunate,
essentially unchristian results of doing so include the instillation of
damaging fear and unworthiness in susceptible people; also insensitive
preaching at intelligent, imaginative, creative people without allowing
them the time, space or encouragement to think things through for
themselves, to integrate what they are discovering from science and the

secular imperatives of the world we inhabit with their innate childlike capacity for spiritual awareness.

Dimmed appreciation of the spiritual dimension leads to restraint in people's development, with a strong concomitant risk of holding them back in the 'conditioning' and 'conformist' stages, adhering blindly to destructive, defensive, dualist, partisan – almost tribal – ways of thinking and behaving. Avoiding this, would-be followers, seeing through insincerity and falsehood, inevitably become alienated at a stage when they need support and guidance most. Even well-intentioned religious leaders adrift of the Holy Spirit, however, come across as either feebly ineffective or arrogant and inflexible. To insist rigidly and aggressively on exclusivity and superiority is to risk serious accusations of misleading those in your charge. Jesus cautioned against this repeatedly: 'woe to you, scribes and Pharisees, hypocrites! For you lock people out of the kingdom of heaven. For you do not go in yourselves, and when others are going in, you stop them' (Matthew 23.13–14).

The entirety of this chapter in Matthew's Gospel is a warning, in Christ's words, against this kind of mistake; specifically, for example, against putting worldly, mercenary commercial values – collecting gold and taxes (see Matthew 23.16–24) – before spiritual imperatives. Jesus' criticism is scathing, calling these false religious leaders 'blind guides', 'whitewashed tombs' (beautiful on the outside but rotten within) and 'a brood of vipers'. The world continues to put strong economic and political pressures on churches and other Christian organizations. They must not be ignored but it remains unwise to allow worldly concerns to take insistent priority over the holy work to be done.

Scripture and sacred music

Reading Scripture carefully, reflectively, taking time both to study it contemplatively alone and to discuss it with companions on the spiritual path, offers one safeguard against mistakes of inflexibility. Remember that the Amish men Ephraim and Jesse (see Chapter 6) accepted banishment in order to do exactly this: to be free to decide for themselves what the Bible was saying to them.

The use of 'creative imagination' while reading Scripture and during the Eucharist also offers protection against rigid, formulaic interpretations. It brings a vital personal feel and focus to the Christian story. It allows for the emergence of what we might call 'spiritual intuition'. The words of psalms and hymns have similar value when savoured, and there is particular benefit from singing and listening to sacred music because of music's powerfully evocative emotional effect. Music has a way of bypassing the (left brain) intellect, striking directly, with immediacy (via the right brain) into our emotions, our hearts and our souls. This is especially the case with beautiful, repetitive chanting.

Prayer

Based on instructions in the Rule of St Benedict, dating from about AD 530,[5] at the Abbey of Gethsemani and many monasteries and convents, the daily office involves connecting to God through the saying of prayers and the chanting of psalms seven times daily,[6] with an additional daily service of Holy Eucharist. There are different kinds of prayer: prayers of praise, of thanks and of supplication, for example. These are prayers in which we are somehow or another addressing God. There are also prayerful states during which we are primarily quietening the restless chatter of our thoughts. A spiritual connection is thus established, the right half of the brain taking control, allowing us better to hearken to God's still, small voice, the voice of the Holy Spirit.

> And he said, Go forth, and stand upon the mount before the LORD. And, behold, the LORD passed by, and a great and strong wind rent the mountains, and brake in pieces the rocks before the LORD; but the LORD was not in the wind: and after the wind an earthquake; but the LORD was not in the earthquake: and after the earthquake a fire; but the LORD was not in the fire: and after the fire a still small voice. (1 Kings 19.11–12 KJV)

In the NRSV rendering of this passage the Old Testament prophet hears 'a sound of sheer silence', and after a voice saying, 'What are you doing here, Elijah?' (v. 13). This evocative passage says something essential about the attitude and conditions required to hear and receive the promptings of the Holy Spirit: silence, stillness and solitude. Sit still, in silence and solitude, and something wonderful happens; especially if you undertake to do so as a regular discipline. This is meditation.

There is an excellent tradition of Christian meditation. However, the practice is not confined to Christianity, so we will explore universal aspects of this topic later. There are other aspects of Christian worship and Christian life to continue considering first.

Seasonal patterns of worship

By operating a seasonal pattern of worship throughout the annual calendar of services, Christian churches retain from Druid, Pagan and Norse precedents a close, mystical connection with earth, sun, moon, planets and stars; with the cosmos. The special day of worship, the Sabbath, is Sunday – the sun's day. It is followed by the moon's day (Monday), by days recollecting the Norse gods Woden and Thor (Wednesday, Thursday) and the goddess Freya (Friday). Saturday is the planet Saturn's day.[7]

Christmas, celebrating the birth of Jesus, falls close to the winter solstice marking the swing of the seasons, after the shortest day, from winter towards spring. The date of Easter, marking the crucifixion and resurrection of Jesus, varies each year according to the phases of the moon, and is held approximately approaching the spring equinox, when day and night are of equal length. For many generations before there were clocks and artificial light, before electricity, globalization and supermarkets, people were much more aware of, dependent on and therefore religiously sensitive to the passing of the seasons. Christianity, like some other religions, serves a valuable purpose, helping to celebrate God's bounty through nature and agriculture, providing a focus for hope (of a good harvest), thanks, and – in adversity, such as when flooding or drought occur – providing a channel for prayers of supplication and mercy. 'For where two or three are gathered in my name, I am there among them' (Matthew 18.20). Only the mature Christian – someone who has experienced the depths of silent prayer and learned how to listen humbly and attentively for that still, small voice – can truly say how helpful connecting to the Holy Spirit of nature in such a way may be, especially when conducted together with others, both in small groups and large congregations.

Fellowship and charity

While wanting to think and act independently, we do not remain exempt from the alternative drive towards belonging; therefore carefully avoiding the dangers of feeling superior and of excluding people seen as different, there remains immense value in Christian fellowship, in the feeling of belonging to both a local and worldwide community. That this community – at all levels – has warm, generous, respectful, fraternal links and relations with other religious and secular humanitarian groups is an important aspect of Christian maturity.

Jesus made clear, for example in the parable of the Good Samaritan (Luke 10.25–37), and in the following passage from Matthew's Gospel, that kindness and generosity are to be extended to people in need, without discrimination:

> I was hungry and you gave me food. I was thirsty and you gave me something to drink, I was a stranger and you welcomed me, I was naked and you gave me clothing, I was sick and you took care of me, I was in prison and you visited me ... Truly I tell you, just as you did it to one of the least of these who are members of my family, you did it to me.   (Matthew 25.35–40)

Christian charity is also mirrored by that of other religious and non-religious groups. It emerges spontaneously from our deep-seated impulses, particularly during the 'integration' and 'universal' stages of development, to recognize our kinship with all other human beings and to honour the compassionate promptings of the Holy Spirit. Jesus is not telling us what to do so much as telling us what kind of beings we are; that our true nature is kind and loving. And he is speaking to everyone.

Christian organizations, like many established similarly in the name of other religions and humanitarian groups, are heavily involved – at local, national and international levels – in education, health care and mental health care. This too speaks of a universal awareness – however subtly or openly felt and acknowledged – of the spiritual dimension, of that which binds us seamlessly and lovingly to one another. It honours the universal principle of reciprocity by which, knowingly or not, we are rewarded for our good deeds: 'We reap whatever we sow'. This is the basic dynamic of compassion and why compassion is the equal companion of wisdom.

Retreats and keeping the Sabbath

Solitude is the opposite of loneliness. In solitude a person feels comfortable, sufficient to oneself, whole, calm and contented. Loneliness, on the other hand, speaks of painful isolation, of a person aware of something or somebody missing, regretful of the absence of meaningful companionship, of feeling valued and loved.

People naturally try to avoid loneliness but many do actively seek peaceful solitude. One way is to go on some form of retreat, particularly – if others are involved, such as on organized retreats – a silent retreat. Time spent alone – whether a short period or an extended one; whether just once or repeated – allows and encourages contemplation. It gives you time to read Scripture, literature and poetry thoughtfully; to pray; to reflect on your life history, relationships and values; to meditate – or learn to meditate. Retreats, like pilgrimages and voluntary acts of charity, are a form of spiritual practice that can be counted on to foster spiritual development.

The Christian practice of keeping Sunday, the Sabbath, as a day of rest honours the seventh day of creation: 'And on the seventh day God finished the work that he had done, and he rested on the seventh day from all the work that he had done. So God blessed the seventh day and hallowed it' (Genesis 2.2–3).

Retreats, then, are a kind of extended Sabbath period, offering rest and respite for biological and psychological recovery, also the time and mental space – through rest and also through worship, fellowship, reflection, prayer and meditation – to grow in spirit, to mature. The 'spiritual self' is given deliberate priority on the Sabbath over the 'everyday ego'.

The Religious Society of Friends is the formal title of the movement better known as the Quakers, which began in England in the 1650s. There are about 200,000 Quakers in the world, 17,000 of them in the UK. According to the 'Quakers in Britain' website:

> Quakerism is a way of life rooted in a transforming experience of the Divine. From this we seek to live out our principles of truth, peace, simplicity and equality, recognising that of God in everyone. Our meetings offer a place of welcome, encounter and spiritual exploration.[8]

There are no priests or ministers. On Sundays Quaker meetings last about an hour. They involve people gathered in both stillness and, 'a silence of waiting and listening to the promptings of truth and love in our hearts, which we understand as rising from God'.[9] Anyone may speak, pray or read aloud during the meeting, if they feel prompted to do so with the aim of enriching the worship. The silence and stillness then resume, as if uninterrupted. This sense of direct contact with the divine is at the heart of Quaker worship, nourishing Quakers through-out their daily lives. In this way the 'Sabbath mind', refreshed on Sundays, is carried with them through the week. The charity and philanthropy associated with the movement is also legendary. The Quaker way seems to offer a commendable example of mature Christianity in action.

Meditation

Stillness and silence

Quakers do not refer to what happens during their meetings as 'medita-tion' but there are obvious similarities with meditation-based practices common to many world religions. Christian organizations like the Julian Meetings in the UK (dedicated to the memory and writings of the fourteenth-century mystic Mother Julian of Norwich)[10] and the World Community for Christian Meditation[11] (started by the Benedictine monk John Main), both founded in the 1970s, exist to promote meditation among Christians.

'Be still, and know that I am God!' (Psalm 46.10). The essence of meditation – also referred to as 'stilling' or 'mindfulness practice' – involves reducing external stimulation. This means choosing a quiet place, becoming calm through stillness or repetitive, rhythmical activity while closing – or part closing – the eyes. This allows the mind to settle so that internal stimulation is also gradually reduced. The mind now focuses naturally upon itself – upon the thoughts, emotions, sense perceptions and impulses that arise. Eventually these too subside, leaving the mind entirely clear.

This sounds easier than it usually proves to be in practice. At the beginning the meditator is easily distracted. Various techniques have been developed to help overcome this problem in the thousands of years that, according to ancient Hindu Scriptures – the Upanishads[12] – meditation has been practised. These techniques involve giving the mind a focus of concentration for its 'spotlight' left hemisphere while allowing the 'flood-light' right hemisphere to remain active and alert. To this end a sacred sound, word, phrase, verse or prayer – known as a mantra – may be used, as may an actual or imagined visual image.

John Main was inspired by the monk John Cassian, who lived in France from AD 360 to 435, before the time of Saint Benedict and the founding of the great monasteries and monastic orders. Cassian wrote: 'The mind casts out and renounces the rich and ample matter of all thoughts and restricts itself to the poverty of a single verse.'[13] The World Community for Christian Meditation (WCCM) accordingly teaches 'mantra meditation', by which repeating a single verse from Scripture – or for example the Jesus Prayer (which goes 'Jesus – have mercy – on me') – is used as the focus of concentration. Other Christian traditions prefer the use of a Christian image or icon as a focus.

During 'sitting meditation' the rise and fall of the chest and abdomen, or the passage of air through the nostrils during inward and outward breathing, offer an alternative, ever-present focus, suitable for a distractible beginner. Those who find themselves restless can try 'walking meditation' in addition; and here the mental focus is on the footsteps as you walk gently and rhythmically along, usually barefoot so as to feel and experience the texture and temperature of ground, floor or carpet. Walking either backwards and forwards or in a circle prevents you being distracted by the thought of going anywhere. During this exercise we are 'simply walking'.

One of the aims of meditation practice is to achieve 'mindfulness' and 'one-pointedness' of focus and concentration. This is difficult while distractions persist, but eventually the 'spotlight', while remaining fixed on the chosen focus, will lose attention as if bored by the sameness, the constancy of the stimulus. This allows merging or harmonization of left- and right-brain activity, so the whole brain becomes engaged, although with a significantly diminished overall level of activity. It stays somewhat alert through the right hemisphere's continuous subtle checking for new input, even when there is little.

The right brain keeps us focused in the here and now of the present moment. Paradoxically, even when the mind seems empty of content, it therefore remains full of energy, filled initially with the single object of concentration, which then fades from consciousness leaving silent stillness and utter simplicity: 'emptiness'. This mental state, devoid of the everyday ego, is expansive. It can seem endless or bottomless yet there is no partitioning and no room within it for anything else.

Meditation, physical health, mental health and therapy

Neurological research confirms many of these points. The structure and function of the brain and nervous system are highly complex and relatively difficult to study. Nevertheless electro-encephalography (EEG) and a variety of neuro-imaging and scanning techniques have revealed numerous insights, as summarized and explained in recent books[14] and an up-to-date article in the *Scientific American* magazine.[15]

The researcher Andrew Newberg and colleagues have shown, for example, that mystical experiences evoked by meditation appear to involve circuitry throughout the entire brain. While a subtle degree of conscious awareness is maintained, meditation decreases compartmental activity in the brain and nervous system, so that it increasingly acts in a unified way, as a whole organ communicating with a whole body.

According to the research author Shanida Nataraja, the stillness associated with meditation causes reduced activity in the *left* orientation association area, resulting in the dissolving of the self/non-self boundary. Reduced activity in the brain's *right* orientation association area gives rise to the sense of unity and wholeness. The closing down of the word-association area, in addition, she says, leaves the meditator struggling to find a way of describing the experience to others.[16]

Reduced sensory input during meditation – from eyes, ears, nose, skin and taste buds – also leads to reduced activity in the brain's parietal lobes. This in turn results in activation of the hippocampus, which in turn stimulates the amygdala: two key structures in the brain's limbic system, the central circuit of neurones mentioned in Chapter 3 that has much to do with processing our emotions. During states of mindfulness these structures linking emotional significance to our experiences switch over, so that significance now becomes attached to the *lack* of sensory input. In consequence the activity of the autonomic nervous system, concerned with arousal, is modified. First a blissful, calm state arises; then a clear state of mental alertness supervenes.

Meditation generates an ideal balance between two interrelated autonomic systems (that is, beyond conscious control): the 'sympathetic' and 'parasympathetic'. This results in a 'relaxation response' characterized by calm, joyful alertness, accompanied by reduced breathing rate, oxygen consumption, blood pressure and heart rate, and by increased skin resistance, blood flow to the internal organs and temperature of the extremities.

In an experienced meditator an optimal balance is regularly achieved and maintained. Meditation therefore enhances general well-being, and research supports that it is beneficial for both physical health and mental health. For example, there is evidence that people who meditate regularly live longer, healthier lives with lower risk of a heart attack. For over 20 years, mindfulness meditation and guided reflection have also been central to the successful programme of the Stress Reduction Clinic at the University of Massachusetts Medical Center, devised by Jon Kabat-Zinn and colleagues, where many people with a wide range of medical disorders have benefited – notably those with chronic pain and enduring multi-organ complaints, often unresponsive to other forms of treatment.[17]

Another successful development has been the use of mindfulness meditation in the treatment of anxiety and depression;[18] and meditation has long been reported as a useful adjunct to some forms of psychotherapy.[19]

Meditation in schools

A report on a programme of meditation introduced into 31 Catholic schools in Australia in 2006, engaging over 10,000 students aged between 5 and 18 years, described many beneficial effects, including increased relaxation and feelings of calm, reduced stress, reduced anger, improved concentration and better interactions with others.[20] Some students described religious experiences during meditation. Others experienced altruistic thoughts and intentions, also a new appreciation of 'such things as food every day'. Teachers and parents interviewed supported the students' reports of mainly beneficial effects. One teacher reported that his students 'were a lot calmer for the rest of the day' after a meditation session, and that they then 'deal better with each other' than at other times.

Other researchers have reported that teaching schoolchildren to meditate regularly, even for short periods daily (no longer than five minutes for younger children), improves their powers of concentration, helps them deal better with stress and reduces conflict between them. Some enthusiasts go further and suggest that meditation – called 'stilling' in some schools – can contribute to improvement in schoolwork and grades, children's sporting abilities, their general levels of creativity and their willingness to co-operate with each other.[21] Recent research makes clear that teachers also benefit, particularly if they learn to meditate too.[22]

These investigations show that meditation appreciably fosters physical and mental well-being among children. They hint too in the direction of spiritual benefits, such as increased gratitude for things previously taken for granted and an increased consideration for the plight of those in difficulty. The UK government, through an All-Party Parliamentary Group (APPG), now supports the Mindfulness in Schools project, founded in 2007 by two teachers with personal experience of meditation.[23] Their course, written 'for teachers by teachers', has been translated into eight languages and is already being used in 38 countries. The similarly named but separate Meditation in Schools organization[24] espouses parallel aims and methods. Already well established in the UK and praised by national newspapers,[25] it offers free resources for teachers to get started, bringing mindfulness, meditation and calm into the classroom, for example by providing a live speaker to deliver a session in school, conduct an assembly or run a workshop for students.

Meditation and everyday life

According to Lord Stone of Blackheath, under the auspices of the APPG on mindfulness, 90-minute weekly classes are currently offered to MPs, Lords and Parliamentary staff in London.[26] The rationale, Lord Stone stated, was based on evidence that: 'Even short periods of mindfulness practice reshape neural pathways, increase the areas associated with kindness, compassion and rationality, and decrease those involved with anxiety, worry and impulsiveness.'

He continued his speech in the House of Lords by drawing attention to other beneficial examples of 'mindfulness practice' in public life, notably in the field of business and philanthropy and in the criminal justice system, where beneficiaries include prisoners, victims of crime and the police.

Meditation, wholeness and spiritual growth

Meditation involves more than simply employing various techniques. It is a mysterious process that occurs spontaneously as a gap opens up when the mind becomes engaged purely with itself, a time during which – to a greater or lesser extent – 'something happens'. It therefore involves an act of faith. The only way to assess the benefits, and to achieve its precious fruit, is to engage and persist with the practice; in other words, to conduct the experiment ourselves.

Proficiency in meditation techniques is advantageous because it allows us increasingly to let go of effort and allow meditation simply to happen. Comparable trance-like states can also occur spontaneously while resting, for example, or during rhythmical repetitive activities like jogging or knitting. Athletes and artistic performers such as musicians sometimes describe this as being 'in the zone'. Meditation techniques can be undertaken deliberately or meditative states can arise naturally; but meditation itself, and the changes involved, cannot be forcibly guided or steered.

This knowledge is important for guarding against 'spiritual materialism' – for avoiding the error of seeing meditation as a means of acquiring physical and mental skills used only for relaxation and enjoyment, for personal gain and worldly success or as a goal in itself as part of some kind of 'spiritual package' of self-development to be purchased and displayed as a trophy by those who are not yet ready, not yet sufficiently mature, to engage rigorously in the processes of surrender and self-transformation. To avoid these mistakes it is best to seek out genuinely spiritually mature people as our mentors, teachers and guides.

For many people the experience of regular meditation practice can be compared to a canoe trip taken by the author with friends along the Spanish River in Ontario some years ago. This is Canadian wilderness territory. At the beginning, unfamiliar with terrain and techniques, faced at different times with shallow water, rock-strewn rapids, baking sun and brief heavy downpours, problems finding safe and suitable campsites before dark, marauding mosquitoes and the night-time threat of hungry prowling bears, the going was not always easy. So it can be when we start meditating. There are usually obstacles, frustrations, dangers and difficulties, low points interspersed with exhilarating uplifts and occasional breakthroughs. It can be dispiriting but often, when things seem to be going badly, we are actually making good progress against a strong countercurrent. That is why there is no easy way to judge our development as a meditator. It is necessary to accept that sometimes the flow dwindles or backs up, just like water in a river. Perseverance is essential. We have only to stay afloat because there is no way off this river, nowhere else to go. As our technique and skills improve, what once seemed against us now seems to work in our favour. We can be reassured that the struggle abates eventually. The flow grows increasingly smooth.

This allegorical comparison between a canoe trip and meditation can be extended further. The water in the Spanish River has fallen as rain on some of the oldest rocks of the earth's crust, beautiful, glacier-sculptured pink granite. It flows in streams through dense spruce and pine forests alive with moose, bears, wolves, eagles, chipmunks and butter-flies, before joining beaver and trout on the banks and in the river. Several timescales are represented here: those of the rocks, of the trees, of the animals, of the canoeists and of the author writing in his study, bringing together into the present, using both intellect and imagination, these different aspects of the past. Now any reader – at a different time – can do the same: build up a picture of that place and those events. This kind of seamless and interdependent continuity reflects a powerful truth about existence. It is not fragmented: it is whole.

The Spanish River is flowing yet. It flows beyond where canoeists can travel, through a dam providing power and electricity for the far-off city of Toronto. The water continues into Lake Huron, over Niagara Falls, into Lake Ontario, then the St Lawrence River and so to the Atlantic Ocean from where it evaporates, falling as rain again: an endless cycle.

When we are proficient, meditation helps us recognize that the activity of our minds is similarly continuous and seamless. In meditation we gradually become aware that there is no 'external' and 'internal', only mind and mindfulness; but the experience of the dualist everyday ego is not like this. During wakefulness our minds are dynamically engaged. Our emotions are active. Our thoughts chatter away. Our bodies are frequently restless. The motor is running. The gears are engaged and we are in motion. In meditation it is different. There are various techniques with the same aim: to leave the motor of conscious awareness running gently, while disengaging the drive.

Meditation and other religions

Many religions promote meditation as a key practice opening up spiritual development. Similar practices involving simplicity, stillness, silence and often solitude – also rhythmical movement, often to the accompaniment of music – are also undertaken in a disciplined way by spiritual seekers of most faiths. All of these activities promote left- and right-brain integration, the harmonization of intellect with creativity and imagination, resulting in improved unitary, holistic thinking and experiences.

Buddhism

Four types of Buddhism – Theravada, Mahayana, Vajrayana (Tibetan) and Zen – all require and teach meditation practice. According to the historical Buddha Sakyamuni,[27] the way to end suffering involves following the Noble Eightfold Path,[28] under the three headings of 'wisdom', 'morality' and 'concentration'. Mental training is vitally important, and so is how people live.

Mahayana and Vajrayana Buddhism, in particular, stress the need to develop compassion; to refrain from harmful intentions, speech and behaviour; and to work intentionally for the benefit of others. During 'loving-kindness' meditation, practitioners are urged to bring loved ones to mind, then acquaintances, then strangers and finally enemies, those who have brought harm. In each case a Buddhist meditator wishes each enemy well, using the accompanying mantra: 'May he/she be well. May I be well. May all beings be well.'

This compares well with both prayerful Christian practice aimed at bringing understanding and compassion to those we habitually dislike and also with Jesus' recommendation:

> You have heard that it was said, 'You shall love your neighbour and hate your enemy.' But I say to you, Love your enemies and pray for those who persecute you, so that you may be children of your Father in heaven; for he makes his sun to rise on the evil and on the good, and sends rain on the righteous and on the unrighteous.
>
> (Matthew 5.43–45)

Jesus tells us, as the Buddha did too, that to develop universal love forms a vital aspect of our spiritual journey.

Zen Buddhism, in addition to sitting meditation (called *zazen*), introduces and promotes another practice for advanced meditators. Aimed directly at breaking through the rational, dualist mode of thinking, this is the study – under the instruction and supervision of a devoted spiritual master – of an impossible riddle or *koan*, such as 'What is the sound of one hand?'

Zen teachers can trace their lineage from pupil to master back for many centuries. The Christian equivalent involves the laying on of hands from one bishop to the next, in an unbroken chain back to St Peter and to Christ. One hand cannot clap or make any noise by itself, so there must be another answer. When the teacher asks you to work on the riddle and present him with a solution, it is taken on faith that he means well and would not ask you to undertake a meaningless task; so you set to work. You meditate and reflect on the conundrum. You hold it in your mind every waking moment and even recall it subliminally during the hours of sleep. What happens is the gradual breaking down of trust in the logical method of thinking as the sole way of addressing such a riddle.

Maybe, eventually, you start to sweat. The effort becomes exceptional. It becomes emotional. You experience bewilderment, doubt and anxiety, then frustration and anger. Next, tempted to let up on the effort, devotion to your teacher makes you feel guilty and ashamed. Finally, cathartic tears flow and the hoped-for breakthrough arrives. You can see through the riddle to the holistic truth at its heart. Relief, joy and satisfaction overwhelm you. The master is smiling as you approach, knowing already from your new demeanour that the hoped-for transformation has occurred.

This is only one possible scenario. According to author Katsuki Sekida a young woman, earnest and experienced in meditation practice, was attending a Zen group some years ago. After a meeting with her teacher, when alone in a garden, she took out her handkerchief to blow her nose. Her existence was suddenly shaken by a sharp shock: 'The curtain of her mind fell down, and the scene changed.' The world in front of her was the same old world but it appeared quite different. She stood mute in amazement then felt an emotional welling up, an outburst of great delight. Everything in the garden – trees, grass, brightly coloured flowers, rock and the adjacent white sand – while retaining their original shape and colour all seemed wonderfully fresh and new.[29]

In Zen circles this experience is known as *kensho*. Until this occurs the person and the world are separate from and strangers to one another. Afterwards, however, there is free communion. The person is harmoniously united to the world. A vital landmark of spiritual development has been reached whereby the everyday ego is reunited with the true, spiritual self.

Koan-like conundrums also arise in many branches of science. Who except the genius Einstein, for example, would have thought that energy and matter, while obviously different, were also fundamentally the same and interconvertible? Furthermore such riddles occur throughout Scriptures from many religions, including the Bible. Moses sees a bush that is blazing without being consumed by the fire (Exodus 3.2); a virgin conceives in her womb and bears a son (Luke 1.31). How can these things be?

Christians do not have a word for this kind of near-indescribable breakthrough event in their lives, but they do have the same kind of experience and must therefore resort to metaphor to explain it. Consider this 'as if' statement of the religious reformer Martin Luther, quoted by William James:

> When a fellow-monk ... one day repeated the words of the Creed: 'I believe in the forgiveness of sins,' I saw the Scripture in an entirely new light; and straightway I felt *as if* I were born anew. It was *as if* I had found the door of Paradise thrown wide open.[30]

Over the centuries, Christian spiritual writers, teachers and mystics have found additional means of promoting such mystical breakthrough experiences. A good example is *The Spiritual Exercises of Saint Ignatius Loyola*, which involve disciplined, guided contemplation and the use of creative imagination regarding the life of Christ.[31]

Hinduism

The word 'religion' has Latin roots in common with a word meaning 'to bind' – think of 'ligature', a tie or binding. The imaginative idea being expressed is of the human soul inescapably bound to the divine.

The spiritual pathway associated with Hinduism, based on the sutras of Patanjali, is called *yoga*. This Sanskrit word is similarly related to the idea of a yoke, another type of binding, again referring to the unbreakable link between flesh and spirit. In the Hindu tradition there are five commonly accepted types of yoga, each representing a major path of spiritual development aimed at awakening consciousness to the seamless connection of spiritual self with the Godhead.[32]

The globally established Brahma Kumaris (BK) organization, which originated in the 1930s with a small group of devout and well-educated Hindus in India, has established the BK World Spiritual University for the primary purpose of teaching meditation and spreading the word about its advantages. According to the BK website:

> Meditation is simple and easy to do. It opens up a treasure of goodness and inner strength. A few minutes' meditation at the start of each day helps you remain positive and calm, even under pressure. It helps you appreciate yourself and others more. Meditation can bring you a whole new perspective on life.[33]

'Vedanta', the mystical form of Hinduism based on the teachings of the mystic sage Ramakrishna[34] and his follower the Hindu monk Vivekananda,[35] also teaches the value of meditation as a means of achieving higher states of contemplation.[36]

Jainism

The ancient Jain religion, also from India, teaches that the way to liberation and bliss is to live lives of harmlessness and renunciation. The essence of Jainism is concern for the welfare of every being in the universe and for the health of the universe itself. Jainism has no priests, rather its professional religious people are monks and nuns who lead strict ascetic lives. They live in small groups of five or six, not in big monastic communities. Lay people are not particularly encouraged to meditate but the monks and nuns do spend their days in meditation and study.[37] One of the principles of Jainism is called 'non-onesidedness', according to which every side of an argument or conflict must be rigorously and impartially examined in order to discover the wisest, most equable way forward. Jain songs and chanting, and Jain temples (each one unique), are exceptionally beautiful.

Judaism

The ancient mystical path of Judaism, known as *kabbalah*, teaches the deepest insights into the essence of God, his interaction with the world and the purpose of creation. According to an authoritative source, two methods of meditation are employed by students of this approach, especially in connection with the study of Hebrew Scripture, the Torah.[38] The first entails centring and settling one's consciousness on the general sense of an idea, while passively withdrawing from all thoughts, feelings and body sensations. The second, in contrast, more like focused contemplation, demands detailed, broad and deep comprehension of the text under consideration.[39]

Islam and Sufism

Sufism is the name of a mystical path associated with Islam by whose beliefs and practices Muslims seek to find the truth of divine love and knowledge through direct personal experience of God. Through *muraqaba*, a practice akin to meditation, Sufis are said to watch over or take care of the 'spiritual heart' within, acquiring knowledge about it and becoming increasingly attuned to the ever vigilant 'Divine Presence'. Dedicated Sufis are constantly meditating on the words of the Islamic holy book, the Qur'an. The statement therein that 'Allah loves them and they love him' became the basis for love-mysticism, championed by the thirteenth-century poet and spiritual master Jalāl ad-Dīn Rūmī, as in the following quatrain:

> Love is here like the blood in my veins and skin,
> It has emptied me of myself and filled me with the Beloved,
> His fire has penetrated all the atoms of my body.
> Of 'me' only my name remains; the rest is Him.[40]

Rūmī also favoured and promoted 'whirling', extended rotatory dancing to sacred music that induces a trance-like state of higher consciousness. It is a central aspect of Sufi worship performed by the renowned Mevlevi Order, or Whirling Dervishes, some of whom are still practising today.

Chanting and poetry, especially love poetry, are also integral to Sufi spiritual practice.

Taoism

Taoism owes its origins to the philosopher-sage Lao Tsu, who lived in China's Honan Province in the sixth century BC. The word *Tao* translates as 'way', 'path' or 'natural law'. Lao Tsu's seminal work, *Tao Te Ching*, however, begins:

> The Tao that can be told is not the eternal Tao.
> The name that can be named is not the eternal name.
> The nameless is the beginning of heaven and earth.[41]

This speaks of a mystical dimension to reality that can only be described by metaphor and poetry. By implication it can only be accessed and appreciated directly, through focused concentration; in other words, through mindful contemplation.

The central tradition of Taoism combines dualism and holistic, unitary thinking and experience in a simple and elegant dynamic, circular metaphor. This involves the entirety of creation being made up of the continual interplay between the complementary attributes of Yin and Yang. These two alternating primal states of being are combined symbolically within a circle divided into dark and light. Yin is the dark, yielding, feminine principle and Yang is light, firm, masculine.

The philosophy of Taoism as developed by Chuang Tsu (also from Honan Province, living in the fourth century BC) in his remarkably expressive work *Inner Chapters*,[42] can be summarized simply:

> Accept what is in front of you without wanting the situation to be other than it is. Study the natural order of things and work with it rather than against it, for trying to change what *is* results only in resistance. Nature provides everything for all, without discrimination. In the clarity of a still and open mind, truth will be reflected.[43]

It is hard for us, as it was for Saul, to kick against the pricks, to act against our true spiritual nature. In contemporary language the message is to discover, listen to, trust our inner guide and – go with the flow! The Taoist version amounts simply to this: 'Obey natural law, and be true to your authentic, most honourable self!'

For Christians the way to follow, the Christian *Tao*, may be rendered as 'Listen attentively, prayerfully at all times, and abide by the promptings of the Holy Spirit within!' How else might we learn to love God with all our heart, with all our soul, and with all our mind – and our neighbours as ourselves? There is no other way.

Notes

1 Each half of Merton's life lasted almost exactly 27 years.
2 Recorded at the Abbey of Gethsemani on 20 August 1965: an excerpt from Merton's final address as novice master before his permanent move to the hermitage. To listen, see websites (Merton audioclip).
3 See websites (Northumbria Community).
4 Northumbria Community (2000).
5 St Benedict (1998).
6 3:15 a.m. – Vigils; 5:45 a.m. – Lauds; 10:20 a.m. – Terce; 12:15 p.m. – Sext; 2:15 p.m. – None; 5:30 p.m. – Vespers; 7:00 p.m. – Rosary; 7:30 p.m. – Compline. See websites (Monastic schedule).
7 Tuesday, in French, is *mardi* – the planet Mars' day; Wednesday is *mercredi* – Mercury's day.
8 See websites (Quakers).
9 Adapted from the 'Quakers in Britain' website.
10 See websites (Julian Meetings).
11 See websites (WCCM).
12 Juan Mascaro (2005).
13 From WCCM website 'What meditation' page: see websites (WCCM).
14 See, for example, Eugene d'Aquili and Andrew Newberg (1999); Andrew Newberg, Eugene d'Aquili and Vince Rause (2001); Shanida Nataraja (2008).
15 Matthieu Ricard, Antoine Lutz and Richard Davidson (2014).
16 Nataraja (2008), p. 89.
17 Jon Kabat-Zinn (1990).
18 Mark Williams, John Teasdale, Zindel Segal and Jon Kabat-Zinn (2007).

19 See, for example, I. Kutz, J. Z. Borysenko and H. Benson (1985); J. L. Craven (1989); G. Bogart (1991); Christopher K. Germer, Ronald D. Siegel and Paul R. Fulton (2005).

20 Jonathan Campion and Sharn Rocco (2009).

21 See, for example, Clive Erricker and Jane Erricker (2001) and David Fontana and Ingrid Slack (2007).

22 Katherine Weare (2014).

23 The founders were Richard Burnett and Chris Cullen. See websites (Mindfulness in schools).

24 See websites (Meditation in schools).

25 Featured in *The Guardian*'s 'Top teaching resources' of 2013.

26 From a BBC Parliament televised House of Lords debate in which Lord Stone spoke on 27 November 2015 on 'The Role of Religion and Belief in British Public Life'. See websites for text (House of Lords debate, text). Between mid-2013 and the end of 2014, 115 people attended one of the eight-week courses, which will be repeated in 2015.

27 The Indian prince Siddhartha of the Sakya clan, 563–483 BC, after a final spiritual breakthrough while meditating in Bodh Gaya, was given the title 'Buddha', meaning 'The Enlightened One'.

28 Wisdom includes right understanding and aspiration; morality includes right speech, action and livelihood; concentration includes right effort, mindfulness and concentration.

29 Katsuki Sekida (1975), pp. 194–5.

30 William James (1982), p. 382; emphasis added.

31 Father Elder Mullan (1914); also published as a PDF document by ixtmedia.com. See websites (Loyola exercises).

32 The five are: *hatha* yoga (postural physical exercises); *bhakti* yoga (devotional practice); *jnana* yoga (wisdom seeking); *mantra* yoga (chanting); *karma* yoga (giving, the exercise of compassion). See David Fontana (2003), pp. 62–79. Fontana includes *raja* yoga (control of the mind) in place of *mantra* yoga.

33 See websites (Brahma Kumaris). 'Brahma Kumaris' translates as 'Sisters of God'.

34 Ramakrishna, 1836–86.

35 Vivekananda, 1863–1902.

36 Christopher Isherwood (1965) and Swami Vivekananda (1948).

37 See websites (BBC on religions).

38 The 'Torah' refers specifically to the first five books of the Bible – Genesis, Exodus, Leviticus, Numbers and Deuteronomy – but can be extended to mean the whole of Jewish teaching, culture and practice.
39 See websites (Kabbalah online).
40 From a poem of Rūmī, quoted by Hüseyin Bingül (2014).
41 Lao Tsu (1972), p. 1.
42 Chuang Tsu (1974). See also Merton (1969).
43 Lao Tsu (1972): back-cover note.

10

Conclusions

—————◆◆◆—————

Everyday spiritual practices

Dissonances seek resolution. The gap between flesh and spirit is constantly seeking closure. If it is true that every child is already imbued with the Holy Spirit – whether baptized or not, whether raised and conditioned within a religious tradition or not – he and she will be influenced accordingly. Many people, consciously or otherwise, respond in adulthood by engaging regularly in universal forms of 'everyday' spiritual practice.

Mindfulness practice and other forms of meditation – more acceptable to many for being stripped of their religious trappings and significance – are increasingly widespread among secular practitioners of all ages. There are a number of additional ways to pursue the goal of spiritual maturity that have religious equivalents. Contemplative reading of great literature, poetry and philosophy, for example, compares favourably with the study of Scripture. Making and listening to inspirational music, and close appreciation of other forms of non-religious art, provide many with more than aesthetic experiences, touching on the sacred.

Look into the lives of people who consider themselves 'spiritual but not religious', and a number of other regular or occasional activities clearly enhance their spiritual sense of connectedness and well-being. Engaging with nature (perhaps by planting and tending a garden, by going for a daily walk or by making pilgrimage trips to beauty spots amid awe-inspiring landscapes); visiting other holy places, sites of special or spiritual interest; exercising creative imagination and ability through art and craftwork; maintaining physical health through adopting

a disciplined regime of exercise (including gym work, yoga classes, T ai
Chi or something similar), through playing sports, eating a sensible
diet, getting enough sleep, and paying attention to dreams: these might
all be included.

At the social level, joining clubs and societies to engage in social and
sporting activities, making friends thereby and discovering a rewarding
sense of fellowship, has something in common with belonging to a
Christian congregation or some other faith community. Making and
maintaining close, loving relationships, both at home within the family
and elsewhere among strangers, is also spiritually enhancing. Acts of
charity, kindness and compassion – directed towards people we do
not know, seeking no payback or reward – are also effective forms of
spiritual work; giving time, skill, knowledge and experience in particular,
but money, material goods and benefits too.

Through such everyday spiritual practices we can confidently expect
people to make progress through the stages towards maturity. The drive
is there within us, both personally *and* collectively. As each individual
moves forward in faith and maturity, so does humanity at large. The
steps may be imperceptible and resistance remains. Nevertheless unless
we destroy ourselves as a race of people, we can hope that – if this is
God's plan – progress will continue through the generations towards
the spiritual fulfilment of consciousness and human personality, towards
Teilhard de Chardin's 'Omega Point' (see p. 70).

As individuals we can do little to prevent catastrophe, to make spiritual development happen at the wider cultural level or to speed it
up, *except* by taking care of our own personal development. We can be
confident that as we do this, everyone else will benefit too. Collective,
social progress is made with every step towards spiritual maturity that
each one of us takes.

Universality

An old parable has it that to cross a river we need to find or make
a suitable vessel. Once across, though, it makes no sense to carry such
a craft around on your back. This is a challenging idea. Not every

Christian or every religious person understands it. Whereas we benefit from structure, guidance and support during the first half of life, while becoming a person in the world, during the transition phase and embarking fully on the second half of life, we have somehow to relinquish attachments and aversions – even religious attachments and aversions – to feel our losses, especially the loss of cherished comfort and security, to grieve and eventually to let go.

The task becomes less one of asserting Christian beliefs, more one of working diligently at spiritual practices that, from the biological perspective, bring both halves of our brains – rational and impersonal, creative and empathic – into harmony. Psychologically speaking, one aim is to develop the capacity for unitary, holistic thinking and experience alongside the more familiar dualist perspective. Another is, through suffering emotional pain, to allow the conversion of desire, fear, doubt, anger, shame and sorrow into contentment, calm, confidence, acceptance, self-worth and joy. In social terms we seek tolerance, kinship and kindness in relations with our neighbours – with the totality of humanity – without division, discrimination or conflict. In spiritual terms we are working towards the embodiment of faith, hope, wisdom, compassion and love.

The life, death and resurrection of Jesus and the words of St Paul are available to connect and guide people in the way of the Holy Spirit. Without exception we are all 'members of the body of Christ'. The mature Christian recognizes, therefore, the universality of faith, the comparable great truth inherent in and expressed through other religions and their practitioners.

Whether surrounded by nature, outdoors in a crowd, in Jain or Hindu temple, in Jewish synagogue, in Muslim mosque, in Sikh gurdwara, in a Buddhist centre or monastery or in a Christian church, prompted by the great and holy spirit of the universe, people come – resonating together – to worship God, the divine being, and his unified, sacred creation. Yet this diversity of worship remains confusing for some people. It may be helpful for these to consider as a metaphor a bicycle wheel, each spoke representing a different religion or religious subgroup, with spokes also for non-religious humanitarian philosophies and communities.

Starting at the wheel's rim the spokes – especially those on different sides of the wheel – are far apart from each other. As everyone gets closer towards the centre, however, towards spiritual maturity, the spokes converge and finally meet at the hub. According to this metaphor the further we travel along any path – Christian, Hindu, Muslim, Jewish, Buddhist, Humanist or whatever – the closer we get to everyone else.

Spiritually mature people recognize mutually the life-giving, wise and compassionate spirit within each other, whatever their background. Thomas Merton and the Dalai Lama, from completely different traditions, admired each other affectionately from the outset. To develop the metaphor, we can raise up the wheel's hub, enlarging the image in our minds to become a massively high, conical island-mountain. The path of each religion and philosophy starts now on the rim at sea level, travels across flat sand and low-lying terrain then starts climbing upwards beside rivers and streams and through thick forest or jungle that obscures most other paths, tricking us into thinking of ours as unique. Beyond the treeline, however, other ways start coming into view.

Our choice is between exploring different routes or remaining on the more familiar one. Either way, going higher we are bound to encounter difficulties: a barren pitted area, perhaps, a steep and smooth rock face or treacherous snow and ice. Cloud cover brings sleet and blizzard conditions, the risk of avalanche, forcing us to bivouac and rest. It is cold. The summit is shrouded, invisible. The altitude makes breathing difficult. Fortunately we are not alone in seeking the summit. Many have gone before us, leaving ropes, guidelines and supplies. Others join and stay with us to show the way and offer support. The routes from all around the mountain are converging. More spiritual seekers and guides arrive, from different directions, from many different traditions. We may discover that, in return, we can help some of them too.

Finally the cloud clears; bright sunshine breaks out illuminating the summit, no longer too far ahead. With our companions, old and new, we make our way now joyfully, free of fear, happy for everyone. Finally reaching the mountain-top, the pinnacle of spiritual maturity, we discover with delight that we have done with gravity, with worldliness, with being bound to earth, time and space. With our spiritual companions, like angels with wings, we are now able to fly.

The only way to describe the goal of the spiritual journey is like this, through metaphor. When the everyday egoic mind and the spiritual mind, never truly separate, are finally fully reunited, we are indescribably free, healed, complete, perfected, whole. Where will we fly, now that we can? Having become natural teachers, healers and mediators, we return surely to where there is ignorance, suffering and conflict. We descend to assist others embarked upon the great climb; encouraging those seeking to remain in the relative comfort and security of the jungle or forest to keep moving, to embark on the greater part of the journey into the second half of life, the more fulfilling half. Until every last one has made it, this is what we find ourselves wanting to do and calmly committed to doing. The whole point of the climb, of the struggle to attain full spiritual maturity, is to be of better service to others. When this is achieved, without making further ado, guided by something – by the Holy Spirit of God, Jesus and the universe – this, our duty and purpose, will also be our delight.

Afterword: My Christian journey

I felt like I was being guided, but without a guide I could point to.[1]

Birth and baptism

Human life is created from dust and ash, from planetary elements that themselves originated in the stars. We are born not so much 'into the world' as 'out of the earth'; and so it was that my mother, beloved instrument of the universe, gave birth to my bodily form on St Patrick's Day, 1950. According to my grandmother, the sun shone and daffodils were in full bloom all around. I was given the name Larry at my baptism nine weeks later, in the Anglican Church of St Mary, Walton-on-Thames.

Very seldom in church, my parents were only nominally Christian. There were no Bible stories at home and prayers were never said. Few references were made to religion and those that were – by my father mainly – tended to reveal a kind of studied indifference; a polite shield, I suspect, for a more entrenched antipathy. He said once, when I was about 16, that accompanying me to a service left him feeling like a hypocrite. 'I realized', he said, 'that I don't believe in any of it.' He tried to respect my position, but on Sunday mornings during school holidays after that, I had to bicycle to church.

Surprisingly, Dad's mother was by all accounts a devoutly religious person who, when widowed, married a former Archbishop;[2] but she died in Canada in the late 1940s and I never knew her.

On my mother's side there was ignorance of Christianity rather than indifference or rejection. My mother's education was truncated by the Second World War and evacuation. Still alive in her late eighties, now in a sweet twilight state of dementia, she appears to recognize the tunes and some of the words to hymns that she will have heard during child-hood, but I do not know with any confidence, for example, that she ever learned to repeat the Lord's Prayer.

It is something of a mystery, then, that I was ever baptized and raised a Christian. I suspect it was because christening was a conventional practice, 'the done thing', rather than through conviction on the part of either parent. The gentle lobbying of one of my godparents, my Aunty Emmy, may also have been instrumental. She was from Switzerland, raised a Protestant and converted to Roman Catholicism when she married my father's oldest friend, Eric. Discovering that she would have to raise their two daughters in the Roman tradition she became the most ardent of devotees, eventually earning herself a *Benemerenti* award from Pope Paul VI for 'long and exceptional service to the Catholic Church'.

Emmy was one of several women who awakened and kindled my Christian awareness and faith. Another had the most appropriate of names for a religious mentor, Roma Christian. Roma and her husband James, who lived next door to us in Holly Avenue, had no children. When my brother was born, my mother was pleased to let Roma take the two-year-old me under her wing. Mum always said it was Roma who taught me nursery rhymes, read to me stories, took me on outings on foot and by bus and generally fostered my imagination. She also started teaching me how to read and write, so that when I first went to the kindergarten, Danesfield, at the age of three, I was substantially ahead of my peers. How impatient at their slow reading, I recall being, always wanting to get on with the story. But I do not actually remember my times with Roma, just as I do not remember the baptism ceremony. I did meet her just once, briefly, as an adult, and corresponded with her towards the end of her life. She remained a staunch worshipper and upholder of the Christian faith. I was pleased to have been able to thank her, before she died, for her early kindness to me.

A Christian education

We moved to New Malden in south-west London when I was about six. I had already started at Gate House, a preparatory school in George

Road. There I was to encounter formidable form teacher Laura Sparshott, a spare, slight, grey-haired, grey-clad woman of fire-like intensity and a beautiful, soft singing voice. Miss Sparshott began every day in class by singing the J. H. Newman hymn:

> Firmly I believe and truly
> God is Three, and God is One;
> And I next acknowledge duly
> Manhood taken by the Son.

It is, of course, the Christian creed put to verse, but what sense could it make to a seven-year-old? It was a complex riddle that she did not try to explain and we did not try to understand. It was a given, every morning, that – once we had learned it from her – we would sing this hymn every day. No Zen master could have prepared us for eventual enlightenment better!

The following year I moved on to a boarding school in Kent, Bickley Hall. For four years, as part of the regular timetable there I studied 'Scripture' with a wonderful teacher, Elizabeth Waddy. Miss Waddy, although younger and more colourful, was as devout as Laura Sparshott. She did not sing but her speaking voice was similarly mellifluous; and she was a master storyteller. Beginning with Genesis and the creation she took us steadily, week by week, through the Old Testament. I was enthralled by the stories – Adam and Eve defying God's instructions, Noah and his ark full of family and animals, the willingness of Abraham to sacrifice his son Isaac, Joseph sold by his brothers, baby Moses in the bulrushes, the flight of the people of Israel from slavery in Egypt and the parting of the Red Sea, the Burning Bush and the Ten Commandments, the boy Samuel called by God in the night, David slaying the mighty Goliath, Solomon and the building of the Temple, the love story of Ruth and Boaz, the healing miracles of the prophets Elijah and Elisha, Daniel in the lions' den, Isaiah's unclean lips purified – and so on. Each tale was gripping in itself but as the magnificent epic unfolded, Miss Waddy gently emphasized the inherent continuity and the constant underlying theme of a creator God, intimately involved with the fortunes of his people in what was always a joint enterprise. Obedience was required, she explained, because obedience to him served them best.

Miss Waddy was a patient teacher. She never got ahead of the story, so it was not until the age of eleven that I really heard about Jesus. Again the stories gripped, enthralled and finally also appalled. Again the continuity was given emphasis: heralded by John the Baptist, Jesus was born to fulfil God's promise of a Messiah; the Ten Commandments were to be forever reinterpreted in the light of new commandments from Jesus, to love God and to love one another 'as I have loved you' (John 13.34). It seemed incomprehensible to me a schoolboy, though, that Jesus should also say, 'Love your enemies, do good to those who hate you, bless those who curse you, pray for those who abuse you' (Luke 6.27–28). These were revolutionary ideas.

Miss Waddy let us wonder at the annunciation and the virgin birth, at the parables and the miracles and at the travesty of justice that led to the crucifixion. What a wise and wonderful man Jesus was, it seemed to me, who, for example, when entrapped by the question of tax to the Romans asked to see a coin and spoke accordingly: 'Render to Caesar the things that are Caesar's, and to God the things that are God's' (Mark 12.17 KJV). I remember how fantastically impressed I was at the time by this skilful response. But I did not then understand why Jesus, the miracle-maker, did not simply rescue himself from the cross. Miss Waddy tried to explain, but not until I was a touch more mature could I finally comprehend the necessity and significance of that most supreme of sacrifices. There was no ram in a thicket nearby to take the place of the Christ. He was not the son of Abraham. He was the son of almighty God.

By then, even though I did not appreciate every aspect of the Christian story, following the examples of Aunty Emmy, Roma Christian, Miss Sparshott and Miss Waddy I had come to love the Lord Jesus with willing devotion. And there were other benefits from the Scripture lessons. Week by week, year by year we listened to each new instalment. Our task as homework was always the same: to recall as many details as possible and set the episode down on paper, consulting our Bibles if necessary. It turned out that I had a talent for this, and I suspect that this was where I discovered and started developing a gift for writing. It involved especially paying careful attention, and it also meant being sure I had understood everything. I was always keen, therefore, and never afraid, to ask for clarification. These same skills were also useful when studying medicine and psychiatry; also later, whenever I had to 'take a clinical history' from a patient. Thirty years after my last lesson from her I am glad to have been able to make contact again with Miss Waddy in the final years of her life, to express my gratitude. It did not surprise me to learn then that another of her pupils had become an Anglican bishop.

In addition to class work we had prayers daily at the school and went on Sundays to a service of matins in the attractive, small chapel. I found the routine of hymns, prayers and a weekly sermon enjoyable. I was seldom bored, unlike some of my friends, constantly fretting to get outside and run around, making fun use of footballs, rugby balls, cricket and tennis gear, depending on the season. I enjoyed those activities too but chapel gave me a different, more reflective kind of pleasure and satisfaction. Attending church services usually still does.

Confirmation

When I moved on at age 13 to Cranleigh, a school in Surrey, my religious education continued. I took O level Divinity, studying especially the Gospel of Mark and the Acts of the Apostles for two years. There we attended chapel daily as well as on Sundays; but there seemed to be so much more pressure on our time, and when the morning service became optional and I often had schoolwork to catch up on, I attended then only sporadically. It was the 1960s, and the broader culture was changing rapidly from conformity, including conformity to the Christian religion, towards individualism and secularization. Several of my most influential teachers – especially the East House housemaster, Iain Campbell, and the science teachers, Paul Connett, Tony West, Ken Wills and Ray Groves – seemed relatively indifferent to religion. Nevertheless at 14, in the school chapel before my parents and godmother Emmy, I was confirmed as a Christian by the Bishop of Guildford. It was a proud moment for me.

This landmark, and being able to take Holy Communion for the first time, the fulfilment of my infant baptism, meant a great deal. I quickly realized, though, that I was in a minority. I suspect that others in my confirmation group had gone through the process 'because it was expected' rather than through genuine engagement with the great Christian verities. Also, when I went to services at Christ Church, New Malden during school holidays there were few other people worshipping there and virtually none of my age group. The liturgy seemed desultory. The atmosphere was gloomy. In addition, my friends either did not believe or did not bother with religion. With no family support it is not too surprising that my faith went underground. This was after, aged 15, I had already felt a definite sense of being called to become a doctor. By the time I started at St Catharine's College, Cambridge to study medicine at the age of 18, I had ceased church attendance altogether. If you had asked me during the following years, I would have said I was a Christian but that medical education and practice formed the central – almost sole – focus of my religious commitment. That seemed all right to me at the time.

Things happen

'Something happened' is a phrase I like to use to indicate any kind of transcendent, 'hard to explain' experience that is meaningful and has a lasting effect in someone's life; and 'something happened' to me in this way when I was 19, teaching me much about God's love and the Holy Spirit. My parents' marriage had failed; a bicycle accident resulting in concussion had impaired my studies and I had been growing increasingly unhappy. To get away from the upsetting situation I decided with two friends to go travelling during the long summer vacation. This resulted in Charlie Gore, Neil Fillingham and me setting off to hitchhike to Istanbul, even though I had never travelled a mile by this method before.

It was a genuine adventure. Because few drivers will pick up three hikers, we travelled independently, meeting up at agreed youth hostels in the evenings. Neil ran out of funds and returned home after a month but Charlie and I continued through Europe to Athens and then by ferry to the island of Rhodes. Later we crossed to Marmaris in Turkey by fishing boat and headed east. At Kayseri (onetime Caesarea) in the middle of Turkey, we eventually parted company. Charlie, who was studying geography, wanted to go further, towards Lake Van. I preferred to spend some time in Istanbul.

It was a marvellous trip, but what happened that stayed with me was the feeling of safety and security that enveloped me, even in precarious circumstances. At the last moment, when despair was setting in – of reaching the planned rendezvous or the ferry terminal on time, of getting something to eat when hungry or of finding somewhere to sleep at night – kind and generous people always appeared to take or show me where I needed to go. I frequently felt blessed and, very often, guided. I had shed my material comfort zone and found a spiritual one, not simply to replace but to better it. My final lift on that trip, incidentally, took me all the way from the Turkish border with Greece to my English front door.

One year later the same search for adventure took me to the USA for three months. A year after that I travelled again through Europe to Greece and then on to the Middle East, to Cyprus, Lebanon, Syria and Turkey, returning through what was then Yugoslavia. Soon after I went from Cambridge to Guy's Hospital in London for three more years' medical training.

Travel

I was in New Zealand the next time 'something happened'. Unsure of what medical career to follow, after getting my medical qualifications and completing my 'house jobs' in medicine and surgery in hospitals in Greenwich and Orpington I had taken a surgical post in the small hospital at Tokoroa in the North Island. However, I soon became unhappy again, this time because I felt I was in the wrong job. There was no obvious way out because the hospital authorities had contributed towards the cost of my air fare and I had signed an agreement to stay in the post for a year. My friend David Gatland was working in Christchurch and said there was a vacancy in a psychiatry training programme there; but I could not simply resign and leave Tokoroa.

One beautiful Sunday afternoon I went for a drive on my own. Parking the car, I took a long walk during which, mulling the situation over, I fell into a kind of reverie and spent an hour or more in deep contemplation. Time passed unnoticed. Eventually, following the track back towards the car I came suddenly out of my trance, becoming fully conscious once more of my surroundings – fields and low hills, scrubby trees – and the warm breeze on my face. I felt uplifted and was almost laughing now because somehow I knew that I *would* be going south to take up that opportunity. I had the feeling that nothing insurmountable could or would stand in my way. And so it was!

Despite its being Sunday, I drove directly to the house of my boss, the hospital superintendent, to lay my cards on the table. Mr Harry kindly told me he would see what he could do. Despite the fact that it would leave him a doctor short for a while, he telephoned his opposite number in Christchurch the following day. A few weeks later I was on my way. The health authority there had agreed to take over my air-fare bond. Although I did not then expect to become a psychiatrist, I have no doubt now that it was all God's will and meant to be.

The next six months were very challenging. One teenage female patient assigned to me, for example, took a near-fatal overdose almost every week, usually just a few hours after her therapy session. Max Brad-field, a wonderful supervisor and mentor, encouraged me to remain optimistic. After Charity's fifth or sixth near-suicide he said:

> She has been very badly damaged in her early life, Larry. She was abandoned by her mother, and misused by all the men she came across. I think you are the first person who has really got through to her. Go and see her in the hospital as she recovers from the overdose. Let her know she has not succeeded in putting you off caring about her. Her attempt at persuading you she is worthless, which is what I think unconsciously she is trying to do, has failed. Let her know you are still there to offer her help if she wants it.

Fortunately he was right. Charity eventually gave up her death wish and was making real progress by the time my six months in Christchurch – and my 12-month New Zealand visa – were up. Her self-esteem was renewed. Max said later: 'I didn't think she would make it, Larry. When you started working with her, I thought her chances of suicide were almost 100 per cent.' It was kind of him – so my self-esteem went up as well!

'Something happened' again – gradually or maybe repeatedly in small increments – during those six months. Because we often worked with entire families in distress I was forced to examine my own family background and history; to make sense of it and my place in it. There were some aspects of the conditioning process – some attachments and aversions – that I needed to shed. This was good for me, but tough, and it was a relief to step out of the crucible of psychiatry for a while at the end of 1976.

My grandfather's gift

Returning to England briefly, I was at my grandfather George's bedside on the day he died. His last words to me, smiling broadly and holding up four fingers, were: 'See you in four years!' Naturally, I spent those four years wondering what he had meant and whether he might have been foretelling my death. It was funny but also slightly alarming. I wondered at first if he might simply have been confused. I remember contradicting him and saying I would return the following day; but this was not to be. He had lung cancer, although no one had told him about it. Earlier, when my grandmother, Violet, asked what he was thinking about, I heard him say without hesitation, 'Six pieces of wood' (in other words a coffin); so we knew he was aware death was close. Amazingly, he seemed really happy about it.

I have written elsewhere about the effect of my grandfather's final words.[3] I will only say briefly here that after ignoring the situation for about a year I began exploring the possibility of an early death, asking myself what goals would I wish to set and how might I live life differently. It struck me that whenever it happened, I was certain to die some day. This helped to get my ambitions and values into focus.

Of course, I did not die at the age of 30. By then, though, I had matured enough to 'see' my grandfather clearly, to see and experience that the bond between us was unconditional, an unbreakable one of love. I see his smiling face in my mind's eye whenever I think of him, and feel again the warmth of his loving affection and approval. It is a wonderful feeling, which I count the most generous gift and blessing.

During none of this time was I going to church, seeking out Christian company or regularly saying prayers. Just days after my grandfather's funeral I returned 'down-under', to live and work in Australia, having obtained an open-ended resident visa. My first job, for a couple of months in Tasmania in 1977, was as locum for a single-handed GP. This was really exciting! I was relatively inexperienced but everything went well there. I was in my spiritual comfort zone again. I moved next to Sydney, continuing to take over single-handed general practices around that beautiful, vibrant city for periods from a week to three months. It was enjoyable and rewarding, but I awoke one morning, about a year later, thinking that while having a good time I was not progressing towards any kind of structured medical career.

I decided that my choices involved staying in Australia or returning to England, doing further training towards a career in general practice or resuming psychiatry. I hesitated, made enquiries and returned to England for a visit; but eventually psychiatry in Australia got the vote, and a number of months later, after a thrilling further three months as a GP in a West Australian town, over 100 miles from any other doctor, I restarted as a trainee psychiatrist, this time in Adelaide. It was early in 1979, and the course was set to last five years.

Return to psychiatry

I was fortunate. The training at Hillcrest and Glenside Hospitals and at the Adelaide Children's Hospital was excellent, and I embraced this new life enthusiastically. More robust psychologically, I was finding the experience significantly less personally challenging than before. Questions raised during my time in Christchurch, together with the quest begun with my grandfather's last words, had encouraged me to think about everyone else's plight as finite human beings on this planet, rather than just my own. When in Sydney I had even written a book, *One Way*, to get my jumbled thoughts into line. It was never published, but some of the principal ideas I have used since came to me then.

One central example is that human lives involve five seamlessly interconnected dimensions of experience – physical, biological, psychological, social and spiritual – and that philosophy, theology and science, to be genuine and fully useful, must take account of all five. This is also true of medicine and especially psychiatry, where there is still a strong emphasis on biology but where biological, psychological and social elements have all long been recognized as contributing to the whole picture.

With others, in recent years I have therefore been involved in recommending an extension of professional thinking to include the spiritual dimension in a new 'bio-psycho-socio-spiritual' paradigm or model.[4] Research has shown that spiritual well-being, living a life full of meaning with a strong sense of purpose, is associated with better physical health, better healing when unwell and greater equanimity in the face of pain, disability and dying.[5] The role of the spiritual dimension and the benefits involved in mental health also seem vitally important but still widely neglected.[6]

I remained a stranger to regular churchgoing while in Adelaide, nor was I thinking or behaving as a typical Christian. However, both psychology and psychiatry were being taught as fairly rigidly secular subjects in the 1970s and 1980s, and my interest in human spirituality – the 'active ingredient' of religion – caused me to begin looking outside the regular syllabus of the training programme. For example, I began taking a serious interest in Carl Jung (see Chapter 4). David Tacey,[7] Julia Fox and I started the Adelaide Jung group, and we twice invited the Zurich-trained Jungian analyst Patrick Jansen from Sydney to conduct weekend workshops in Adelaide. On the second occasion he brought along Scott, an American who had 'taken robes' and become a monk in the Dalai Lama's Gelugpa order of Tibetan Buddhism. This was unexpected.

Learning from Buddhist monks

Scott – who also had a Tibetan name that I no longer recall – was then based at Tara House in Melbourne. At the workshop he immediately invited us to put away our notebooks and pens, sit with a straight back, rest our hands comfortably, half-close our eyes and pay attention to our breathing, registering each in and out breath as it passed through the nostrils. Whenever distracted, he said, we were simply to return our focus of awareness to the breath. Twenty minutes later – when Scott invited us to open our eyes – how still we had become! The sweet calls of Australian bell-birds in the garden outside flooded my consciousness. Looking around, every face wore a smile. 'Meditation', said the maroon-robed teacher eventually, 'is just this ... Bringing the mind home to its pure, natural state ... reflecting each passing moment. Practise it when you can.'

I have been heeding this advice ever since. It was God's will for me to meet Scott, a man of about my own age, learn to meditate and take an interest in the teachings and practices of Tibetan Buddhism – and this has never felt like betraying my Christian roots at all. Like the spiritual writer Thomas Merton, I felt intuitively that there were many paths to God's truth, therefore the knowledge and wisdom I was learning from the East would in time prove valid and valuable. Nor have I been the only mental health professional to take note of the possible benefits of Buddhist insights – and especially meditation practice – for people experiencing anxiety, depression, psychosomatic and other psychological problems. As mentioned in Chapter 9, Jon Kabat-Zinn and his colleagues at the Stress Reduction Clinic in Massachusetts used Buddhist ideas and practices to develop a 'mindfulness' programme in the 1980s that has spread widely and been of proven benefit to very many people.[8]

Scott was the monk who, a few days later, also taught me something vital and valuable about myself.[9] I was telling him how concerned I was about a distressed patient whose condition had not responded to treatment. Scott showed me, first, that the only pain I could really do something about was my own; second, that I should accept rather than fight it; and third, that I would only then be in a position to have it heal. He then patiently explained that the remedy involved wisdom. It involved understanding that I suffered because I cared, and that it was therefore a noble pain. He said:

> This is the nature of compassion. It hurts to care. But this is what our true selves are like. We cannot escape this predicament. We can only learn from it. You are wise, therefore, to make such a patient your teacher.

These noble words, kindly spoken, changed my working life immeasurably for the better, and changed my view of humanity too. Compassion is involuntary and it is innate. We can try and ignore the suffering of others but, seamlessly interconnected within the same sacred whole, this is impossible. We will feel it sooner or later. We may try exciting distractions and dampening agents – sex, drugs and rock 'n' roll, wealth, status and power – to mask or dull the effect but these only lead away from truth and our true selves. Our suffering and the knowledge of others' suffering will not go away. We are left with only one satisfactory solution: to acknowledge our pain and allow it to work upon us. The pain, in other words, is the remedy. This was how I started developing the theory of emotions and personal growth that appears in this book.[10]

I discovered that people grow towards maturity mainly *through* adversity, not by seeking to avoid it – both through suffering loss themselves and through sharing in the losses of others. This is the basis of many a vocation. At some deep level people know that we will be better off by dedicating our lives in the service of others. I also discovered that wisdom and compassion go together: wisdom without compassion is false; compassion without wisdom leads only to exhaustion. As well as loving our neighbours, in other words, we are wise to learn how best to love ourselves. This shift in priorities – from a self-centred existence to a form of universal and unconditional self-directed love – marks a key point of transformation towards personal and spiritual maturity. It sounds like a boast, I know, but the only boast belongs not to the person affected but to the divine cosmic breath, the great Holy Spirit within.

Further transformation

This was an important development period, these few years in Adelaide. I was living alone, meditating daily, recording my dreams in a notebook, struggling with my grandfather's riddle, making new friends, developing new interests and learning to become a psychiatrist. I remember having a dream about being shot repeatedly in the head yet surviving and transcending death, living on. Another dream, which triggered a kind of breakthrough experience, concerned a very dear former girlfriend who was terminally ill at that time. The dream was again about love, and seemed to signify that my friend and I were forever bound by love, unconquerable by the death of either. This, though wonderful, was only half of it. There were other people in the dream and, on waking and reflecting on it all, I knew totally that just as my friend and I were deeply and seamlessly connected within the wholeness of God's loving universe, so is everyone equally and lovingly connected to everyone else. This, I have remained convinced, is a central fact of the universe.

The wonderful sense of a loving connection to all others, even those who do harm, resonates with me still. For several days after the dream I felt blissful. Afterwards I understood even more clearly that my grandfather's message had also been about the highest form of love. His fearless smile in the face of death said everything. Following these dreams and some other experiences, I lost all fear of my own death and began living much more in the present moment, less troubled by the past or concerned for the future.

In addition this spiritual breakthrough was accompanied by a change at the biological level. I felt somehow more complete in my body. I am right-handed and was now more aware and in control of my left side than before. The two hemispheres of my brain seem to have begun communicating more freely with each other. This also allowed me to see things better, both rationally and poetically at the same time. This was the emergence of a holistic form of vision and understanding, and the simultaneous recognition of how dominated by dualist thinking my mind had previously been. I could now see people and their pre-dicaments from every angle, aware of the tensions affecting them and better aware, therefore, of how these might be eased. I could see how every negative was balanced by a positive; every up by a down. The opposites, it was suddenly so obvious, need and define each other. I had been studying the oracular book of Chinese wisdom, the I Ching,[11] and could now see clearly how, like Yin and Yang, all complementary pairs interpenetrate each other dynamically. The only constant throughout the cosmos is change.

The change in me was also helpful; for example, I now felt several degrees more empathic towards others than before, especially my patients. By 'empathy' I mean that moment by moment while with them, I did not need to guess but could actually feel how they were feeling. It was a form of direct emotional telepathy, so I had an instant and intuitive grasp of their emotional state as it unfolded. This, of course, was of great assistance but it did take getting used to. In the company of a sad person I once found myself weeping openly, for example; usually, though, I felt the same emotion as the other person but with the volume turned low. This meant I could say with confidence to a patient something like 'You seem sad' or 'You seem angry – please tell me about that', which would help establish a beneficial rapport between us, often leading to a spontaneous and very healthy emotional unburdening on the part of the patient. Sometimes it was as if I could tell how a patient was feeling better than he or she could.

I also benefited, before I left Australia in 1981, from the teaching of an elderly Tibetan lama and his translator at Tara House in Melbourne. Our texts were from the eighth-century Buddhist teacher Shantideva[12] and the tenth-century master Atisha,[13] both available in English translation. The teaching concerned Tibetan thought transformation, which strikes me now as having many similarities to the cognitive behavioural therapy developed by Aaron Beck from the mid-1970s onwards, especially as described in recent textbooks.[14]

The key practice for the Tibetan involves meditation: learning to observe calmly the transient thoughts, emotions, sense perceptions and impulses that fill and flit about in one's mind from moment to moment, while staying calm and allowing the energy behind them to dissipate. In this way the mind becomes still and perfectly clear – just as the sediment in a stirred glass of fruit juice eventually settles to reveal the clarity of the liquid above. For example, when someone attacks you, the teaching says, rather than retaliate there is a better way to respond. Eight stanzas summarize thought transformation. Here are two of them:[15]

> Examining my continuum (of mental content) throughout
>   all actions,
> As soon as an emotional affliction arises that endangers
>   myself and others,
> By facing it I shall strictly avert it. (Stanza 3)

> When someone whom I have assisted and in whom I have
>   placed great hope
> Inflicts me with extremely bad harm,
> I shall view him as my supreme spiritual friend. (Stanza 6)

The teacher, Geshe-la as we called him, made very clear to the three or four of us in his daily classes that there was no point simply reading the texts. To understand and benefit you had diligently to practise the advice. Stanza 6 brought directly to mind Christ's commandment: 'Love your enemies, do good to those who hate you, bless those who curse you, pray for those who abuse you' (Luke 6.27–28). In that moment I knew my Christian journey was unfinished.

Homecoming

After three years in the Adelaide training programme I became eligible to sit the British psychiatry qualifying exams. It was an option, but I was not sure how to proceed. Another break from training was a possibility. Then I heard by telephone that my 70-year-old father had collapsed with a stroke. The next day I decided to resign and go back to England.

It was clearly the right thing to do but I was obliged to work a three-month resignation period. I also had to sell the house I had bought a year earlier. My father was recovering well so I was free to make my way back to England gradually, visiting South Africa, Egypt, the USA and Canada on the way. I was still assimilating recent experiences and felt no urgency to resume psychiatry. I had written a novel, *Moving Pictures*, and was rewriting it on advice from a London agent in the hope of publication. I soon knew my life was at a crossroads again but had no clear inclinations. Briefly, I did entertain thoughts of becoming a Buddhist monk but also knew intuitively that this was not my true path. I had learned much from and fully respected Buddhism but never really counted myself as a Buddhist.

About a year after leaving my post in Adelaide I visited the Manjushri Institute, a Tibetan Buddhist centre in Cumbria. By coincidence or synchronicity, there was a visit that weekend from a highly respected monk who was teaching about meditation. During the long silences, sitting in the meditation room I found the Lord's Prayer insistently on my lips and the words and tunes from hymns familiar from my school-days running through my mind. The thought immediately came: 'I am in the wrong place!' But what was the right place for me?

The next day, with nothing better to do, the teaching lama having returned to London, I took a short stroll through woodland to the banks of Morecambe Bay. Here I found a smooth bench on which to sit and meditate. It was a sunny, warm, peaceful day. By now I was used to sit-ting still, my mind at rest. Thoughts and feelings settled quickly. I was unaware of any thought content for the next 20 minutes or so, when 'something happened'. Something like a quiet but insistent voice came into my head, passing on a cosmic message: 'You are a psychiatrist, Larry. That's what you have trained to be – go and do that!'

This was not a psychotic hallucination. I was experiencing the Holy Spirit as my guide, and this seemed like a wonderful acknowledgement that I could again be counted among the children of God. This was exactly as St Paul had said to the Christians of Rome: 'For all who are led by the Spirit of God are children of God' (Romans 8.14). When my life was apparently deeply uncertain, I had been in my spiritual comfort zone all along.

The next day I left for London in a very positive mood. Another day later and I was being interviewed and encouraged to apply for a vacant training post by Arthur Crisp, eminent professor and head of the

Department of Psychiatry at St George's Hospital Medical School. After a more formal interview later I was duly appointed. A few months further on I managed to pass both parts of the qualifying exams for membership of the Royal College of Psychiatrists. It was the summer of 1983. I was to become a Senior Psychiatric Registrar at St George's the following year, and a Consultant Psychiatrist in Brighton in 1988.

In 1984, though, something else to mention had happened. I owned a small house in Ashleigh Gardens, close to All Saints Church in Sutton. One day I decided to attend a service for the first time in many years. When I got there the building was completely full. A lightning strike had damaged it some time previously. Repairs complete, the local bishop was attending now to give the renovated edifice a blessing. I knew nothing about this, and arrived in time only to squeeze into a pew at the back, hear the organ start to play and see the long procession of choir and clergy enter the church. Bringing up the rear, carrying his ornamental shepherd's crook, was the bishop. Having been nicknamed 'Larry the Lamb' when younger, this immediately gave me the wonderful feeling that, on this sunny day, I was the lost woolly creature being gently returned to the fold of Christ's Church. This homecoming experience was very moving. I did not become a regular and frequent churchgoer until later, when I moved to Sussex, but was no longer in doubt about my Christian roots and identity.

The heart of God's love

For over 25 years I have regularly attended the local Anglican Church of St Andrew and St Cuthman. I have served on the Parochial Church Council, the Deanery Synod and have been a representative on the local ecumenical Churches Together committee. Until taking a break recently I have also continued reading lessons, leading prayers and acting as a licensed Eucharistic Minister, helping administer the chalice at Holy Communion. In about 1990 a group of us started a Julian Meeting in the town, a Christian meditation group that continues to meet regularly. I went to several national Julian Meeting and other Christian retreats. I also began attending a regular interfaith meditation group, which used to host monks and nuns who had taken robes in the Thai Buddhist Theravada tradition, based at Cittaviveka monastery, Chithurst. I also went on meditation retreats at their sister monastery of Amaravati in Hertfordshire. In this way I have continued my spiritual practice, puzzling some people by appearing to follow two religions; but Christianity and aspects of Buddhism complement one another well.

I had heard relatively little about the contemplative tradition of Christianity before going to the 1994 gathering of the World Community for Christian Meditation,[16] the 'Good Heart' seminar, lasting three days at Middlesex University. The principal speaker was the Dalai Lama of Tibet, who had been given two short texts from each of the four Gospels as the basis for talks on Christian Scripture, 'from the point of view of a simple Buddhist monk'. He began by saying that his respect for Christianity was due largely to his conversations over several days in 1968 with the monk Thomas Merton.

Merton's account of those meetings can be found in his *Asian Journal*,[17] a copy of which was soon afterwards in my hands. I had already, somehow presciently, signed up with Kenneth Wilson's Soul of India tours for a pilgrimage trip to various sacred sites in India. As a fortuitous result I found myself reading Merton in some instances in the very location, even in the same building, where he had written an entry in his journal. Merton's open attitude to ideas from Buddhism and Zen, and from other Eastern faith traditions like Hinduism and Taoism, especially his thirst to learn more about the practice of meditation, immediately endeared him to me.

'Something happened' yet again on this pilgrimage, liberating me for all time from any anxieties and ambivalences I could have about an obligation to make a binding choice between two – or more – world religions. We went to Bodh Gaya in India's impoverished Bihar State, where in about 500 BC the historical Buddha Shakyamuni, originally a Prince of the Shakya clan, had stayed in meditation under a Bodhi tree until becoming enlightened.[18]

We arrived late at night. The following morning I decided to go alone to the Bodhi Temple, where the site of the Buddha's awakening is commemorated. Slowly I circumambulated the temple precincts in a kind of walking meditation for about an hour before being eventually drawn within the central building's portals. The interior there was dark. In front of me I could make out a man prostrating himself in traditional Buddhist fashion before a large Buddha-figure. I did not know whether to follow suit or whether to kneel, hands clasped together and recite the Our Father. I felt on the brink of having to make a desperate choice, but suddenly then felt as if forcibly pushed on to my knees, and forced again to move my hands towards the statue in deeply humble obeisance – not to an effigy of a once-living prince and spiritual teacher, but to the ineffable Holy Spirit of the eternal almighty God.

It was as if all dualities were suddenly and magnificently fused together into one within my mind. There were no longer either/or thoughts or decisions. There was only the underlying wholeness of both/and non-duality. And this, I instantly knew, was at the heart of God's love. 'Something happened', but not from my own will or actions. I felt only a responsibility to acquiesce meekly, to submit, surrender and obey. This was another irreversible, transformative step towards spiritual maturity. It was another great liberation and, for a second time in consequence, I was to enjoy three days of bliss.

After the India trip I joined the Thomas Merton Society of Great Britain and Ireland, also the International Thomas Merton Society,[19] and have since attended many meetings, conferences and pilgrimage trips in Thomas Merton's footsteps in UK, the USA, Canada, France, Cuba and Italy. I have also been on a refreshing week-long retreat at the Abbey of Our Lady of Gethsemani, the monastery in Kentucky where Merton spent the second half of his life. As for many others, through his many books and recorded lectures, Merton has been a kind of spiritual friend and mentor for me.

On a later pilgrimage tour of the Holy Land I was blessed with further deeply affecting spiritual experiences, bringing home with utter certainty that Jesus of Nazareth is indeed my personal lord and master. Mindful of the many who remain estranged from the Holy Spirit, from the spiritual dimension of their lives, I have felt committed since to try and rectify this in some way. I retired from the National Health Service in 2007 and from all clinical practice in 2011, to focus on this endeavour.

An earlier step, in 1999, was to combine with Andrew Powell, Andrew Sims, Sarah Eagger and others to set up, within the Royal College of Psychiatrists, the Spirituality and Psychiatry special-interest group[20] and to co-author a public leaflet, published by the college and available online under the title 'Spirituality and mental health'.[21] This led to publications already mentioned[22] and to the course I offered to third-year medical students at the Brighton and Sussex Medical School between 2005 and 2007 on spirituality and health care.[23] Since January 2011 I have also regularly posted an essay on spiritual wisdom as a blog on the website of the US magazine *Psychology Today*.[24]

I list these matters, not seeking admiration or congratulations in any way but simply offering them as my credentials, so to speak. Previously it has seemed best to develop and use a language of spirituality that deliberately avoids reflecting the beliefs or practices of one or other religion. My articles and books so far[25] – on happiness, on love and spirituality – have thus been directed towards a readership that includes people from different world faiths, those identifying with no particular religious background or beliefs and even those opposed to religion. I am a disciple of Christ, however, and am pleased now to have the opportunity of closing the circle, reinterpreting what I have learned about human spirituality, and the path towards maturity, in terms of the Holy Trinity and the sacred whole of God's creation. We are all kin, worthy of each other's love and respect, sharing a spiritual journey. I hope that point, at least, has been made.

Notes

1 Lloyd Jones (2013).
2 Adam de Pencier, of New Westminster, the arch-diocese centred on Vancouver.
3 Larry Culliford (2007b), pp. 181–9, 199–207.
4 For example, Culliford (2002) and (2007a).
5 Harold Koenig, Dana King and Verna B. Carson (2012).
6 See, for example, Christopher Cook, Andrew Powell and Andrew Sims (2009).
7 David Tacey, former professor at Latrobe University, Melbourne, later wrote the influential book, *The Spirituality Revolution* – Tacey (2004).
8 Jon Kabat-Zinn (1990).

9 Culliford (2007b), pp. 146–7.
10 Under a pen-name, Patrick Whiteside, an earlier version of the theory appeared in Culliford (2001).
11 Richard Wilhelm (1967).
12 Acharya Shantideva (1979).
13 Geshe Rabten and Geshe Ngawang Dhargyey (1977).
14 For example, Zindel V. Segal, Mark G. Williams and John D. Teasdale (2012).
15 Rabten and Dhargyey (1977), pp. 16–17.
16 The WCCM was founded by Benedictine monk John Main (1926–82). See websites (WCCM).
17 Thomas Merton (1973).
18 A beautiful account of the Buddha's life has been written by the Vietnamese Buddhist master Thich Nhat Hanh (1991).
19 See websites (Thomas Merton).
20 See websites (Spirituality special interest group). This group now has 3,000 psychiatrist members.
21 See websites (Mental health leaflet).
22 Culliford (2002 and 2007b).
23 Culliford (2009).
24 See websites (Author's blog).
25 See websites (Author's website) for details.

References, further reading and other sources

Asterisked items in the following list are particularly recommended.

Amir Aczel (2007), *The Jesuit and the Skull: Teilhard de Chardin, Evolution, and the Search for Peking Man*, New York: Riverhead.

Kate Adams (2001), 'God Talks to Me in My Dreams: The Occurrence and Significance of Children's Dreams about God', *International Journal of Children's Spirituality* 6:1, 99–111.

Kate Adams, Brendan Hyde and Richard Woolley (2008), *The Spiritual Dimension of Childhood*, London: Jessica Kingsley.

*Adyashanti (2014), *Resurrecting Jesus: Embodying the Spirit of a Revolutionary Mystic*, Boulder, CO: Sounds True.

Alcoholics Anonymous (2001), published by Alcoholics Anonymous World Services Inc., 4th edn.

A. Reza Arasteh (1975), *Toward Final Personality Integration: A Measure for Health, Social Change, and Leadership*, 2nd edn, New York and London: Wiley.

Karen Armstrong (2014), *Fields of Blood: Religion and the History of Violence*, London: Bodley Head.

St Benedict (1998), *The Rule of Saint Benedict*, ed. Timothy Fry, New York: Vintage Books.

Hüseyin Bingül (2014), 'Ecstasy in the Song of the Reed's Plaintive Notes', in *Rumi and his Sufi Path of Love*, ed. M Fatih Çitlak and Hüseyin Bingül, New York: Tughra Books.

G. Bogart (1991), 'The Use of Meditation in Psychotherapy: A Review of the Literature', *American Journal of Psychotherapy* 45:3, 383–412.

Jonathan Campion and Sharn Rocco (2009), 'Minding the Mind: The Effects and Potential of a School-based Meditation Programme for Mental Health Promotion', *Advances in School Mental Health Promotion* 2:1, 47–55.

*Chuang Tsu (1974), *Inner Chapters*, trans. Gia-Fu Feng and Jane English, London: Wildwood House.

Robert Coles (1990), *The Spiritual Life of Children*, London: HarperCollins.

Christopher Cook, Andrew Powell and Andrew Sims (eds) (2009), *Spirituality and Psychiatry*, London: RCPsych Publications.

*Phil Cousineau (1998), *The Art of Pilgrimage: The Seeker's Guide to Making Travel Sacred*, San Francisco: Conari Press.

J. L. Craven (1989), Meditation and psychotherapy. *Canadian Journal of Psychiatry*, 34:7, 648–53.

*Larry Culliford, as 'Patrick Whiteside' (2001), *Happiness: The 30-day guide*, London: Rider Books.

Larry Culliford (2002), 'Spiritual Care and Psychiatric Treatment: An Introduction', *Advances in Psychiatric Treatment* 8:4, 249–61.

Larry Culliford (2007a), 'Taking a Spiritual History', *Advances in Psychiatric Treatment* 13:3, 212–19.

*Larry Culliford (2007b), *Love, Healing and Happiness: Spiritual Wisdom for Secular Times*, Winchester: O Books.

Larry Culliford (2009), 'Teaching Spirituality and Health Care to Third-Year Medical Students', *The Clinical Teacher* 6:1, 22–7.

*Larry Culliford (2011), *The Psychology of Spirituality: An Introduction*, London: Jessica Kingsley.

*Larry Culliford (2014), 'The Meaning of Life Diagram: A Framework for a Developmental Path from Birth to Spiritual Maturity', *Journal for the Study of Spirituality* 4:1, 31–44. (Available online at: <http://essential.metapress.com/content/h312v54765504q30/fulltext.pdf>.)

Eugene d'Aquili and Andrew Newberg (1999), *The Mystical Mind: Probing the Biology of Religious Experience*, Minneapolis, MN: Augsburg Fortress.

H. H. the Dalai Lama (1996), *The Good Heart*, ed. Robert Kiely, London: Rider.

*Neil Douglas-Klotz (1999), *The Hidden Gospel: Decoding the Spiritual Message of the Aramaic Jesus*, Wheaton, IL: Quest Books.

Clive Erricker and Jane Erricker (2001), *Meditation in Schools: A Practical Guide to Calmer Classrooms and Clearer Minds*, London: Continuum.

Peter Fenwick and Elizabeth Fenwick (1995), *The Truth in the Light: Investigation of Over 300 Near-Death Experiences*, London: Headline.

Gustave Flaubert (1950 and 1979), *Madame Bovary: A Story of Provincial Life*, trans. Alan Russell, London: Penguin.

David Fontana (2003), *Psychology, Religion and Spirituality*, Oxford: BPS Blackwell.

David Fontana and Ingrid Slack (2007), *Teaching Meditation to Children: The Practical Guide to the Use and Benefits of Meditation Techniques*, London: Watkins.

Frieda Fordham (1953), *An Introduction to Jung's Psychology*, London: Penguin.

*Jim Forest (2007), *The Road to Emmaus: Pilgrimage as a Way of Life*, Maryknoll, NY: Orbis.

Jeff Forshaw (5.08.2012), 'The beauty of the Higgs boson', *The Observer*.

*James Fowler (1981, new edn 1995), *Stages of Faith: The Psychology of Human Development and the Quest for Meaning*, San Francisco: HarperSanFrancisco.

Anna Freud (1937), *The Ego and the Mechanisms of Defence*, trans. Cecil Baines, London: Hogarth.

Christopher K. Germer, Ronald D. Siegel and Paul R. Fulton (eds) (2005), *Mindfulness and Psychotherapy*, New York: Guilford Press.

Tobin Hart (2003), *The Secret Spiritual World of Children*, Makawayo, HI: Inner Ocean.

David Hay (2006), *Something There: The Biology of the Human Spirit*, London: Darton, Longman & Todd.

David Hay and Kate Hunt (2000), *Understanding the Spirituality of People who Don't go to Church*, Final Report of the Adult Spirituality Project, Nottingham University.

*David Hay and Rebecca Nye (2006), *The Spirit of the Child* (revised edn), London: Jessica Kingsley.

*Etty Hillesum (1999, reprinted 2007), *An Interrupted Life: The Diaries and Letters of Etty Hillesum 1941–1943*, (trans. Arnold J. Pomerans), London: Persephone.

Brendan Hyde (2008), *Children and Spirituality: Searching for Meaning and Connectedness*, London: Jessica Kingsley.

Christopher Isherwood (1965), *Ramakrishna and His Disciples*, Calcutta: Advaita Ashrama.

*William James (1982), *The Varieties of Religious Experience*, London: Penguin.

Lloyd Jones (2013), *A History of Silence*, London: John Murray.

Carl Jung (1933), *Modern Man in Search of a Soul*, London: Routledge & Kegan Paul.

*Jon Kabat-Zinn (1990), *Full Catastrophe Living: Using the Wisdom of your Body and Mind to Face Stress, Pain and Illness*, New York: Delta.

Harold Koenig, Dana King and Verna B. Carson (2012), *The Handbook of Religion and Health*, 2nd edn, Oxford: Oxford University Press.

I. Kutz, J. Z. Borysenko and H. Benson (1985), 'Meditation and Psychotherapy: A Rationale for the Integration of Dynamic Psychotherapy, the Relaxation Response, and Mindfulness Meditation', *American Journal of Psychiatry* 142:1, 1–8.

*Lao Tsu (1972), *Tao Te Ching*, trans. Gia-Fu Feng and Jane English, London: Wildwood House.

Pim van Lommel (2010), *Consciousness Beyond Life: The Science of the Near-Death Experience*, New York: HarperCollins.

*Iain McGilchrist (2009), *The Master and his Emissary: The Divided Brain and the Making of the Western World*, New Haven, CT and London: Yale University Press.

*Juan Mascaro (trans.) (2005), *The Upanishads*, London: Penguin.

Thomas Merton (1948 and 1998), *The Seven Storey Mountain*, 50th anniversary edn, New York: Harcourt, Brace & Co.

*Thomas Merton (1962), *New Seeds of Contemplation*, New York: New Directions.

*Thomas Merton (1966), *Conjectures of a Guilty Bystander*, New York: Doubleday.

Thomas Merton (1968), 'Final Integration: Toward a "Monastic Therapy"', *Monastic Studies* 6, 87–99.

Thomas Merton (1969), *The Way of Chuang Tsu*, New York: New Directions.

Thomas Merton (1971), *Contemplation in a World of Action*, New York: Doubleday.

*Thomas Merton (1973), *The Asian Journal of Thomas Merton*, New York: New Directions.

Thomas Merton (1985), *The Hidden Ground of Love: Letters of Religious Experience and Social Concerns*, New York: Farrar, Strauss & Giroux.

Thomas Merton (1989), *The Road to Joy: Letters to New and Old Friends*, New York: Farrar, Strauss & Giroux.

*Thomas Merton (1990), *The Intimate Merton: His Life from His Journals*, New York: HarperCollins.

Thomas Merton (1993), *Courage for Truth: The Letters of Thomas Merton to Writers*, ed. Christine Bochen, New York: Farrar, Strauss & Giroux.

Thomas Merton (1997), *Learning to Love: Exploring Solitude and Freedom – The Journals of Thomas Merton, Volume Six: 1966–1967*, San Francisco: Harper SanFrancisco.

Thomas Merton (1999), *Merton and Sufism*, Louisville, KY: Fons Vitae.

Thomas Merton (2003), *Merton and Judaism*, Louisville, KY: Fons Vitae.

Thomas Merton (2004), *Peace in the Post-Christian Era*, Maryknoll, NY: Orbis.

Thomas Merton (2007), *Merton and Buddhism*, Louisville, KY: Fons Vitae.

Thomas Merton (2014), *Merton and The Tao*, Louisville, KY: Fons Vitae.

Thomas Merton and Lawrence Cunningham (1996), *A Search for Solitude: Pursuing the Monk's True Life – The Journals of Thomas Merton, Volume 3: 1952–1960*, San Francisco: Harper SanFrancisco.

Father Elder Mullan (1914), *The Spiritual Exercises of St. Ignatius Loyola*, translated from the Autograph, New York: P. J. Kennedy & Sons.

*Shanida Nataraja (2008), *The Blissful Brain: Neuroscience and Proof of the Power of Meditation*, London: Gaia.

Andrew Newberg, Eugene d'Aquili and Vince Rause (2001), *Why God Won't Go Away: Brain Science and the Biology of Belief*, New York: Ballantine.

Northumbria Community (2000), *Celtic Daily Prayer: Inspirational Prayers and Readings from the Northumbria Community*, London: Collins.

Barack Obama (2008), *Dreams from My Father*, London: Canongate.

Diarmuid O'Murchu (2012), *In the Beginning Was Spirit: Science, Religion and Indigenous Spirituality*, New York: Orbis.

Bruce Parry with Mark McCrum (2008), *Tribe*, London, Penguin.

*Swami Prabhavananda and Christopher Isherwood (1987), *Bhagavad Gita: The Song of God*, 4th edn, Hollywood, CA: Vedanta.

Geshe Rabten and Geshe Ngawang Dhargyey (1977), *Advice from a Spiritual Friend: Buddhist Thought Transformation*, ed. Brian Beresford, trans. with Gonsar Tulku and Sherpa Tulku; New Delhi: Publications for Wisdom Culture.

*Walpola Rahula (1959, repr. 1997), *What the Buddha Taught*, ch. 8, New York: Grove.

Matthieu Ricard, Antoine Lutz and Richard Davidson (November 2014), 'Mind of the Meditator: The Neuroscience of Meditation', *Scientific American*.

*Richard Rohr (2012), *Falling Upward: A Spirituality for the Two Halves of Life*, London: SPCK.

Siegfried Sassoon (1930), *Memoirs of an Infantry Officer*, London: Faber & Faber.

Victor Schermer (2003), *Spirit and Psyche: A New Paradigm for Psychology, Psychoanalysis and Psychotherapy*, London and New York: Jessica Kingsley.

Daniel G. Scott (2004), 'Retrospective Spiritual Narratives: Exploring Recalled Childhood and Adolescent Spiritual Experiences', *International Journal of Children's Spirituality* 9:1: 67–79, p. 69.

Zindel V. Segal, Mark G. Williams and John D. Teasdale (2012), *Mindfulness-Based Cognitive Therapy for Depression*, New York: Guilford.

Katsuki Sekida (1975), *Zen Training: Methods and Philosophy*, New York: Weatherill, pp. 194–5.

William Shakespeare, *As You Like It*.

William Shakespeare, *King Lear*.

William Shakespeare, *Much Ado About Nothing*.

William Shakespeare, *Othello*.

William Shakespeare, *Romeo and Juliet*.

William H. Shannon, Christine M. Bochen and Patrick F. O'Connell (2002), *The Thomas Merton Encyclopedia*, New York: Orbis.

Acharya Shantideva (1979), *A Guide to the Boddhisattva's Way of Life*, trans. Stephen Batchelor, Dharamsala, India: Library of Tibetan Works and Archives.

Nikki Slade (2004), 'Heavenbound', also Larry Culliford, 'A Commentary on "Heavenbound"', in Phil Barker and Poppy Buchanan-Barker (eds), *Spirituality and Mental Health: Breakthrough*, London: Whurr.

*David Tacey (2004), *The Spirituality Revolution*, Hove and New York: Brunner-Routledge.

Steve Taylor (2009), *The Fall: The Insanity of the Ego in Human History and the Dawning of a New Era*, Winchester, O Books.

*Steve Taylor (2011), *Out of the Darkness: From Turmoil to Transformation*, London: Hay House.

Pierre Teilhard de Chardin, with Julian Huxley (1955), *The Phenomenon of Man*, London: Collins.

Pierre Teilhard de Chardin (1964), *Le Milieu Divin (The Divine Milieu): An Essay on the Interior Life*, London: Collins.

*Thich Nhat Hanh (1991), *Old Path, White Clouds: The Life Story of the Buddha*, London: Rider.

George Vaillant (ed.) (1992), *Ego Mechanisms of Defence: A Guide for Clinicians and Researchers*, Washington: American Psychiatric Press.

Swami Vivekananda (1948, 20th impression 2004), *Teachings of Swami Vivekananda*, Calcutta: Advaita Ashrama.

Katherine Weare (2014), *Evidence for Mindfulness: Impacts on the Wellbeing and Performance of School Staff*, © Mindfulness in Schools Project; <www.mindfulnessinschools.org>.

*Ken Wilber (1991), *Grace and Grit: Spirituality and Healing in the Life and Death of Treya Killam Wilber*, Boston: Shambala.

Richard Wilhelm (1967), *The I Ching or Book of Changes – The Richard Wilhelm Translation* (German), rendered into English by Cary F. Baynes, Foreword by C. G. Jung, 3rd edn, Princeton, NJ: Princeton University Press.

Mark Williams, John Teasdale, Zindel Segal and Jon Kabat-Zinn (2007), *The Mindful Way Through Depression: Freeing Yourself from Chronic Unhappiness*, New York: Guilford.

Howard Worsley (2009), *A Child Sees God: Children Talk about Bible Stories*, London: Jessica Kingsley.

Relevant and recommended websites

(Dates given in brackets when most recently accessed.)

Author's blog: <www.psychologytoday.com/blog/spiritual-wisdom-secular-times> (09.02.15)

Author's website: <www.ldc52.co.uk> (20.02.15)

BASS (British Association for the Study of Spirituality): <www.basspirituality.org.uk> (17.01.15)

BBC on religions: <www.bbc.co.uk/religion/religions/jainism> (14.01.15)

BBC2 'Soul of Britain' programmes: <www.facingthechallenge.org/soul.php> (20.02.15)

Brahma Kumaris: <www.brahmakumaris.org/uk> (14.01.15)

House of Lords debate, text: <www.publications.parliament.uk/pa/ld201415/ldhansrd/text/141127-0001.htm#14112781000360>. (Lord Stone between 1.27 – and 1.33 p.m.)

Julian Meetings: <www.julianmeetings.org> (10.01.15)

Kabbalah online: <www.chabad.org> (14.01.15)

Loyola exercises: <www.companionofjesus.com/se-mullan.pdf> (13.01.15)

Meditation in Schools: <www.meditationinschools.org> (12.01.15)

Mental health leaflet: <www.rcpsych.ac.uk/healthadvice/treatmentswellbeing/spirituality.aspx> (09.02.15)

Thomas Merton: <www.merton.org> and (in UK): <www.thomasmertonsociety.org.uk> (both accessed on 09.02.15)

Merton audioclip: <http://merton.org/Research/AV/audioclip.aspx> (03.01.15)

Mindfulness in Schools: <www.mindfulnessinschools.org> (12.01.15)

Edgar Mitchell: <http://noetic.org/directory/person/edgar-mitchell> (11.08.14)

Monastic schedule: <www.monks.org/index.php/about-us/daily-schedule> (12.01.15)

Northumbria Community: <www.northumbriacommunity.org> (14.01.15)

Quakers: <www.quaker.org.uk> (10.01.15)

Scientific and Medical Network: <www.scimednet.org> (20.02.15)

Nikki Slade: <www.freetheinnervoice.com> (24.02.15)

Spirit Release Foundation: <www.spiritrelease.com> (03.02.15)

Spirituality special interest group: <www.rcpsych.ac.uk/spirit> (09.02.15)

Teilhard de Chardin: <www.teilhard.org.uk> (26.01.15)

WCCM (World Community for Christian Meditation): <www.wccm.org> (10.01.15)

Index

Did you know that SPCK is a registered charity?

As well as publishing great books by leading Christian authors, we also . . .

. . . make assemblies meaningful and fun for over a million children by running www.assemblies.org.uk, a popular website that provides free assembly scripts for teachers. For many children, school assembly is the only contact they have with Christian faith and culture, and the only time in their week for spiritual reflection.

. . . help prisoners to become confident readers with our easy-to-read stories. Poor literacy is a huge barrier to rehabilitation. Prisoners identify with the believable heroes of our gritty fiction. At the same time, questions at the end of each chapter help them to examine their choices from a moral perspective and to build their reading confidence.

. . . support student ministers overseas in their training. We give them free, specially written theology books, the International Study Guides. These books really do make a difference, not just to students but to ministers and, through them, to a whole community.

Please support these great schemes: visit www.spck.org.uk/support-us to find out more.